4

D0558371

CONQUEST AND CATASTROPHE

The Triumph and Tragedy of the Great Northern Railway Through Stevens Pass

By

T. Gary Sherman

authorHOUSE™

1663 LIBERTY DRIVE, SUITE 200
BLOOMINGTON, INDIANA 47403
(800) 839-8640
WWW.AUTHORHOUSE.COM

© 2004 T. Gary Sherman.
All Rights Reserved.

No part of this book may be reproduced, stored in a retrieval system, or transmitted by any means without the written permission of the author.

First published by AuthorHouse 10/13/04

ISBN: 1-4184-9575-1 (sc)

Printed in the United States of America
Bloomington, Indiana

This book is printed on acid-free paper.

Table of Contents

Acknowledgments

This manuscript was too big for me to handle on my own. What started off as a simple short feature story for a local historical museum publication soon became overwhelming. For every one question answered, three more arose. It did not take long before I found myself seeking the assistance of one person after another. The list continued to grow for nearly two decades. Everyone is listed in the Index of Resources at the back of the book. Every one of them helped in a great way to get this story completed as best as possible. However, I would be remiss if I did not mention certain people who made a special effort to go out of their way to assist, guide, and at times, push me to get it done.

First, I must thank Ruby El Hult whose book "Northwest Disaster," published in 1960 is 'the source' for anyone interested in or researching the Wellington avalanche disaster. Her guidance on how best to do historical research, and her ideas for my manuscript were invaluable. She also gave me Basil Sherlock's 26-page letter to her, which provided such detail at Wellington before, during, and after the avalanche. The late Murray Morgan, probably the Northwest's premier historian, author of "Skid Road," for his reviewing of my research and advice on how best to approach the Japanese connection to the Great Northern. Professor Albro Martin of Bradley University, who wrote "James J. Hill and the Opening of the Northwest," for his invaluable help in the different ways the Great Northern coded their telegrams and help with answering so many questions. His selfless time that he provided me, helped shorten my efforts in researching so many areas of the railroad's impact on Seattle.

I also owe a debt of gratitude to Thomas White, curator of the James Jerome Hill Reference Library in St. Paul, Jon Nakagawara of the King County Medical Examiners Office, Ruby Shields and Dona Sieden, of the Minnesota Historical Society, Jun Yoshida, of the Consulate-General of Japan Office in Seattle, Former Mayor of Tacoma, Doug Sutherland, Professor David R. Knechtges of the University of Washington Asian Language Department, William N. Edwards, retired President of Mount Pleasant Cemetery in Seattle, and the late Frank Hatori, Seattle's 'unofficial' historian for the Japanese community in Seattle. Mr. Hatori helped me so much in understanding the way things really were for immigrants and aliens in the early 1900's in this country.

Thanks also to my friends and acquaintances, Stan Staniforth who never gave up pushing me to get this project finished. My sister, Linda Lindstrom, for her help, understanding, and support. Shawn Guthrie, for his critical analysis, ideas, and proof reading. And Chuck Meding for his much needed and appreciated technical expertise.

Finally, I must offer a sincere, yet posthumous thanks, to Edward William Topping, who lost his father, Ned, at Wellington. The letters we exchanged and the telephone conversations we had, brought home to me, as nothing else could have, the human tragedy of the country's worst avalanche disaster.

Prologue

They are one of the most terrifying and destructive forces of nature. Avalanches are caused by the added weight of fresh snow, or by the gradual weakening of older snow that has built up over time on a cliff, hillside or mountainside. They occur most often on slopes that exceed 30 degrees.

Snow can act like a plastic material that exhibits both elastic and viscous properties. Because of this nature, any snow cover situated on a sloping surface, tends to deform internally by downhill flow under the influence of gravity. This is known as "creep." The snow cover also slides slowly over the surface of the ground, a phenomenon called "glide." Both "creep" and "glide" are highly dependent on temperature, as snow has low viscosity near the freezing point, but becomes increasingly brittle at lower temperatures. The shear stress produced by uneven "creep and "glide" of the snow cover are an important factor in understanding the nature of avalanches.

These slides can be set off by a combination of factors including, as mentioned above, temperature changes, the constant impact of falling snow, freezing rain, or rain. Sudden vibrations, including loud noises such as thunder are also major causes of snow slides.

Depending on high up the peak the avalanche begins, it can gain speeds exceeding 100 miles an hour. Depending on the conditions and as described earlier, there are two major types of snow slides. One is a loose snow avalanche, which gathers more and more snow as is descends a mountainside. The other is a slab avalanche, which is made up of more compact snow, cohesive snow and ice that suddenly breaks away from a slope.

During the winter, the Cascade Mountains of Washington State are frequently visited by these slides. They pose a constant danger to skiers and hikers, and cause the highways that run across them to be closed regularly for avalanche control.

The Cascades are the northern extension of the Sierra Nevada Mountains of Northern California. Rising between the Pacific coast and the Rocky Mountains, the Cascades roughly parallel the Washington and Oregon coastline, 110 to 140 miles inland.

The loftiest peaks are volcanic cones that are the most imposing mountains in the United States. Several river valleys cut through the Cascades, such as the Klamath, Frazier, and most importantly, the Columbia. The foaming rapids of these rivers, called "cascades," give the mountain range its name. The valleys also provided for, in the late 1800's, the location of passes for a number of transcontinental railroads to be built from the east, to Puget Sound.

The last of the railroads to be built across the Cascades was the Great Northern. It crossed the mountains farther north then any of the other railroads. It was also the shortest route through the mountains. Just what the owners wanted. However, they failed to see the dangers this crossing would present in the future. Dangers that would result in the most tragic avalanche disaster in the history of the United States.

Every winter, it was a constant battle between nature and the railroads to keep their lines open to traffic, both freight and passenger. No railroad had more trouble with the elements then the Great Northern. As successful as the railway was, its large army of snow fighting equipment and thousands of workers seemed to wage a continuous war against the weather, winning some and losing others.

In 1910, nature unleashed her fury and power in a manner no one had ever imagined. A thirty feet deep avalanche, more then one mile long, broke away from Windy Mountain on the western slope of the Cascades, and carried with it, into the gorge 200 feet below, two stranded trains and their passengers, as well as part of the town of Wellington, Washington.

Author's photograph: 1992

View of Windy Mountain from "Old Faithful" pullout a few miles west of Stevens Pass summit. The massive double-track, concrete snow shed can be seen skirting the base of the mountain. The town own of Wellington was located just to the right of the snow shed, which was constructed where the trains stood when the avalanche hit.

The story of Wellington is the central story of Stevens Pass and the Great Northern Railway in Washington. The Great Northern's enormous economic impact on Seattle and the entire state of Washington cannot be overstated or denied. But railroading in the late 1800's and early 20th century was also extremely dangerous to both workers and passengers. However, their vision, work, and sacrifice have resulted in the booming economy that the Pacific Northwest enjoys today.

This book is an attempt to piece together, as best as possible, the coming of the Great Northern to Puget Sound. To tell the story of the people responsible for the legitimate success, as well as (by today's standards), the unethical, and at times, illegal actions taken by these men. This book also details the discovery of the pass, the construction of the rail line, and how it was kept in operation under all conditions; purely in the interest of profit, both for the region's economy and for the financial gains of the powers that owned and ran the Great Northern.

What follows is true. Sadly, however, the story has some gaps. Gaps that cannot be completely filled in. The Great Northern did an excellent job of covering up (as much as it could), what really happened at Wellington. Now, with the passage of nearly a century, only partial records and other written correspondence can help put the story together. One of the richest sources of information are the corporate papers of the Great Northern and Northern Pacific housed at the Minnesota Historical Society in St. Paul. Interestingly enough, many records of this tragedy no longer exist.

Nor do many of the records of the Japanese laborers exist. This is another sad truth in trying to put together as accurate a historical account as possible. The story of the Japanese worker's great contribution to the railroad's construction and maintenance, and the shameful treatment that these early immigrants endured, has never been told until now. But again, there are gaps.

Twenty years of research, including personal interviews and correspondence with relatives of the Wellington avalanche disaster, and employees of the Great Northern has helped to piece together (as best as possible), the true story of the Great Northern Railway and the history of Stevens Pass. The reader will find much information never before published. It is the hope of the author that this book will peak interest in this overlooked, but extremely important chapter in American railroading history. Perhaps some reader or readers will be interested enough to pursue the story even more; and with some hard work and luck, be able to fill in the gaps to this historical enigma.

Introduction

"So far as loss of life and damage to property is concerned, I believe this is the worst experience we have ever had." (61)

This is the tragic observation made by H. R. Parkhouse, a Great Northern Railway official on the scene at Wellington, Washington on March 4, 1910. His telegram was sent to Louis Hill, president of the Great Northern, who was vacationing at the Casa Loma Hotel, enjoying the warmth and sunshine of Southern California, more than a thousand miles south of where this country's greatest avalanche disaster had occurred just three days earlier. Hill wanted to know exactly what happened during that fateful early morning hour of March 1, 1910, on Stevens Pass in the Cascade Mountains of Washington State. Nearly a century later, his inquiry has still not been completely answered, and probably never will.

What follows, however, is the closest account that has ever been assembled about the Wellington disaster. It is also the story of the discovery and construction of Stevens Pass, the dreams and foresight of the management of the Great Northern Railway who knew how important the Pacific Northwest would become to the rest of the nation's economy, and it's important ties to the Orient, especially Japan. The story is filled with stouthearted men and women of courage, bravery, and determination. It is the story of feats of engineering that are remarkable even by today's standards. However, it is also a story of treacherous and unscrupulous individuals who would use any means at their disposal, including the illegal importation, specifically Japanese, to achieve their desire for wealth and power. Many of these Japanese laborers were held prisoners by the railroad and literally worked to death.

The story centers around Wellington, Washington, as it was the focal point for most of what went on in the development, construction and maintenance of Stevens Pass and the Great Northern for its first thirty-five years. Through interviews, personal papers, the many publications that include books, magazines and newspapers, as well as the discovery of the Great Northern coded telegrams (and their translation), the true story of Stevens Pass, the Great Northern Railway, and the Wellington disaster, can now be told (as closely as possible).

The four primary words that make up the title of this book were not chosen at random. 'Conquest,' it most certainly was. The ability to locate and then build a major railway pass through some of the most difficult terrain across one of the most formidable mountain ranges in this country was indeed an enormous challenge that was successfully met. 'Catastrophe,' because of the many natural and manmade accidents that regularly occurred on Stevens Pass. Blizzards, avalanches, forest fires, train wrecks, injuries and deaths, were all too common until the Great Northern finally decided to abandon its original route for a more safer one. 'Triumph,' it certainly was too. The arrival of the Great Northern was, without question, the defining moment in the economic growth and success that resulted on Puget Sound. And finally, 'Tragedy.' It is a word that best illustrates the inhumane nature of how people of different races were treated and exploited in those days, simply for the riches gained by others at the cost of their labors and sacrifices. The untold number of dead Japanese workers and the mistreatment they endured is an unforgivable blight on what otherwise is a magnificent piece of Americana.

Two last bits of information. Many of the statements, recollections, and other historical observations are keyed to the Index of Resources at the back of the book. They are offered for anyone who is interested enough and willing to further pursue the subject matter. Secondly, the telegrams, newspaper and magazine articles, and all other forms of written correspondence are written here in the original way they were written decades ago. No attempt was made to change spelling, grammar, or punctuation.

Chapter 1:

The Empire Builder and the Engineer

What really happened at Wellington and why, cannot be adequately explained or understood unless it is set in context with the discovery of Stevens Pass, and the construction of James J. Hill's Great Northern Railway. To do this, one needs to know the two major characters involved in the drama. Jim Hill and John Stevens.

The Empire Builder

"I will make my mark on the face of this earth and no man will ever wipe it out."

-James Jerome Hill-

One person who knew Jim Hill well, Stewart Holbrook, described him as, "a legend while he lived, a legend in death…(he was) the Little Giant, the Devil's Curse of the northern plains, the barbed-wire, shaggy headed, one-eyed old sonofabitch of Western railroading."(57)

"Mr. Hill was a hard taskmaster," so explained John Frank Stevens (88), who would at the order of his boss, James Jerome Hill, discover the pass that bears his name in the Cascade Mountains of Washington State.

"The Empire Builder," as he came to be called, James Jerome Hill, was born near Rockwood, Ontario, Canada on September 16, 1838. He was the second child of a poor, struggling farming family, the son of James and Anne Hill. In order to help make financial ends meet, young Jim took a job at a dry goods store in Embro (probably where the station stop in the Cascades got its name), not far from Rockwood. He was an all around clerk, cleaning the store, keeping the barrels filled, and measuring out the merchandise to be sold. Seeing no future remaining there, the adventurous young man headed for the eastern United States, ending up in New York City in his later teens. (57)

Here, he heard about and was captivated by numerous and exotic stories of men of wealth who had made their fortunes in the Orient. He listened intently to businessmen such as Asa Whitney, who predicted some day in the near future, the United States would be crossed by railroads from Atlantic to Pacific, and that these steam powered trains were without doubt the cheapest way of transporting goods throughout the country. More importantly thought young Hill, the riches of the Orient that he had heard so much about, could be greatly enhanced by shipping the merchandise, such as silks and teas, to the newly settled ports in the Pacific Northwest. They could then be hauled back east (where the real money was), by rail. The idea fascinated his quickly expanding entrepreneurial mind. When Hill's idea finally took root, it would lead him to become one of the most successful railroad tycoons of all time.

But that was still sometime in the future. Hill ran out of money in Syracuse and could not find work. He headed for St. Paul, Minnesota hoping to catch on with an expedition heading for the west coast. To his dismay, when he arrived in St. Paul, he had discovered the expedition had left only days earlier. Hill was forced to spend the winter in St. Paul, making a living anyway he could. It was a meager existence, to say the least, and the industrious lad promised himself that he would never spend a winter in near poverty like that ever again. (41)

The following years spent in Minnesota were filled with numerous jobs. Young Hill spent time as a shipping and receiving clerk, a night watchman, and held a number of different jobs aboard Mississippi steamboats. Jim Hill was learning much from his experiences (he was very much a visionary). He quickly came to realize that St. Paul, located on the Mississippi River, offered great economic potential as a railroad terminus.

When he first arrived there, Hill noticed that the population consisted primarily of Native Americans. During the first decade he spent in St. Paul, he witnessed a great influx of immigrants, primarily Scandinavian and German. Here was the abundant labor needed for the construction of the new, but small railroads that were beginning to sprout up around the upper Midwest. Hill probably became aware of the fortune and power that railroads afforded people willing to work and invest in them when he got a job as an agent for the small St. Paul & Pacific railroad. True, it was losing money. In fact by 1878 it was nearly bankrupt. Here was his opportunity to get hold of a railroad for himself. A railroad that was granted, by Congress, almost 3,000,000 acres of land, if it could be completed from St. Paul to St. Vincent, Minnesota by January, 1879.

He had assembled a few wealthy businessmen and convinced them that there was plenty of money to be made by investing in this railroad and other lines. Hill explained these trains would become the primary movers of the cargo that landed at St. Paul and other ports on the upper Mississippi to all the communities away from the river. It was cheaper to continue the transport of freight over land to their destinations by railroad, after the river boats arrived with their merchandise.(57) Together, they raised the $9,000,000 necessary to purchase the St. Paul & Pacific, and the railroad was completed on time.

They immediately reorganized the corporation, changed its name to the St. Paul, Minneapolis & Manitoba Railroad, and sold the nearly 3,000,000 acres of land that came with the deal for nearly $16,000,000! Under Hill's leadership, it did not take long to get their investment on sound financial footing.

Hill, however, was still looking at the Pacific Northwest, where he believed his real fortune waited. The fact that the Union Pacific had been completed to the west in 1869 and the Northern Pacific in 1883, made Hill all the more anxious to construct a rail line to Puget Sound as quickly as possible. Hill also kept a close eye on the Northern Pacific. He liked its location, but he liked even more the fact it was deeply in debt. The NP crossed through areas of the Northwest, which contained enormous amounts of timber, minerals, and hundreds of thousands of acres of prime agricultural land.

He envisioned a railroad that would reap incredible profits from these natural resources, while creating settlements and towns from North Dakota to Washington. There was no way to lose and so much to gain, Hill convinced his investor friends. Their railroad would bring farmers, timber workers, and miners to this land that had yet to be developed, but could not be possibly ignored much longer by other railroads. Besides, the growing Pacific Northwest, especially along Puget Sound, needed plenty of already manufactured goods from the eastern part of the country. Their railroad would haul this too. No doubt, Jim Hill was also thinking the riches of the Orient and the strategic locations of the ports on Puget Sound. Here was Hill's and his partners' opportunity to settle and develop the Northwest, and they would be the fortunate benefactors.

In Hill's own words, from his book "HIGHWAYS OF PROGRESS," the 'Empire Builder' explained, "When the railways reached Puget Sound (the Great Northern in 1893), they found there the largest supply of standing timber in the world. It reached the outer world only in small quantities, that sailing vessels carried up and down the coast, or to foreign ports. The freight rate to the East, where alone it could be sold extensively, and where the demand for it was greatest, was ninety cents per one hundred pounds. This was prohibitive. The question was how to make this rate low enough to bring this timber to the prairie country and the Mississippi Valley. It could be done only by securing an ample and steady volume of cargo to be transported in **both** directions, so that both eastbound and westbound cars, moving in each direction, are loaded."

In 1893, when the Great Northern had finally arrived on Puget Sound, the westbound business of the Northern Pacific and other railroads, was considerably more than their eastbound business. When their trains returned to the east, they were practically empty of any cargo. Hill could not understand this. He saw it as extreme economic folly. He would make sure the Great Northern cars, when they returned east from Puget Sound, would haul plenty of timber, and later costly imports from the Orient.

One of Jim Hill's neighbors on Summit Avenue in St. Paul, was Frederick Weyerhaeuser, head of the largest lumbering business in the United States. (40) He had made his first fortune from the forests of Minnesota and Wisconsin just after the Civil War. In the evenings, whenever the two got together, Hill would rave to his friend about all the timber out in the Northwest. The timber, he told Weyerhaeuser, was the best quality he had seen anywhere in the country. And the trees, the trees were so enormous…well he'd just have to take Hill's word for it, or go out West to see it for himself. Hill seemed particularly obsessed by the spectacular forests of Northern Idaho and Washington. But Weyerhaeuser wasn't interested at the time.

Later, when Hill gained control of the Northern Pacific, along with its tens of thousands of acres of government granted forest lands, Hill stepped up the pressure on his neighbor. He offered the lumber baron all the forestland, ninety thousand acres, covered primarily with Douglas Fir, for six dollars an acre. When Weyerhaeuser still showed some reluctance, Hill made a final offer that his friend could not refuse. After the timber was cut, Hill would charge Weyerhaeuser, the smallest freight rates in the country, to haul the timber east, via the Great Northern Railway. Frederick Weyerhaeuser capitulated. It would become one of the largest land transfers in this country's history.

This all took place in 1900. Finally, after Weyerhaeuser had seen for himself the timber that covered his new acreage, he could not wait to embark on his new enterprise. Saw mills went up by the hundreds, both in Washington and Idaho. By 1909, there were over three hundred working mills in operation. The timing was perfect. There was a current construction boom in the Dakotas. In 1906, the great San Francisco earthquake and fire caused that city to be almost completely rebuilt. The Bay area was still in desperate need of materials even three years later. Extra shifts were put on at all the Weyerhaeuser mills to meet the overwhelming demand for lumber in California.

The Weyerhaeuser family had investments in a number of other mills in the Northwest. In Potlatch, Idaho, one of many towns created by these lumber camps, Weyerhaeuser purchased the Boise Potlatch Company, which became Boise Cascade. With this acquisition, Weyerhaeuser gained control of just about all the western white pine forests, and complete dominance of lumbering in the country.

Frederick Weyerhaeuser had become wealthy beyond his imagination, and James Hill would be guaranteed the profitability for the growth of the Great Northern. He was also able to acquire the necessary financial capital to purchase more rail lines to add to his growing railroad empire.

The St. Paul, Minneapolis & Manitoba Railroad was soon able to advance enough money to construct the Montana Central Railroad, which would run between Great Falls, Helena, and Butte. Meanwhile, the St. Paul, Minneapolis & Manitoba was steadily moving westward at breakneck speed. Hill's crews averaged 3 ¼ miles of track laid per day. In one spectacular day of railroad construction, his crew completed just over 8 miles of laid track![35]

It was not difficult constructing President Hill's new railroad westward, in fact in 1886 his crews built over 120 miles of track all the way to Minot, North Dakota. Maybe the winters were bad, but the track was straight (very little curvature), and even more importantly, the ground was flat. This is how the construction continued, with thousands of workers employed as track layers, grading crews, as well as surveyors and bridge builders, for the next 600 miles, to Great Falls, Montana.[58] There the terrain changed dramatically. The railroad would have to be completed over two imposing mountain ranges, the Rockies and Cascades, with curves and grades that would slow down progress considerably before they reached the ports on

Puget Sound. From Great Falls to completion in Seattle would take the next two years, beginning in 1891.

In 1889, with the purchasing and connecting of numerous smaller lines, and under the authority of Federal legislative action, James J. Hill filed notice of a name change for a number of rail lines now under his control. Thus was born the Great Northern Railway Company.(32)

Unlike other railroads in the United States, the Great Northern was built without any government funding. Hill and his associates secured the needed capital from private institutions, both within the U.S. and abroad. Those who ran the Great Northern, led by Hill, ran their new line so successfully the GN was one of the few railroads that was able to weather the Panic of 1893. The depression sent many of their competitors into bankruptcy.

Many historians believe that this severe economic downturn began with the collapse of the Philadelphia & Reading Railroad Company. Railroads in the late 19th century had such powerful influence on the nation's economy that the troubles with this one railroad may have caused the sudden drop in the stock market. In 1893 alone, more than 700 banks and other financial institutions closed down. Business failures reached more than 15,000. In "ECONOMIC HISTORY OF THE PEOPLE OF THE UNITED STATES," Fred Shannon states, "For the next five years the situation remained bad, reaching another low level in 1899. In 1894 there were 156 railroads with 39,000 miles of track in receivership, including the Erie, Northern Pacific, and Union Pacific. They represented a valuation of 2 ½ billion dollars, or a fourth of the total railroad capital in the country. Basic industries showed a great decline in output, the production of pig iron falling off a third. All this involved widespread unemployment, reduction in wages, lockouts, and social distress in general. Farm prices plunged to new low levels, and Populism gained new converts." But not for the people operating the Great Northern Railway.

As the line progressed toward the west, Hill encouraged immigrants in the upper Mississippi River Valley that they could avoid the terrible results of the depression and actually profit much better by relocating along the Great Northern line and begin raising crops and livestock. His idea appealed to many who heard him. Thus the Great Northern helped to create and develop, not only large, successful ranches and farms across the northern plains, but entire towns all the way to Washington state.

It didn't take long for his dream to pay off. Grain elevators sprang up all along the line. Soon could be heard the thunder of large Great Northern trains rushing westward across the flat terrain, filled to capacity with wheat and other crops. Hill was also thinking about his trains returning from the west. The GN, he believed, could make even greater profits from the timber the Pacific Northwest had, and what the burgeoning Northeast needed. This was before his talks with Weyerhaeuser. Always in the back of Hill's mind, however, was the Orient, with its teas, silks, and other precious commodities that offered a fortune to the first railway to take advantage of it. That is why he needed to get the Great Northern to Puget Sound and the towns of Everett and Seattle without delay. The Northern Pacific had already arrived at Commencement Bay in Tacoma, but failed to see, thus far, the economic opportunities in the Orient the way he did. Hill also surmised this was another example of the lack of vision on the part of the Northern Pacific people. Another reason, perhaps, for the Northern Pacific's near economic collapse.

The Engineer

John Frank Stevens was born April 25, 1853 in West Gardiner, Maine. Strangely enough, he had no formal technical training as an engineer. He spent only two years at a teacher's college in Farmington, Maine. He had plans for becoming an educator, but like his future boss, James J. Hill, he was fascinated with railroading, but in a different way.

Albro Martin in his book, "JAMES J. HILL AND THE OPENING OF THE NORTHWEST," described Stevens as "wiry and athletic." A self-taught New Englander who would become the prime mover in establishing the route that the Great Northern would follow across the two great mountain ranges "that stood between Pacific Junction and Puget Sound."[57]

By 1873, he was working for railroads in the Midwestern and Western United States. In 1874, Stevens moved to Minneapolis and accepted a job in that city's engineering department. Within three years, he got himself another job, this time with a small railroad in the Upper Midwest. This was the type of work that Stevens was looking for, and for the next six years he spent this time learning first hand the science of railroad engineering. His first big break came in the spring of 1883 when he was given the job as assistant to the chief engineer responsible for locating a route for the Canadian Pacific Railroad through the Rockies.

In 1889, the Great Northern Railway had just completed its line to Havre, Montana. It was another, major leg in Jim Hill's quest for the shortest transcontinental line in the United States. The Union Pacific and the Northern Pacific were already operating as far west as Puget Sound. Hill's vision of the wealth and opportunities the Pacific Northwest offered, both in natural resources and its connection to the Orient, would be lost to these competitors if he did not complete building his Great Northern to Puget Sound as rapidly as possible. This would require that the rest of the railroad to be built over the shortest possible line, with the smallest grades through the imposing mountains of the Rockies and Cascades. The line had to be located farther north than any other railroad in the United States. Hill was perplexed about what to do with these mountain barriers. After all, they were the last stumbling block that were left to conquer, and what stood in the way of him becoming one of the country's richest and most powerful railroad barons.

John F. Stevens' successful surveying for the Canadian Pacific probably caught the eye of the "Empire Builder." Hill believed his transcontinental needed to follow as straight a path as possible to the west. He also wanted the shortest passes that could be found through the Rockies and Cascades. Stevens seemed to be just the right man for the formidable job of discovering these passes.

Jim Hill instructed his chief engineer, E. H. Beckler to contact Stevens and offer him the job of finding the passes needed for the Great Northern through the two mountain ranges. Beckler quickly located Stevens and brought him immediately to meet Hill. Stevens remembered Hill's first words to his new employee. "We don't care about Rocky Mountain scenery...what we want is the best possible line, shortest distance, and the least curvature that we can build between the points covered."(88)

With these orders, Stevens began his new assignment in November of 1889, just a few miles west of Havre, Montana. A team of mules, a covered wagon, a saddle horse, a driver, and a Blackfoot Indian (who would also act as guide), were all he took with him as he started his journey of discovery westward...in a blizzard.

Studying the best maps he could find, Stevens determined that the best route through the Rockies would begin somewhere near the Marias River in Montana and end in the Kootenai River Valley of Northern Idaho. He had heard the Indian legend of a "hidden" pass near the headwaters of the Marias River. True, it had never been discovered, but that was what Jim Hill was paying him to do. Find the easiest pass through the Rocky Mountains.

One hundred and eighty miles later, Stevens arrived at the Blackfoot Indian Agency seeking whatever information he could about this "mystical pass" through the Rockies. To his dismay, all he heard were superstitious folklore and legends of how the pass was the home of evil spirits and no one in their right mind would dare venture that way. Certainly no Blackfoot.(3) Stevens wasn't certain of his next step until he ran across a Flathead Indian who was on the run for murdering a member of his own tribe. He would be glad to escort Stevens through the pass. After talking with this more than willing guide, he easily determined that the Flathead knew nothing about the mysterious pass, but decided to bring him along anyway, just in case he (Stevens) met with disaster. This way, there was a chance that the newest member of his party might take time to leave a message with someone regarding what happened to Stevens, while he (the Flathead) was still on the lamb.

It wasn't long before they found the entrance of what appeared to be the pass Stevens was looking for. As they continue their hike into the mountains, the snow got so deep they constructed a type of snowshoe needed to continue, sent the animals back with the driver, and carried all of their provisions on their back. However, it turned out not to be the entrance to the elusive pass. It seemed like a dead end. Stevens recounted that, "something, possibly a sixth sense, urged me to keep going."(88) That "sixth sense," was not felt by his Indian friend who decided this was as far as he wanted to go. Stevens hiked the rest of the way up the mountain by himself.

On December 11, 1889, John Frank Stevens, the man who had no formal training as an engineer, laboriously hiked a few more miles and was astounded to see he had reached a somewhat low summit near the Continental Divide. He was now viewing with wonderment and relief, the downward, western side of the Rockies. He had found "the pass." Even better, there would be no need for a tunnel to be built at the summit.

What happened next gives a great deal of insight into the kind of man John Frank Stevens was. As he recalled it, he started back down the slope in the exact same direction he came. It was now dark, and the temperature was rapidly dropping, while the winds were picking up, and the snow was falling harder then ever. There was no way for him to build a fire, and he didn't dare fall asleep. His only chance for survival was to remove his home made snowshoes and to keeping walking back and forth while his weight dug a groove in the snow. Stevens continued to pace back and forth all night long; to stay awake and keep from freezing to death.

The next morning, as soon as light in the east appeared, Stevens could now see his way down the slope. Stumbling, sliding, and falling, he finally reached his Indian friend who had remained behind. According to Stevens, the Flathead was almost frozen to death, and Stevens had to nearly beat him up to wake him up. The two made it back to the Blackfoot Indian Agency where the Indian, remembering his felony, took off for places unknown. Stevens telegraphed Hill the good news. Hearing this, Hill was overjoyed, then wired Stevens to head for the Cascades and do the same thing there.

The pass through the Rocky Mountains would eventually become known as Marian Pass. At the summit, the Great Northern, in later years would honor John Frank Stevens by constructing a larger than life bronze statue of the man, by himself, in the dead of winter, discovered the easiest mountain crossing for America's northern most rail line.

Stevens, upon receiving Hill's telegram immediately set out for Spokane, where he would begin his last and most difficult task; the task of discovering the best route for the Great Northern to Puget Sound. The boss, Jim Hill, had left instructions with Stevens to locate the route somewhere north of the Northern Pacific line and south of the Canadian border. The Great Northern Railway's engineer was perfectly aware of the fact that in 1870, engineers and surveyors for the Northern Pacific, led by D. C. Linsley, spent nearly the entire summer searching for the best pass for their railroad to Tacoma. They were obviously familiar with the area Stevens was considering, but they had located their route many miles to the south and named it Stampede Pass. The fact was that all of the mapping the Northern Pacific people did, convinced them that there were no good locations for a railroad north of where they built their line. Despite the fact that the Cascades where not as high as the Rockies, they presented a far greater challenge to Stevens. Their mountainous barriers had far steeper grades and more curves, something Jim Hill had originally insisted he wanted to avoid.

But now, with the discovery of a pass though the Rockies, Hill's dream of a transcontinental railroad, that would greatly challenge the others already in service, grew so intense that he was willing to negotiate and sacrifice some of his ideals. This was something completely foreign to his nature, but he was not about to let this one last barrier stand in the way of his dream, and Hill told Stevens that.(40)

In the spring of 1890, John F. Stevens set out once more to conquer another mountain range, the final barrier for the Great Northern. In his memoirs, Stevens wrote, **"On one of my cruises up the Wenatchee River, I noted a large creek (Nason Creek) coming into it from the south, well up into the mountains. I knew that its course could not long continue from the south, and so followed up a short distance to where it turned abruptly, coming from the west. Realizing that it must head at a summit in the main range, I filed that mental picture away in my head for future investigation. A short time afterward when I was cruising the top of the main range, I found a comparatively low place in it, against which a creek flowing east had its head. I felt certain that it must be the beginning of the same creek that I have noted above."** (88)

Stevens explained all this to head of his engineering party, C. F. B. Haskell. He instructed Haskell to head up Nason Creek and "develop its head." Following the path Stevens' told him, he found the creek, which emerged in the pass at just above 4,000 feet. The watercourse was surrounded by steep mountain peaks towering 2,000 to 4,000 feet above. This was, no doubt, the pass that Stevens would want for the Great Northern.

The story goes that at this point in the expedition, Haskell carved into huge cedar tree the words "Stevens Pass."(38)

Charles F. B. Haskell's contribution to the discovery of Stevens Pass and his work with the Great Northern has been given little recognition. Records show he was performing surveying work for the railroad in Montana in 1889. He wrote many letters to his wife back home in St. Paul, Minnesota. Mrs. Haskell kept her husband's letters and they are now available for researchers at the New York City Public Library. They were not well off financially and from his letters, he did not expect to grow rich and comfortable working for the railroad.

In one letter, he wrote to his wife, Haskell detailed what it was like surveying in the Northwest. "We took one blanket apiece and carried all our provisions and cooking utensils on our backs. We wore heavy dutch socks and overshoes. Our cooking utensils consisted of a frying pan, coffee pot, and half pints. Our supplies consisted of 100 lbs. of flour, 15 lbs. of sugar, 4 lbs. of coffee, 1 lb. of tea, and 40 lbs. of bacon, some baking soda and salt."(38) He went on to describe how he and his people made large biscuits from the doughy mixture and fried them over a log fire. They called these flattened biscuits 'pone.' It became a staple of the men's diet. He also shared with his wife of how "our fingers make first-rate forks, and jack-knives are good enough for culinary purposes. Our coffee mill consisted of a deer skin and an axe. We pounded the coffee in the corner of the deer skin until it was sufficiently broken up."

One other letter, written at Waterville, Washington on July 18, 1890, told his wife of his first experience at Puget Sound. "I believe the last time I wrote you a long letter I was in Seattle. From there I went to Tacoma on a steamer. We had a lovely ride on Puget Sound. It was one of those soft warm afternoons and we had a beautiful view of the city. Seattle is on a side hill something like Burlington, Vermont, only the hill rises up from the water...and there are few trees. The country was all covered with timber once but has been cleared up and very few shade trees left." He described his trip into the Cascades, aboard a Northern Pacific train on his way to Ellensburg in Central Washington. The conclusion of this particular letter to his wife is a bit personal and describes the relationship they had and their financial woes.

"I wish I could see you Pet but we can visit when we can't work. I am very glad to have a chance to work at fair wages. I hope we shall never again be so short as to be worrying when we are together as we were when I was at home last. When I am at home I would like to feel that I had not got to hurry away again to avoid starvation."

They were separated for nearly three years as Charles Haskell worked, nearly fifteen hundred miles away, to support his wife and save enough for her to join him in November of 1891 in Eastern Washington where they would finally be able to spend their lives together.

Haskell went into business for himself in Wenatchee, but later became part of the U. S. Army Corps of Engineers as a civilian employee in charge of improvement of navigation on the upper Columbia River, between Wenatchee and the mouth of the Okanogan River. Family life was wonderful, and things were looking up for the Haskells. But it all ended too suddenly when on May 20, 1895, C. F. B. Haskell drowned in the Columbia River while performing his duties for the Corps of Engineers.

By now, spring had turned to autumn, and winter was rapidly approaching. Stevens organized another engineering expedition to survey the western slope of the newly discovered pass. The surveying of the Skykomish River Valley on the west side was a disappointment to say the least. It became obvious almost at once to Stevens that there was no possible way to continue the rail route along the line on the western slope. Both Stevens and Haskell had concluded they could not stay within the 2.2 per cent grade dictated by Hill. The only possible way to continue, Stevens finally determined, would be to bore a tunnel through one of the peaks. He knew Hill would not go for the idea. It would take too long and cost too much. In addition, with the primitive equipment in those days, Stevens himself wasn't sure a tunnel would be possible. By his calculations, the tunnel (again if it could be built at all) would have to be two miles long, probably longer. He did not look forward to telegraphing his boss of the problem they were now up against.

Stevens decided to take one more look. By now winter had set in, but Stevens would not be deterred. After all, the Rockies had not stopped him, why should the Cascades? He strapped on his snowshoes and headed back up to the summit. Too much time and energy had already been spent finding this route. Stevens was determined as ever to come up with something positive to offer Jim Hill back in St. Paul.

Standing with his snowshoes, on top off the normal winter deposit of 30 feet of snow, Stevens kept staring at one particular peak. The more he looked at it, the more he could envision a series of switchbacks that would zigzag back and forth climbing, up and down that peak. Hill would go for this, Stevens knew.

James J. Hill hit the ceiling when he received the telegram from his engineer in the Cascades. Four per cent grades, and thirteen degree curves! What the hell was the problem out west? The always impatient, hard to please Empire Builder ordered his special train to take him personally out there to see for himself what was the problem. The Rockies were so easy to survey. Surely the Cascades could not be anymore difficult to conquer.

In the meantime, Stevens had already ordered the work to begin, as winter was now coming to an end, and time was of the essence. The grading was still going on when Hill arrived. He instructed Stevens to show him this thirteen degree curve mentioned in his telegram along with whatever else he had planned. Hill also reminded Stevens he didn't like having to travel all the way out her for this, and that he just simply was not happy with the results in the Cascades so far.(41) But Stevens was never easily intimidated, and took his boss on a hike to see what needed to be done to get the Great Northern to Seattle and Puget Sound as soon as possible. Hill studied the terrain, gave it some thought, and then gave his approval for the work to continue. "You could have done nothing else," he told Stevens and raised his salary from $200 to $300 a month, right there on the spot. (40)

The two of them did not discuss the eventual need for a tunnel during this meeting in the mountains.

John F. Stevens tells the next step of completing the line to Puget Sound. **"As soon as all necessary location engineering was completed, the line was put under construction, and I was given charge of it from the summit to Puget Sound. The work was completed, and the track laid over it, mostly from the west, connecting with that laid from the east. In January, 1893, at a point 12 miles west, by rail, from the west portal of the old tunnel. It is here that the last spike was driven in the line of rails which Jas. J. Hill's genius and untiring energy had stretched across prairie, plain, and mountain, nearly 1,800 miles from St. Paul to the Pacific Ocean.** (88) (Stevens mention of the tunnel, even though not yet constructed, was to give his readers a reference point where the track was completed).

Such an event as the completion of Jim Hill's transcontinental line would dictate a stupendous ceremony, with as much hoopla and fanfare as possible. It was, after all, what Jim Hill and his people had labored to long and hard for, and what Seattle and Puget Sound had been waiting for. Such was not to be, however. In fact Hill was not even on the scene when the final iron (not gold) spike was hammered down. He was back home in

St. Paul in bed with the flu. Stevens was not there either. He was doing some surveying work along the Columbia River.

Stevens stayed with the Great Northern until 1898. He felt the need for a change after his experiences in the Rockies and the Cascades. As he states in his autobiography, **"I had been working almost literally day and night for three years. I asked Mr. Hill for a vacation, but did not get it, as he said I could not be spared at that time."** (88) At that, John Frank Stevens tendered his resignation, which was accepted by Hill, but not after a verbal assault on him by the "Empire Builder" who predicted he would be back asking for his old job within a year. (57)

If the ceremony was unassuming in the mountains, it was not the case at Puget Sound. The completion of the railroad was celebrated by all the business people in Seattle and Everett. The local newspapers herald the completion of the railroad with blazing front page headlines. **LAST NAIL DRIVEN, THE GREAT NORTHERN RAILROAD IS COMPLETED,** read the banner headline on Saturday, January 7, 1893 in the Seattle Post Intelligencer.

AT THE LAST SPIKE. Jan. 6 – (special) The last spike of the Great Northern tracklaying was driven this evening, 13 miles below the summit of Stevens Pass, on the western slope of the Cascades. The only officials present were Superintendent C. Shields and Superintendent J. D. Farrell. As the last rail was brought forward by the workmen and laid in position, Mr. Shields and Mr. Farrell took the spike-manus from the spiker's hands, and with alternate blows drove home the last spike.

It was not golden, but only iron. So unpretentious was it done that the laborers, ten rods away, were not aware of it until the little group on the spot sent up a wild hurrah. Foreman Benson grasped Superintendent Shields by the right hand, and with his left hand emptied into the air, a six-shooter. The engineers took the cue, and the whistles of the great Moguls sounded and reverberated through the canyon of the Skykomish. The occasion was Thanksgiving, Christmas, and New Years combined. (69)

Photo courtesy of Minnesota Historical Society

J.H. Farrell, driving last spike to complete the Great Northern line across Stevens Pass, connecting Minnesota with Puget Sound.

Although there was plenty of snow on the ground, it was not snowing when the event occurred. Why the businessmen of Seattle and Everett were not on the scene also, is a bit of a question. It was this coming of the Great Northern to Puget Sound that would put Seattle and the other cities of Puget Sound on the map. No executives of business and industry knew this. No other enterprise then as now has had the economic impact on the growth of Western Washington as the Great Northern. It gave Seattle the financial shot in the arm it needed to become the banking and commercial center, as well as the primary port in the Northwest. It may have been the tough weather conditions that businessmen and other dignitaries expected to encounter that kept them away. However, as stated earlier, the weather was unusually mild that day in the mountains.

The great enterprise of building the Pacific extension of the Great Northern began October 20, 1890 on the cold, northernmost plains at Havre, Montana, continued westward from Spokane on July 19, 1892, and had now been completed near the summit of the Cascades. It caused Superintendent Shields to declare that Friday would always be the Great Northern's lucky day.(79)

Chapter 2:

Wellington

It was the most disastrous avalanche in terms of loss of life in the history of the United States. During the last seven days in February 1910, a crowded westbound passenger train, the No. 25 Spokane local, headed for Seattle, and the No. 27 fast-mail train, both of the Great Northern line, had been stranded at the remote railroad hamlet of Wellington, about 80 miles east of Seattle, at the western portal of the original cascade tunnel. The two trains had been kept there by a relentless snowstorm of a magnitude never before experienced by the locals. At times, the horrific blizzard dropped snow at the rate of more than one foot per hour.(83) The snow would get so deep that in order for the switchmen to move the trains around the yard, the snow had to be shoveled onto flat cars and hauled to a cliff, then dumped in the Tye Creek ravine, hundreds of feet below. For most of the train's passengers, and many others who lived at Wellington, these were the conditions they could not escape, and this is where they would spend the last week of their lives.

Named for William E. Wellington, a successful Minnesota business tycoon who greatly supported the fledgling, yet up and coming railroad baron, James J. Hill, the town served a major role in the construction of the Great Northern across the Cascades. (40) His association and influence on Hill can not be understated. William Wellington was one of the most prominent steamboat operators on the upper Mississippi when Jim Hill met him in the early 1860's. Wellington was already a popular and well established steamboat operator in numerous river towns. As Albro Martin points out, "Wellington…had endeared himself to the people of the river towns below St. Paul by rescuing a rhinoceros which had fallen overboard during a collision between Dan Rice's circus boat and the *Key City.*" He was very impressed by what he saw in Hill. Here was a young, aggressive, tough, and prudent businessman. Hill had foresight, an ability to see future opportunities where most men didn't. Wellington liked this. He tutored and counseled Hill on how to go about getting what he wanted. Wellington instructed him in the tough, hard, stubborn, and uncompromising ways of business. He gave Hill inside tips on future business ventures, such as bids for contracts so Hill had the opportunity to outbid everyone and get the contract for himself. He would write letters of instruction to Hill constantly advising him on how to get what he wanted from others. Most of these letters were marked "confidential" and Hill was ordered to destroy them after reading them. However, Hill did not destroy them all.

Jim Hill was also useful to Wellington. An example was when business began to pick up along the Minnesota River, a tributary of the Mississippi just above St. Paul. Wellington saw plenty of financial opportunities in this rich, fertile valley. When he decided it was time to put his steamship *Julia* into service in the spring of 1865, he asked Hill for assistance. Wellington needed two pilots for the *Julia*, and Hill got them by taking two pilots away from a rival steamship line.(57) His association with Hill would last the rest of his life.

Constructed in 1893, Wellington, Washington served as the western terminus for the infamous switchbacks that traversed the 5,300 foot mountain to Cascade Tunnel Station on the eastern side. A few years later, when Hill finally admitted that the switchbacks were too slow, too dangerous, and not cost effective, Wellington became headquarters for the construction of the first Cascade Tunnel.

The Switchbacks

Situated on a flat, narrow shelf between the base of Windy Mountain and a steep cliff several hundred feet above the Tye River, Wellington was constructed to host both the workers and passengers of the Great Northern at the base of the infamous switchbacks at the summit of Stevens Pass. These switchbacks were a series of legs that zigzagged back and forth, up one side of the mountain and down the other side.

The terrain that the eight switchbacks originally crossed was covered with dense forest. That was the first task for the contractor, to clear out the trees so the engineers, laborers and other workers constructing the line, could at least see each other. Much of the cut timber was then used to construct several trestles, which were used on the switchbacks. The actual work of laying the track on the switchbacks was done during the months of November and December 1892.(80)

When the switchbacks were first opened, a train of eight cars, would head up the mountain on one length of track, and then pull onto a "spur" track that was up to one thousand feet long. Later the "spur tracks" would be increased in length to handle a train of up to 23 cars. It would then begin the next leg of the journey with the pulling locomotive now pushing.

The engine that had pushed the train on the first leg was now pulling. This would continue until the train reached the summit. It was there the difficult and dangerous process began all over again, as the train descended to the other side of the mountain. In the winter, after each snowstorm, two heavy locomotives would be coupled, tender-to-tender, with a snowplow attached to the front of each locomotive. This combination would then work its way up one side of the switchbacks and then down the other side. It was a costly and dangerous operation, but it was the only way to keep transportation moving during the winter months.(80)

These trains had to travel nearly thirteen miles of track to go just three miles between Wellington and Cascade Tunnel Station. The switchbacks reached a height of 4,059 feet, more than 800 feet above the two station stops. If all went well, which it rarely did, the crossing would take from one and a half to two hours. It was a terribly inefficient way to run a railroad. These switchbacks made no sense if they were to stay in keeping with Jim Hill's belief, "maximum ton-miles with minimum train miles." (40) But his obsession of reaching Puget Sound as quickly as possible, dictated the construction of these four per cent grade switchbacks, though it made it nearly impossible to operate the line economically. Hill was already experiencing trouble with the locomotives he used to cross the 1.8 per cent grade of Marias Pass to cross the Rockies. He knew he needed larger and much stronger engines, with heavier motive power if he were to be able to cross the summit of Stevens Pass via his switchbacks. He contracted with the Brooks Works Company of Dunkirk to build the heaviest motive power locomotives possible. They developed the 26,080 pound-tractive-effort Consolidation. An engine with 120,000 pounds on drivers and others with as much as 132,000 pounds on drivers. (80) these monstrous engines should do the trick, Hill and his engineers believed. However, due to the cost of these locomotives, the Great Northern could not at the time, order enough to solve their difficulty in the Cascades.

The three and one half to four per cent grades with maximum curves of twelve per cent on the Cascade swithbacks were still a problem. The powerful new engines could haul over twenty cars across the summit, but the switchbacks had still not been extended to accommodate that many. The trains still needed to be reduced in size to seven or eight cars to cross the summit. The solution to time reduction and cost effectiveness also remained a problem. It would be several more years before the tracks on the switchbacks were lengthened to handle a twenty three-car train at one time. Even so, the expense of operations through the Cascades was still enormous. Each of these longer trains burned at least 3,000 pounds of coal to negotiate the switchbacks. The cost to the Great Northern for this operation was nearly prohibitive. In addition, under the most ideal conditions, the crossing over the eight switchbacks from Wellington to Cascade Tunnel Station took 1 ½ to 2 hours. Ideal conditions were rarely the case, however. Snow slides in the winter, rock and mud slides during most of the year, and derailments nearly all the time, could increase the crossing time up to 36 hours.

A more descriptive account of what it took for these trains to travel thirteen miles to reach a distance of just three miles helps to understand why the switchbacks were out dated as soon as they were completed. When a train reached the switchback, two 110-ton consolidation engines with fifty-four inch diameter driving wheels, and cylinders 20 x 30 inches, were coupled on, one at each end of the train. A special train crew took charge, and movements at the different switches were governed by whistle signals from the engines. Passenger trains averaged nine cars, or 350 tons, and freight trains averaged 18 cars, or 700 tons, behind the tenders. In the winter, Leslie rotary snowplows traveled in front of two coupled-together consolidations to keep the line open. They were run over the tracks as frequently as necessary to excavate the deep snow and to keep these snow cuts open and the tracks clear. (24)

One incident in particular occurred in January of 1897, when a westbound passenger train was stalled on the second leg of the switchback at Wellington for over 36 hours. The train had been stopped by a huge snow slide, and while it waited for the rotary snowplows to arrive, a larger slide came down behind the train, trapping it and everyone on board. Over two hundred workers and several more rotaries worked feverishly to free the stalled train. The snowstorm, typical on the west side of Stevens Pass, continued to build its obstreperous white blanket at a relentless pace. Crewmen measured the snowfall at nearly three feet in four hours. In addition to clearing the track (an almost impossible job in itself), the wheels of the stranded train froze to the rails.(71) The switchbacks were still a problem for employees and passengers. Second thoughts about their functionality and safety had begun. As one passenger put it, "in that one spot, on the second leg of the switchback, we spent two whole days and nights." (69)

In fact, the switchback problem was ominously foretold immediately after the Great Northern was completed in 1893. The very first westbound passenger train from Seattle to St. Paul was scheduled to leave the Seattle & Montana Depot at the foot of Marion Street at 8 o'clock on the morning of Sunday, June 18, 1893. The departure was delayed several hours, however, as the cars to make up the new train (coming east from St. Paul), were detained on the switchbacks for ten hours due to an "unexplained accident," as reported in the Seattle Post Intelligencer. All of Seattle was excited in anticipation of viewing this brand new passenger train. From all the news that came to the residents of Seattle, the train's elegance was without parallel. It consisted entirely of all new equipment, made up of first and second class coaches, a buffet car, library, parlor and dining cars, along with first class sleepers.(71) But all the beauty and luxury of the train made little difference to those stranded for hours and sometimes days in the mountains.

It took a sturdy soul with a strong heart (whether a railroad worker or passenger) to have the courage to cross the switchbacks. One of these hardy individuals was a Great Northern employee who stated, "From one end of the continent to the other, man cannot find another such piece of eccentric railroading as experienced in crossing the Cascades on the famous switchback."(80)

"The signal for starting is given. Two engines - one pulling, the other pushing - with much puffing and labor, carry the train slowly up the first grade, which rises steadily before us for nearly one half mile." This is a more detailed description of the venture on the switchbacks as expressed by another Great Northern worker. His vivid account is remarkable. "Here, having passed a switch connecting with a track leading in exactly the opposite direction - but ascending with the same steep grade - we stopped, and started backwards. The rear locomotive now becomes the 'forward one.' This was done three times ascending the mountain. Thus a track runs up the side of a mountain, where it's impossible to have a continuous line around it. The road consists largely of steep embankments, braced with logs and timber, and long, high trestles." (95)

He goes on to explain how snow sheds protect the track from "numerous avalanches" which come tearing down mountainsides in the winter. This trip over the summit between Cascade Tunnel Station and Wellington may have offered this fellow all the thrills he could stand, but the Great Northern Railway's Public Relations Department knew it had to someway convince would be passengers that they had nothing to fear.

On the GN's itinerary for travelers to and from the Pacific coast, the PR people painted a different scene. One of beauty and reassurance. From a schedule of May 11, 1898, the Great Northern Public Relations Department had printed right next to the timetable, the following:

"From Spokane, the Great Northern track leads out through the Big Bend wheat country, thence to the mighty Columbia River, with its canyons and gorges, by the town of Wenatchee, whence entry is made into the Okanogan Country. Then the way is up the Wenatchee River, with ever changing scenes, through the famous Tumwater Canyon, to and over the Cascade Mountains, via the marvelous Switchback. This is one of the most wonderful journeys in the country. The track is cut into the mountain side, and the feeling of the passenger is one of perfect security, for every precaution possible to model management is faithfully observed. The interest of the traveler flags now all the way down the west side , along dancing rivers, waterfalls, sky-piercing peaks, and giant trees, to the cities of Snohomish, Everett, where tidewater in Puget Sound is reached, and Seattle, where the train meets ships from Alaska and Asia." (83)

Translation: close your eyes and hold on! The simple truth was that the Great Northern management decided the "marvelous switchback" was only temporary. A tunnel between the two station stops was badly needed. In fact, the people at the St. Paul headquarters for the railroad went to work almost immediately after the switchbacks were constructed on surveying and designing the first Cascade Tunnel.

The First Cascade Tunnel

John F. Stevens, along with engineers Beckler and Haskell, were all disappointed from the very beginning when the boss, Jim Hill ordered the switchbacks be constructed across the pass. They all hoped he would abandon his obsession of getting to Puget Sound in such a hurry and wait for a tunnel to be built. The three of them knew a tunnel had to be bored eventually, not just for costs but also for safety purposes. In July of 1891, Assistant Engineer C. F. B. Haskell wrote, "We expect to have the tunnel located in two days or more." (38) He assumed that Hill would understand and go along with Haskell's recommendation. Stevens, the Chief Engineer of the Great Northern's Pacific Division, thought the same and submitted a plan for tunnel construction to Hill in September of 1892.

To their astonishment, he refused to consider it. He told them that the rail line to Puget Sound was still in its infancy and not yet making that much money. The cost of constructing a tunnel would be enormous. In addition, Hill was a very astute businessman and at the time, he was fairly sure he saw a nationwide economic depression on the horizon. This was no time to accrue any more debt.

Stevens, being an engineer and not the businessman his boss was, had no idea of the depression that was coming, the Panic of 1893. So he continued to argue with Hill that the switchbacks were more of a problem than what they were worth to the railroad. The most common problem was delayed trains due to slides of every kind throughout the year, and runaway trains as well. This tied up the movement of freight, costing the Great Northern a lot in revenue, and just maybe its reputation. The biggest snow slides also contained much timber and rock, so there were frequent derailments in the winter and major damage done to their trains, as well as to the very expensive rotaries and snowplows. There was also the need to keep hundreds of laborers at both Wellington and Cascade Tunnel Station during the winter months just to shovel and clear the tracks. It was a continuous job all winter long, and winter came early and stayed late in the Cascades. The cost to the Great Northern operations finally became too much, if Hill insisted on running his trains across the switchbacks. Fortunately, the Great Northern survived the 1893 depression, and by 1896, was finally making enough money so that orders finally arrive from the "Empire Builder" to begin at once to update the original 1892 plan for a tunnel.

The Seattle Post Intelligencer's edition of Friday, January 29, 1897 released the news that everyone doing business with the Great Northern was waiting to hear. **THE BIG TUNNEL**, the front page headline blazed, **THE GREAT NORTHERN WILL SOON BEGIN THE IMPORTANT WORK.** The article went on to explain, but lacked in accuracy, just what was ahead for the railroad in construction of the Cascade Tunnel.

The arrangements for building the Great Northern tunnel through the Cascades are being rapidly pushed ahead and active work on the construction may be begun almost any day. As has been previously stated in the P.I., the contract for the construction of the approaches has been let to H. C. Henry of this city, and all other preliminary arrangements have been completed. A large force of men will be employed and the work will be carried forward to completion

as rapidly as possible, as it is the intention of the company to have the tunnel ready for service early in 1898.

The tunnel will be one of the greatest engineering feats of its kind ever known in railroad history, and the cost of this construction has been estimated at $2,000,000. It is to be run in a straight line...and will have a grade of 90 feet to the mile, sloping to the west. The tunnel will be 13,283 feet in length, 18 feet in width and 23 feet high. A very large portion of this length will be driven through solid rock, and such portions, of course, will require no lining, but where ever necessary, it is to be lined with brick and stone.

In its excitement to report the beginning of construction of the much needed tunnel, the Post Intelligencer was far more optimistic in its belief of how quick and easy it would be to build the Cascade Tunnel. The article gave no thought to the difficulties of surveying, the excessive water problems (especially on the east side of the summit), danger of cave-ins, and even labor problems.

The tunnel would be bored through a mountain with two peaks. Engineers erected transit point towers, each sixteen feet high on both peaks. The length and direction of the bore were obtained by direct measurement using a steel tape measure of four hundred feet. Measurement points were marked with signs on trees, markings on large stumps, or signs driven into the earth, between the two transit points. By today's standards, this was a very crude and extremely time consuming method, but the ultimate result would make railroad engineering history.

The mountain consisted of a medium to hard granite, and the earth at the west portal (Wellington) was very soft. Gravel and crushed boulders would be used to eliminate the soft terrain problem at the Wellington end, but construction workers, once the actual blasting began, discovered that the granite would quickly disintegrate either after being blasted or drilled. This gave rise to concern as to the stability of the tunnel once trains began running through it. The engineers determined that the entire length of the tunnel would have to be lined with timber, as a temporary measure. (86)

Drainage at the east end was also more of a difficulty than first thought. The constant flow of water inside the bore needed a quick solution. To handle the water problem, a six thousand foot, eight inch pipe was built to pump the water out of the tunnel. This only helped, but did not eliminate the situation. Many times during the long winters, work had to be halted when the air valves on the pumps would freeze. Water and drainage were not a problem for those working from the west as the water was naturally carried away in side ditches down the 1.7 per cent grade.

To complete the Cascade Tunnel would take much longer than had originally planned. After all the preliminaries, actual excavation started on August 20, 1897, at both the east and west portals. Despite what the Seattle Post Intelligencer claimed in its article, the truth is the entire project was carried out completely by Great Northern employees, without any outside contractors.

Before the actual work of boring the tunnel could begin, large powerhouses had to be constructed at both portals, to house the compressors, generators, and fans. Eight 300-kilowatt dynamos (generators for producing direct current) were built to supply electricity to the camps as well as for the actual construction of the tunnel. (81)

By April of 1898, progress of construction was about one foot per day. Hoists had to be brought in to lift the rock and boulders (some weighing as much as 12,000 pounds) onto flatcars for removal. As the barricades to the building of the tunnel were systematically eliminated, and more men were added to the around-the-clock construction crews (there were 800 men working 3-eight hour shifts, seven days a week), progress increased to more than eleven feet per day. The two headings met in September of 1900. Even by today's, high-tech, computer standards, the result was when east met west, the alignment, grade, and distance errors were almost perfect. The engineers and workers were astounded to find the error of alignment to be just 0.0201 feet! Even more amazing were the error in grade, only 0.019 feet, and the error in distance, just 0.0170 feet. (22) It was consider a "perfect score." The original Cascade Tunnel was over 2 ½ miles long, with both portals being 16 feet wide and just over 21 feet high.

LAST BLAST IN GREAT NORTHERN CASCADE TUNNEL FIRED YESTERDAY, read the special dispatch in the Seattle Post Intelligence on September 22, 1900. A portion of the article is reprinted here:

WELLINGTON, Sept. 22 – The last blast in the Great Northern tunnel which pierces the Cascades was fired at 4 o'clock this afternoon.

The obstruction which separated the working gangs fell, and after the smoke had cleared away, congratulations passed between those who were on hand to witness this final performance in one of the greatest pieces of engineering work that has been entered in the West.

The last blast was set off by General Foreman A. McIntosh. The officials in charge of the tunnel present were Superintendent A. L. Andrews, Resident Engineer H. W. Edwards, and M. E. Reed, assistant engineer. John F. Stevens, chief engineer, was also present. The error of alignment was less that one-forth of an inch. No formal ceremony attended the opening.

It would still be two months before the tunnel went into operation. The entire interior of the Cascade Tunnel had to be lined with concrete, two feet thick. This work had been taking place several hundred feet behind the actual drilling of the bore, and needed a month or more to complete. Jim Hill believed that when completely finished and in full operation, the Great Northern had the finest railroad tunnel in existence. The 13,253 foot tunnel, built at a cost of about $4,000,000, shortened the track mileage between Cascade Tunnel Station and Wellington by nine miles. It reduced time and danger, the hazardous climb of some 700 feet over the switchbacks, and the increasing cost of coal. Still, it was not long before the problems and dangers of the new tunnel began to plague the Great Northern.

Wellington was more than a station stop in the mountains. It was headquarters for construction and repair of track, maintenance of equipment, a major rest stop for passengers and crew, for coal and water for the steam locomotives, and would prove to become the most important location for railway snow removal equipment in the Great Northern's Cascade division. At the time of the opening of the Cascade Tunnel, Wellington consisted primarily of barracks to house railroad workers, a dining hall and kitchen, along with a hospital, commissary, powerhouse, timber shed, a concrete plant, and a train car repair shop. Cascade Tunnel Station, on the east side of the tunnel, was similarly equipped, except for a hospital.

Railroad people of that era always considered Stevens Pass to be the weakest link in the Great Northern's iron chain from St. Paul, Minnesota to Puget Sound. Due to its precipitous terrain and severe winters, Wellington was definitely the most fragile and dangerous part of that link, mainly due to the possibility of avalanches. When the town was constructed, at the base of Windy Mountain, the fear of snow slides, in the minds of railroaders, was remote. After all, Windy Mountain was thickly covered with large evergreens, including Douglas Fir and Pine. Many of these mammoth trees had diameters over three feet at their base, and stood so close together it was nearly impossible to walk between them. It seemed at though nature had done it's very best to protect travelers and inhabitants that were to come from the danger of snow slides. After the trains started making their regular crossings of the Cascades, however, Windy Mountain quickly lost its protective foliage. Forest fires rapidly depleted the mountain slope of its enormous evergreen, primarily due to the sparks from the passing trains in the summer, when the mountains and surroundings were timber dry.

From the very beginning, Great Northern employees who were sent to work and live at Wellington considered it more of a sentence than an assignment. In fact, railroaders and their families referred to the town as "the end of the world."(96) For many, it was. Wellington quickly became, after the trains started crossing Steven Pass, the location for most of the accidents along the Great Northern's entire 2,000 mile route.

Runaway trains were constant on the switchbacks, as well as derailed rotary snowplows in the winter. These recurring mishaps maimed and killed many Great Northern workers from the start. The opening of the Cascade Tunnel in 1900 helped reduce time and distance over the pass, but not casualties to both passengers and laborers. Before the tunnel was electrified, steam trains would regularly break down inside the two and one half mile-long bore, and passengers and crewmembers would be overcome by smoke and gas fumes. A number of these accidents resulted in the death of many riders on the trains.

In those days, with the motive power that the Great Northern used, trains rarely exceeded eight miles an hour heading east through the tunnel. Its 1.7 per cent grade was a slow, steady climb through the entire tunnel. Wellington rested in the Cascades at an elevation of 3,136 feet while Cascade Tunnel Station was sat over 200 feet higher at 3,382 feet. It was a small difference in elevation, but that made it all the more difficult for eastbound trains. This slow rise eastbound brought about another problem that the designers of the tunnel failed to realize. The concrete subterranean passage was very damp due to the constantly wet rails from condensation, causing the locomotives to slip regularly on the soppy, sooty rails. Some way, they had to get the trains through faster. But the solution to getting the trains through the tunnel quicker, brought about another problem that had to be solved. They would use two or three engines to pull the train through the tunnel from Wellington to Cascade Tunnel Station. The engineering staff believed this would be the solution. However, the amount of steam power needed for this operation in the tunnel often created unbearable heat inside the train cabs. Regardless of the season, the heat inside the tunnel, generated by this approach of using more than one locomotive, caused near deadly temperatures to occur whenever an eastbound train went through. (23)

Just six months after the opening of the Cascade Tunnel, the smoke and gas fumes from a stalled train inside the tunnel, caused the death of two crewmembers by asphyxiation. A third member, not yet completely overcome by the toxic vapors, struggled out of the tunnel, only to collapse and drown in a large mud puddle before anyone at Wellington noticed. (26)

In an effort to prevent these fatal mishaps, a railroad fireman would make sure the flues (pipes or tubes through which hot steam, gas, and smoke could pass) were clean with barely enough coal on what was left of the fire in the engine to get through the tunnel to Cascade Tunnel Station. As the 1.7 per cent grade was uphill going east, this problem was almost nonexistent with westbound trains. They could, in fact, coast through the tunnel to Wellington. Regardless of all the precautions taken, however, many Great Northern workers insisted that there were too many times when the temperature inside the engine would reach 200 degrees! (24)

As mentioned earlier, the rails inside the tunnel were frequently wet with condensed steam. On a large pull, the wheels of the train's engine(s) would have little if any traction. The flames and heat, cinders and smoke from the locomotives made breathing nearly impossible. A year or so after the tunnel opened, gas masks became standard equipment in the engine cabs, but not for passengers. The Great Northern had installed in the tunnel, telephones every quarter mile, but even they were rendered inoperable by the heat, gas, and smoke. Few people, besides the workers and passengers, knew of the problem in the tunnel. But by the spring of 1901, the railway could no longer keep the perilous predicament from the public. Jim Hill sought to assure everyone, passengers and companies doing business with the Great Northern, that he and his engineers had come up with a solution to the problem. The railway would begin using "Crow's Nest" coal. It was "free of sulfur and gas-forming materials," they were told. (86) But for whatever reason, the railway never got around to using this type of coal.

The Seattle Mail & Standard, a weekly magazine of that era, was the first to take the Great Northern and Jim Hill to task. In a blistering front page article, entitled "THE CASCADE TUNNEL," the Seattle Mail & Standard of April 27, 1901 declared:

When Mr. James Hill built the cascade tunnel as a means of doing away with the switchbacks, it was clearly not in his mind to construct a mantrap. This much is self-evident; but one need not look further that the columns of the daily press to learn that the mantrap exists nevertheless.

We are certain that two, and are informed that three fatalities have occurred in the tunnel within the tunnel the past two months. In each case, several men have been overcome with gas and smoke, and fatalities have occurred.

The cascade tunnel is three miles long. Its grade upward towards the east in 100 feet to the mile. This naturally creates a steady draft of air from west to east through the tunnel, which carries the smoke backwards from the westbound train, but carries it in a body with any train going up the grade.

The trouble exists only in the case of freight trains, which cannot outrun the smoke. Passenger trains go through swiftly, and the coaches carry sufficient air for respiratory purposes during the passage. The frequency with freight trains is alarming.

As a matter of fact, all the dangers attending the passage through so long a tunnel were known to Mr. Hill at the time of the tunnel's construction. He promised a remedy, and that remedy has at all times been within his easy reach. The reason why he does not stretch his hand and take it is because it will cost him a few thousand dollars.

The remedy Mr. Hill promised in this case, electric locomotives to pull trains through the tunnel. In the absence of these, he promised to use Crow's Nest coal, a comparatively smokeless fuel. But thus far he has arranged for neither, as the repeated deaths in the tunnel indicate.

Long experience has persuaded us that Mr. Hill may trifle indefinitely with the patience of Seattle people. But he certainly cannot with impunity, take the lives of Washington citizens.

If Mr. Hill still refuses to remedy this worse than evil, then the people have their recourse. They should send him through his own tunnel on a freight train.

It would not be long after this article appeared that passenger trains would also become victims of Jim Hill's lack of follow through on his promises. One of the more well known incidents happened on February 5, 1903, when an eastbound passenger train from Seattle was stalled in the tunnel long enough for nearly all the passengers and crew members to be rendered unconscious by the smoke and fumes. A fireman on board the train was able to release the brakes before he passed out, and the train coasted backwards down the 1.7 per cent grade into the Wellington yard. In this case, no one died, but many were sent to hospitals. The tunnel urgently needed to be electrified to prevent these continuing mishaps.

Another incident that impressed on everyone the danger in this area of Stevens Pass occurred in December of 1907. Train No. 4, led by a rotary snowplow, left Skykomish for Wellington. The train and its crew were again battling another windy snowstorm rapidly covering the tracks. Even with the rotary, the going was so slow that it took nearly five hours to reach Scenic, only twelve miles to the east. There the crew argued to keep the train there and not attempt the final nine miles to Wellington. However, the trainmaster ordered them on. The No. 4 got within two miles of Wellington when an avalanche came down, blocking the entrance to the snow shed up ahead. But the rotary had already entered the shed. Throwing the train into reverse, the engineer backed the train into the snow shed from which it had just emerged. It was only in the shed for moments before another large slide came down, blocking both entrances of the snow shed. Incredibly, the train remained trapped there for ten days as the crew tried to dig it out. Finally giving up, they hiked into Wellington. It was another two days before the train could be dug out.

Just as management and head engineers of the Great Northern knew from the start that the switchbacks would need to be replaced by a tunnel, they also admitted that the completion of the Cascade Tunnel was not the answer they hoped it would be to the railways's difficulties across the summit. To prevent accidents as the one just described, electrification of the tunnel was the only answer left them. ENGINEERING NEWS, in an editorial on February 19, 1903, blasted the Great Northern for the delay in electrifying the tunnel:

There have been repeated reports that the Great Northern Ry. was to adopt electric traction for the movement of trains through the Cascade tunnel; and we trust that the recent accident in the tunnel, in which a passenger train became stalled and a large proportion of those on board were rendered unconscious by gas, will have the effect of inducing the management to take prompt action in the matter.

Engineering News, as its readers know, has maintained a very conservative position respecting the application of electricity to steam railways; and has also advised the use of fans for tunnel ventilation where circumstances favor such a system. But for such long railway tunnels as the Cascade tunnel...where the conditions prevent the use of ventilating shafts, and particularly where steep grades make necessary the use of large amounts of power in hauling trains, there can be no question that a change to electric locomotives in the only prudent course to adopt. From the accounts which reach us of the conditions on the stalled train, the railway company narrowly escaped have to pay damages for loss of life which might easily have amounted to more than the entire cost of equipping the tunnel for electric power. (27)

This was not the first time Engineering News and the Great Northern publicly fought over the tunnel's safety. In the March 14, 1901 issue of Engineering News, the editors clearly described the troubles with the tunnel as they saw them.

The operations of the Cascade Tunnel on the Great Northern Railway is said to be attended by serious difficulties, due to defective ventilation. This tunnel opened to traffic on December 15, is 13,500 feet long and the temperature is generally high at all times. A strong air current sweeps through it from west to east, and carries the smoke and gases from the engine with the train going in the same direction, with serious affects upon the trainmen. As the eastbound trains have an upgrade of 200 feet to the mile to overcome, two and sometimes three engines are used with heavy trains, and this increases the trouble. The authorities are now planning to work this tunnel by

electric power, and to generate the power, the flow of water from the tunnel - amounting to **1,250,000 gallons daily** – will be utilized. By carrying this water a short distance beyond the west end of the tunnel, a fall of several hundred feet can be secured. The original plans for this tunnel contemplated the use of electric power in operating it. (22)

Two weeks later, in the issue of March 28,1901 appeared this letter to the editor:

"Sir: I notice in your issue of March 14th, an article which says that the operation of the Cascade Tunnel on the Great Northern Railway is hampered by serious difficulties, due to defective ventilation. I will say there is no truth whatever in the statement that we are experiencing difficulties in the operation of this tunnel from smoke and gases. We are more than pleased with the results which we have achieved, and are not planning to operate it by electric power; at least not at present, and all such statements as those contained in the article in question are absolutely false. They were undoubtedly originated by some irresponsible daily newspaper correspondent, and I wish to deny them in every particular.

Truly yours,

John F. Stevens, Chief Engineer
Great Northern Railway
St. Paul, Minn. March 21, 1901 (25)

The truth was that the Great Northern engineers were already working on plans to electrify the Cascade Tunnel. They knew that the railroad could not continue to operate efficiently and safely as long as these accidents continued on a regular basis. And these accidents would continue until the eventual electrification of the tunnel. Stevens' letter to ENGINEERING NEWS was more of a public relations ploy rather that an adequate and honest answer to the concerns posed by the dangers inside the tunnel.

Not long after this exchange between Chief Engineer Stevens and the editors of ENGINEERING NEWS, the Great Northern began work on electrifying the tunnel. In July of 1909, the Great Northern accomplished this amazing task with a unique three- phase system of electrification to pull its trains safely and swiftly through the Cascade Tunnel, using General Electric and American Locomotive Company built electric engines called "helpers." This was the first and only three-phase system in America.

The characteristics of this process of electrification was distinctive in that the construction of a three phase motor, permitted it to act as a generator to bring the trains up the 1.7 per cent grade, and then return the power to the distribution system when the trains were operating downgrade. The consulting engineers to the Great Northern chose this three-phase, 6,000-volt alternating system as it had already been used successfully in Europe, especially in Italy.

Photo courtesy Minnesota Historical Society

Cascade Tunnel Station at east portal of Original Cascade Tunnel. Photo displays new G.E. built Electric "Helpers" used to pull trains through the tunnel to prevent buildup of toxic gases and smoke.

The job of designing and constructing the catenaries (the uniformly dense and thick cables that would be strung above the rail lines to power the four electric engines) was awarded to General Electric. The company would also build the four electric engines. All four would be extensively damaged in the avalanche to come. In fact, the four helpers and two of the steam engines were just about all the railroad decided to salvage after the Wellington disaster. The rest of the trains were left in the ravine.

Officials of the railway now believed that had finally solved their difficulties in conquering the Cascades regarding safety for both passengers and employees. But they had forgotten about nature, and how strongly it could and would control the tragic events that would begin in less than a year.

Wellington

Officials of the Great Northern knew they had made a mistake by sending the No. 25 Spokane Local and the No. 27 Fast-Mail trains into the mountains the last week of February 1910. The weather in the Cascades had been terrible all winter. On January 3, 1910, it was announced in Wenatchee, Washington that all westbound trains would be delayed at least two days or until weather conditions improved. All trains and their passengers would either be held at Wenatchee or returned to Spokane.

Maybe it had been these numerous days all winter long that prompted the Great Northern people to chance getting their trains through to Seattle and Everett. This particular winter disturbance was costing the line a fortune, something that Jim Hill could not, and would not tolerate. Perhaps it was their belief that the company's massive army of rotary snowplows, and the 75-men teams assigned to each one of them, could successfully battle the storms and keep the tracks cleared of slides so that their freight and passenger trains would be able to cross the mountains safely and quickly, with little or anymore delay. Whatever the reason, the fatal decision would result in a cataclysmic nightmare that would haunt the Great Northern for decades to follow.

The Northern Pacific (later to become one of Hill's lines) and the Milwaukee Road, had stopped their trains from crossing over Snoqualmie and Stampede Passes, both lower in elevation than Stevens Pass. The Northern Pacific already had one train stalled in the Cascades, and the Milwaukee Road people decided against even attempting to get their trains across Stampede Pass. The two railroads held their through-trains in the lowlands. But not the Great Northern.

Late in the afternoon of February 22nd, the Great Northern's six-car train, from Spokane to Seattle, with it's more than 100 passengers, left Wenatchee to begin its fateful ascent into the ominous weather conditions in the Cascades. It was followed one hour later by the No. 27 Fast Mail. No one aboard either trains had any premonition that they were embarking on one of the most terrifying trips by rail in the history of America. At each station stop, the crew and passengers heard disquieting reports of the unusual and relentless snowfall taking place higher up the grade. To those passengers who expressed apprehension and fear of continuing the trip, the railroad people and veteran travelers, who had made this run many times before, reassured the anxious passengers that the trip would be safe. After all, most of the trouble with snow slides, stuck trains, and derailments happened on the switchbacks which were no longer in use. The passengers were reminded of the great Cascade Tunnel that now took the place of the once dangerous switchbacks. It was a wonderful engineering marvel, built to make it quite safe crossing the summit in all types of weather. They were also informed of how the Great Northern had constructed huge walls made of rock and enormous snow sheds all along the route to protect the trains from slides. If the railroad officials had any concerns about sending the trains through, they would certainly have held them at Wenatchee or Leavenworth.

Through the blizzard and into the night, the trains finally arrived at Cascade Tunnel Station at the east portal of the Cascade Tunnel. The passengers and crew were met by a big, broad shouldered man who had worry and concern written all over his rugged Irish face. He was Superintendent James H. O'Neill, head of the Cascade Division of the Great Northern Railway. At the age of 38, he was a man who enjoyed life to the fullest. When it came to his work, he was all business. O'Neill had rightfully gained a reputation with the Great Northern as a man who gave complete attention to his duties with boundless energy, and had complete confidence in his own ability and judgment to get things done.

James Henry O'Neill got his first job with the Great Northern at the age of 14. It did not take long for him to work his way up from a track laborer, to brakeman, then conductor, and on up to yardmaster. In 1902, he became the Superintendent of the Montana Division and was transferred to head the Cascade Division in 1907.(35) In the three years that followed, he had sent more than 4,000 trains through Stevens Pass, with none of them being delayed for more than twenty-four hours. O'Neill believed he knew his division better than anyone. He knew how treacherous winter weather conditions could be every year. It was just a matter of degree as to how much of a challenge each winter would throw at him and his people to keeping traffic moving across the Cascades. But he was also completely confident in the strength and number of snow fighting equipment and the large force of manpower the Great Northern had available at his request.

Ultimately, it was James O'Neill who would be responsible for the final decision to send the two trains across the mountains to Seattle. Despite the events that were about to occur, he would always maintain that all the decisions he made during that fateful week, were the correct ones and in the best interests of the passengers and the railroad. Right now, however, as he greeted the trains at Cascade Tunnel, O'Neill was thinking it might have been best if he left the trains at Wenatchee or Leavenworth (a small Great Northern station stop that was the division point where O'Neill's responsibilities began).

It was snowing in Wenatchee when they left, and snowing even harder at Leavenworth. O'Neill and Trainmaster Harrington had so far been successful in keeping the line open through the Cascades, with the use of four powerful rotaries at their disposal. As of now, O'Neill believed their efforts were paying off, as the Great Northern's plush Oriental Limited passenger train had just recently made it safely through the mountains on its easterly journey to St. Paul. A westbound freight had reached Scenic, west of Wellington, and reported no major slides or line closures. The Superintendent was cautiously optimistic at the moment, yet was acutely aware of how quickly conditions can deteriorate in the winter. His cautious optimism would not last long. As the trains pulled into Cascade Tunnel Station, O'Neill did not know that at about the same time frightening events were taking place on the western slope of the pass. Conductor Homer Purcell and Engineer William Courtney, aboard rotary snowplow X-807, had just run into a large slide near Windy Point, a few miles west of Wellington. It was a big slide, and they were in trouble. There were not yet any shovelers assigned to their rotary. (61) Purcell, who had been working this section of the Great Northern lines for the past three years, had never been in a situation like this before. He did not know what to do.

O'Neill had just arrived from Wellington, on the other end of the Cascade Tunnel, three miles to the west, when the Nos. 25 and 27 trains arrived. Even though Wellington was such a short distance away, these three miles made a tremendous difference in weather conditions. Wellington was the first eastbound stop for the Great Northern located at the top of the western slope of the railway line. The blizzard conditions were far more severe there, as the western side of the mountains caught the bulk of the storm's fury. O'Neill knew that it was not only the snow piling up that was a predicament, but the real problem was the ice forming on the tracks. Ice, two and three inches thick had already derailed some of the rotaries. Ice would become a formidable and frustrating menace to everyone in the dreadful days ahead. O'Neill decided that the trains should spend the night at Cascade Tunnel Station, with the hope that morning would bring encouraging news from Wellington. Thinking about news, O'Neill was also wondering why Purcell and Courtney had not called in from Alvin, another station stop less than one mile east of Windy Point.

Windy Point was his biggest concern. In O'Neill's mind, that was the most likely place for a major avalanche, if there should be one, to happen. If a major slide occurred before he got his westbound trains over the hump and on their way to Puget Sound, how long would they be stranded at the summit? To add to his anxiety, neither train had a dining car. With no ability to deliver supplies, food would become quickly scarce at Wellington if they were stranded too long.

The morning of February 23rd only brought word of numerous new slides over the tracks west of Wellington. News finally arrived from Alvin that rotary-807 was stuck in a huge slide at Windy Point. Telegraphers had wired O'Neill of Purcell's plight. He was informed that crews with shovels had finally arrived to extricate the rotary. But whenever the slide was cleared from the rails, another would follow. In addition more rotaries were being trapped by snow slides. It was non-stop, backbreaking work to keep the tracks cleared. However, it was becoming obvious to all the snowplow teams that the battle with the mountain and the snowstorm was being lost.

That morning, the passenger hiked from their train through the snow to the cook shack at Cascade Tunnel Station for breakfast of pancakes, eggs, hot oatmeal, and canned fruit. (67) The food, along with the warmth of the spacious cookhouse helped to ease their nerves, if only temporarily.

O'Neill nervously paced the tracks behind his two, stalled trains. He gazed up at the steep slopes above and told the engineer of the Spokane Local, "Maybe a slide here," and pointed towards one of the peaks.(19) He was right too. A few hours later, a huge mass of snow came thundering down onto the tracks just behind the trains. In demolished a bunkhouse, killing two men sleeping inside.

The passengers were becoming anxious and asked trains officials why the delay. O'Neill, along with Conductor Pettit, walked through the cars to reassure all of them that they would indeed be on their way to Puget Sound very shortly, just as soon as the tracks were cleared west of

Wellington. But it was difficult for them to convince the passengers. The chilling fact was they were trapped. O'Neill knew it, but to avoid any panic he refused to inform either the passenger or the railroad workers at Cascade Tunnel Station. The slide that narrowly missed the trains forced him to make the decision that the trains had to be sent through the tunnel to Wellington. Entering the telegrapher's office, O'Neill was about to wire Wellington that the trains would be coming through very soon. But he was informed, before he tried to send the message, that word had been received from the Wellington side that a deep mass of snow had just plummeted onto the tracks near the west portal of the tunnel. The dispatcher at Wellington stated though the snow was deep, it contained little debris and the men were already working to clear the tracks. He also mentioned that Wellington desperately needed more men and more plows.

By now, many of the passengers were near panic, and a delegation of them confronted the Superintendent with an ultimatum to move the trains through the tunnel now! "We won't stay here trapped like this, you've got to move the trains," they told him. (19) O'Neill promised them they would all be moved early the next morning, and explained the blockage at the other end of the tunnel.

The travelers spent the rest of the day and night of February 23, 1910, nervously pondering their fate. The steep, snow covered mountains stood thousands of feet above and all around them. It was a foreboding sight indeed. But even more disturbing was the continuous, distant rumbling of avalanches that began in the late afternoon of the 23rd and could be heard and felt throughout the following night as they tried in vain to get some sleep. The constant roar of thousands of tons of snow and debris crashing down the mountains made it impossible in their efforts to get any rest.

Sixty-nine year old Mrs. M. A. (Sarah Jane) Covington, a passenger on her way home to Seattle to be with her ailing husband for their golden wedding anniversary, kept notes during the ordeal. Mrs. Covington would not survive the Wellington avalanche, but her writings which were found in her purse, paint a very vivid and descriptive picture of what it was like in the Cascades during that last week in February, 1910. Her writings are stored at the Washington State Historical Society in Tacoma. A portion of them follow:

"Feb. 23, We are snowed in at the mouth of the tunnel. They say we may be here all day, the cars are warm and very nice. The place to

get food is down about two blocks. **On board are about 130 men, 13 women with children...they do not think we will get out of here before night."**

"Thursday, 24ᵗʰ, 10:00 AM. They are clearing the snow from the top of the roundhouse, it is about 8 feet high, they say it has snowed 13 feet in 11 hours. The mountains loom up thousands of feet. Two boys get their horns and play, they keep saying the provisions are getting low and they can't get water for the trains."

(Later) "February 24 on in the mountains, the Cascades, the telegraph wires are down, no communication with the world."

Another passenger whose notes and letters help to understand the predicament and plight of those stranded in the blizzard was Edward W. Topping, a hardware salesman from Ashland, Ohio, known as Ned. Like Mrs. Covington, he would not survive the avalanche disaster either.

Prior to this tragedy, Ned's wife had died in childbirth along with their baby daughter. Mr. Topping still had a surviving son named William. Even though a baby, young William would figure prominently in the aftermath in the search for answers for what happened at Wellington. His father, Ned, was not scheduled to travel to Puget Sound. The assignment was meant for another salesman. But it was thought by his parents and his company that perhaps the trip to the west coast would help to alleviate some of his sorrows. A number of Ned's correspondence made it back to his mother and father, and some notes were found in his clothing at Wellington. His accounts are as vivid and disturbing as Mrs. Covington's.

"Feb. 23, 1910.
Dear Mother and all of you,
I wrote you last night from Spokane that I expected to reach Seattle this AM. Here I am at the summit of the Cascades snowed in since 6:30 this morning. Such a snow you never saw. It's banked up to the top of the window here and we can't go or come. Can't get any information as to when we'll get out...now 5:00PM. Have been in this spot for nearly 12 hours."(91)

On February 24ᵗʰ, Superintendent O'Neill decided that both trains had to be moved through the tunnel to Wellington. It was now past noon and he believed it was only providence that the trains had not been destroyed by the numerous snow slides the night before. Late that afternoon, he telephoned Wellington station (the phone lines had not yet been knocked out) and told the telegrapher there that the trains were on their way and to put them in the safest place possible. The telegrapher, Basil Sherlock, and conductor J. L. Pettit (who would also be killed in the avalanche) decided to place the trains about one thousand feet to the west of Bailets Hotel, at the base of Windy Mountain.

Basel Sherlock would play an integral part in the rescue. His recollections offer unique insight about the week leading up to the disaster and the rescue efforts that followed. He wrote about his experiences at Wellington in a lengthy letter to Ruby El Hult in 1960. She had been doing research of the tragedy for her book, NORTHWEST DISASTER. The book was published before Miss El Hult received Mr. Sherlock's letter to her. As a result, none of the information he provided was contained in her book. She gave a copy to this author and a copy exists at the Washington State Historical Society in Tacoma.

Sherlock and his wife were instructed to report for work at Wellington in August, 1909. He recalled immediately after arriving at Wellington, seeing the shelves carved into the mountainside that were once the Great Northern switchbacks. It wasn't long after moving in that he started hearing stories from the old timers. They told him disturbing tales about the switchbacks and the tunnel. He listened to stories of numerous accidents on the switchbacks and during the construction of the tunnel. He recalled being told of many people being killed inside the tunnel while it was being built, and that many more died after its opening. He was told how the Great Northern Railway avoided paying any liability for most of these deaths by claiming that the worker(s) who had been killed had no known relatives. This was easily accomplished, as many of the laborers for the railway were illegal aliens from Japan, who had no family in this country. The long time residents also told Sherlock that the mountainside around Wellington was covered with their graves. Whenever an accident happened that took the life of a Japanese laborer, a hole was dug and the body thrown in, then immediately covered over. There was never any marker placed where the workers was buried.

The Japanese connection with the Great Northern will be explored in depth later, but perhaps a letter between two Great Northern officials is appropriate at this place in the story. The letter is part of the Great Northern Corporate papers, housed at the Minnesota Historical Society in St. Paul. It helps set the stage for future events in the life of Japanese workers on the railroad. Written on "Great Northern Railway Line" stationary, it reads as follows:

Great Northern Railway Line.

ASSISTANT GENERAL SUPERINTEDENT'S OFFICE

Spokane, Wash., Feby. 15th, 1900.

Mr. F. E. Ward,
    General Superintendent, St. Paul.
Dear Sir:-
    Replying to your letter of the 5th inst. relative to white laborers being employed on sections on both sides of Leavenworth and at coal chutes at Cascade Tunnel and Wellington, I beg to say that the Japanese have a reputation of not desiring to get out in deep snow or during severe weather and it was thought best to not place them on section work in that particular locality until the winter is over. They can then get broken in to the weather conditions in time for next winter. I think it is not advisable to place Japanese laborers in the coal chutes s Cascade Tunnel or Wellington until the tunnel is finished and the large force of white men are moved away from those points. If we should place the Japanese laborers at either of those points under existing circumstances, I believe that the tunnel laborers would make all the trouble they could for them and perhaps it would result in intimidating the Japanese at other points.

    However, if you think differently, I will arrange to have them put on at Cascade Tunnel and Wellington. The Japanese laborers were placed handling coal at East Spokane January 22nd in place of white laborers.

                           Yours truly,
                           Mr. Downs
                           Asst. Genl. Supt.

    Mr. Ward did think differently and Japanese workers were sent to Cascade Tunnel Station and Wellington.

Photo courtesy of University of Washington Special Collections Division-Pickett 4176

Japanese laborers working on tracks of Great Northern Railway near Cascade Tunnel in early 1900's.

One day in the late 1940's, a Japanese businessman, visiting Seattle made a trip to Mount Pleasant Cemetery atop Seattle's Queen Anne Hill. He told the owner and president, Mr. William Edwards, Sr., that he wanted to visit the gravesite of a number of Japanese who helped to build the first Cascade Tunnel. He explained to the president of the cemetery that these workers were killed in an explosion when they were sent into the tunnel before all the volatile gases had escaped from the bore. One of the Japanese swung his pick ax onto a large boulder, creating a spark that set off a deadly explosion that killed all the workers inside the tunnel. Because of the great number killed, the businessman from Japan estimated twenty to thirty, and the large number of witnesses to the tragedy, the Great Northern arranged for a common burial plot at Mount Pleasant.(16) This would not be the first time that the railway would contact Mount Pleasant to handle the burial of another large number of disaster victims.

In his written reminiscences, Basil Sherlock detailed the layout of the town of Wellington as it was in 1910. For the first mile west of the mouth of the tunnel stood many of the railroad's buildings, such as the motor shed, coal dock, water tank, and the depot. Just to the east of the depot was the largest and busiest structure in town, Bailets Hotel. This was the focal point of most business and social activities at Wellington. The hotel was surrounded by a number of houses, a general store, post office, and the town's saloon. There was also Fogg Brothers, a restaurant with rooms for rent upstairs. Many Great Northern employees from Cascade Tunnel Station would travel through the tunnel to cash their paychecks at Fogg Brothers.

Sherlock described the terrain surrounding Wellington and Windy Mountain in particular.

"From the depot to one mile west of the south mountain (Windy Mountain), [which] was two thousand feet above the track, the slope of which was 60 or 70 degrees. That was where the slide came. Above the west side of Bailets the mountain tapered off from two thousand feet to where it joined the east mountain at about seven hundred feet with a slope of from 60 or 70 degree to about 40 degrees."(96)

On arrival at Wellington, the Spokane Local rested on No. 2 track, and next to it the Fast Mail on No. 3 track. The first track, nearest the base of Windy Mountain, was occupied by O'Neill's private car. There was also a fourth track that bordered s 300-foot precipice above the Tye River. Here is where officials of the Great Northern believed the trains and their passengers would be the most comfortable and safe while waiting out the blizzard and the rail line to be cleared.

On the morning of Friday, February 25th, came word from the east side of the tunnel that a terrible snow slide occurred at Cascade Tunnel Station at 4 o'clock that morning and destroyed the cook house where the stranded passengers, now at Wellington, had eaten dinner the night before. The slide killed the night cook, John Olson, and waiter and dishwasher, Henry Ellerker.(74) The news was extremely unnerving to everyone. Had the trains remained on the east side of the tunnel, they too would have been destroyed. Superintendent O'Neill's judgment to move them through the tunnel had saved them from disaster.

It was snowing hard on Friday, February 25th, and O'Neill was with one of the rotary snowplows a few miles west of Wellington. As he helped with the feverish work of trying to clear yet another slide that had come down the previous day, it was becoming more apparent that the rotaries and their crews of snow shovelers were losing the battle with nature. It was not just the snow, but the huge rocks, boulders, and evergreen trees that made it impossible to keep the tracks cleared. The chances of getting the trains through to Everett and Seattle were becoming more and more remote. Despite all his years of fighting snow slides, O'Neill had no idea of the immensity of the slide he and his men were dealing with. And this was only one of many on both sides of the summit. A front page article in the evening edition of the Seattle Times, Thursday, February 24th, graphically detailed what O'Neill and his men were fighting.

10-MILE SNOW SLIDE BLOCKS GREAT NORTHERN TRAFFIC

A snow slide 10 miles in length, extending from Wellington to a point some distance east of Alvin and about 10 feet deep has put the Great Northern in the worst predicament in which that road has found itself in years.

For three days, in unabated fury, the Cascade Mountains have been lashed by a mighty blizzard and thus far the Great Northern has expended $6,000 in a vain endeavor to clear the track and resume traffic...from all signs the blizzard may be expected to rage several days longer.

O'Neill was becoming more alarmed at what the near future held for everyone, as the storm continued to rage, and the slides continued to fall. For the first time in his experience in the Cascades, he had to consider what might happen if they all had to wait out the storm, as no progress was being made in clearing the tracks in either direction. He had more than three hundred men assisting nine powerful rotaries and snowplows. But all attempts by this large army of workmen and snow fighting equipment, thought by himself and other Great Northern officials to be the finest in the country, were proving futile. By now the storm was unbelievably fierce. Snow had been falling at the rate of three inches an hour since the previous day. O'Neill calculated that it was even heavier now. He had never been in this type of predicament, nor felt so helpless. How long would the storm last? How much coal, water, and food were left at Wellington? How much longer could they survive stranded in this tempest? Too many questions and not enough answers. This was without question the most vicious storm he had ever encountered. O'Neill ordered the rotary he was on and its men back to Wellington for more coal before another slide came down between them and the town.

Aboard the No. 25 Spokane Local, some of the passengers simply waited in numb hopelessness. Some tried to sleep in the improvised beds that had been rigged up in the coaches, while others paced the corridors in endless worry. Some stoically played cards and told jokes in an effort to keep up the courage of their fellow passengers.

Another note written by Edward Topping on Friday, the 25th helps to better glean the scene at Wellington.

"Have not moved an inch since last night, just out of the tunnel on the west side. Glad we moved from where we were though, a snow slide hit the camp about four this morning and smashed the building to kindling across two tracks and buried the night cook and waiter, think they are dead as haven't heard of their rescue. This is place where we've been eating.

Perched on the side of a mountain now, a wooded hill to my right and deep valley on the other side."
                    -Ned Topping (91)

On February 22nd, the people at the Seattle Times were aware that no Great Northern trains were leaving Seattle or Everett for Spokane and points east. The editors also knew that a number of passengers were staying at Scenic Hot Springs Hotel, as that was as far east as the trains could get. Scenic was only two miles to the west of Wellington as the crow flies and lower in elevation, but nine miles by train. They had also heard that some snowbound tourists were making the best of things in Skykomish. The reporters at the Times were curious that they had heard nothing official from the Great Northern of any stranded passenger trains on Stevens Pass, and that seemed a bit odd. The newspaper, however, had a reporter staying at Scenic Hot Springs, only a few miles east of Skykomish. J. J. Underwood would find himself to be the first, and for many days, the only reporter to reach the scene of the avalanche to come. His reports from Wellington contain some of the most valuable descriptions of what happened there, and the rescue efforts that followed.

Skykomish

Skykomish, often referred to by railroaders and its citizens as "Sky," is another town that still exists along Stevens Pass today. It also got its start in life as a major station stop and rail yard for the Great Northern Railway.

When John Frank Stevens was surveying the Cascades for what would become the original route of the Great Northern railway, he met John Maloney who had a homestead just 17 miles east of the summit. Steven hired Maloney to help his engineers with the surveying and construction of the railroad. He also advised Maloney to increase the size and development of his homestead, as Stevens could see by the location that it would become and important locale in the operation of the Great Northern.

In 1892, a boxcar was put on a sidetrack on John Maloney's homestead to be used as a depot. The new settlement was called Maloney's Siding. After completion of the line a year later, a post office was built and the town was official named, Skykomish. It was platted in 1899, and incorporated on June 5, 1909. Mr. Maloney built a store just before the turn of the century to supply the needs of the railroad workers and their families that were moving into the area.(72) It was here that for many years to come, the railroaders would spend their idle time around the old pot-bellied stove near the back and swap stories of their adventures with the Great Northern. As Brian Thompson, in his mid 90's, told Seattle Times reporter, Diane Brooks, "(in 1908) the last bag of mail was delivered on the train at 8 o'clock, and all the old liars would sit around the stove and tell stories about what they used to do." It was an enjoyable past time for the children of the town too. They would gather there to listen wide eyed at the tall tales of the train workers. The last train to stop at Skykomish in the evening was referred to as "the Dinky," as it was made up of one locomotive, one passenger car, and one baggage/mail car.

Frank Wandschneider arrived shortly thereafter and saw a need for a hotel to accommodate the large number of temporary railroad employees. Sadly, the hotel he constructed turned out to be only temporary too, as it was destroyed by fire in 1904.

On June 18, 1893, Patrick McEvoy drove the first scheduled Great Northern freight train through Skykomish. The engineer later settled in "Sky" and opened a saloon in 1897. It also rapidly became a favorite gathering place for Great Northern workers in those early years. Originally known as the "Olympian," it continued to prosper throughout most of the twentieth century under the name, "The Whistling Post Tavern."

The first permanent depot, roundhouse, coal chute, and water tank were all built in 1894. In 1922, the original depot what was built on the south side of the tracks, was moved to the north side, where it remains today. What else remains in Skykomish is the Skykomish Hotel and Restaurant built in 1905. When it first opened, and for many years to come, both hotel and restaurant were opened 24 hours a day as the railroad continued to grow and prosper. The town grew as the Great Northern grew. The hotel hosted all night card games. Poker and panguingue (pan) were the favorites of the railroad workers as they passed the time between calls to work.

The years 1922 and 1923 were years of change for Skykomish. In addition to the major chore of relocating the depot, a new hotel was constructed to replace a boarding house. The Cascadian Hotel still operates in "Sky." Many of the shacks and other run down structures that stood along the south side of the tracks, were destroyed to clean up the area. Later, a small park was built just west of the depot and maintained by the Great Northern. Today, the Skykomish Lion's Club takes care of the town's only park.

The primary reason for relocating the train depot and other railroad structures was in anticipation for the eventual electrification of the Great Northern into Skykomish, after the completion of the 7.79 mile long, 2nd Cascade Tunnel in 1929.

The first Great Northern electric engines began operating eastward from Skykomish on March 5, 1927. Trains pulled by the huge force of steam engines, used the town's new railroad yard as the western stop to convert the trains to electric power. Skykomish became one of the busiest and largest station stops in the Great Northern Cascade Division. On July 31, 1956, the last electric engine left Skykomish, as a new ventilation system was completed inside the new Cascade Tunnel. This new system allowed for the operation of diesel-powered locomotives to safely haul the largest of trains through the tunnel.

Most of the town's folk saw that this was the beginning of the end of the glory days of railroading in Skykomish. With the ventilation system installed in the new Cascade Tunnel, few trains needed to stop there. For some of the smaller trains, the use of the electric helper engines would continue for a few more years. Eventually they too were eliminated all together. By the mid 1930's, the growth of Skykomish slowed as the use of diesel power grew.

At one time, eight passenger trains a day stopped in Skykomish. These were the prestigious days of passenger train travel in the United States, and some of the country's finest trains stopped in Skykomish – the Great Northern Flyer, The Oriental Limited (the Great Northern's top of the line passenger train until The Empire Builder took its place), as well as The Cascadian and The Western Star. There was also one local that ran daily between Seattle and "Sky." It was The Dinky mentioned earlier. The last regularly schedule passenger service ended in May of 1971.

Today, about twenty freight trains a day pass through Skykomish, hauling their cargo from all over the world. Amtrak's "Empire Builder" still passes through the town, one heading west in the morning and east in the evening. It runs between Seattle and Chicago.

The business district of Skykomish was nearly completely destroyed by fire in 1970. Many of the buildings' facades, that gave a true old west look to the town are now gone, as are the steam and electric engines and rail yard that kept the town constantly buzzing with noise and activity. But for anyone who stops at Skykomish (population about 250), just off U. S. Highway 2, west of the summit, the romance of the glory days of the Great Northern still lingers, whether the traveler is a railroad fan or not.

Wellington

By sending coded telegrams (as long as the telegraph lines stayed up) to its offices in Everett and St. Paul, the Great Northern was able to keep from the outside world the plight of their marooned passengers and employees. The local newspapers did not get wind of the true situation until just three days before the disaster when the Great Northern attempted to send an eastbound No. 2 Oriental Limited across the mountains on its way to St. Paul. That was the GN's mistake. The train could only get as far as Skykomish. It had to turn around and go back to Seattle. Why the officials of the Great Northern even made the attempt is still a question. This particular incident was all that was needed to alert the newspapers just how serious the conditions were on Stevens Pass, and as mentioned earlier, only the Seattle Times had a reporter near the scene.

At Wellington, there was one other reason, besides safety, for placing the two stranded trains at the base of Windy Mountain. The location made it easier, despite weather conditions, for the passengers to walk to

Bailets Hotel for meals. By Saturday, February 26th, food supplies on the train and at the local eateries (including Bailets) were beginning to run out. In addition, coal for heat was nearly depleted. A haggard O'Neill kept sending messages to Everett over the recently restored telegraph lines. When would the snowplows (either from the east or west) break through all the slides to get the beleaguered trains and their cargo off the mountains? Did anyone know just how large and how many these slides were? The replies were always the same and frustrating. The railroad had large work forces all across Stevens Pass, digging away at the snow slides as quickly as possible. More laborers were on their way, and the extra snowplows borrowed from the Northern Pacific should soon be arriving. But there was nothing definite in any of the telegrams as to when the stranded passengers would be rescued. O'Neill was now suffering from a disturbing sense of fear and pessimism; feelings he had never had before. They were emotions had never experienced due to the confidence he always had in his own judgments and his trust in the Great Northern.

The truth was that most of the rotary snowplows were, themselves, trapped in slides and worse, some had been derailed. Those that were still operating were ineffective. They could bore through slides, making an opening of 13 feet, but that did little when faced with slides 20 feet deep.(74) Much of the tracks were covered with snow, rocks, broken trees, and other debris for miles on both sides of the summit. But nowhere was it as bad as the line west of Wellington. The weary passengers and exhausted workers would just have to wait for the storm to subside before any hope of rescue could take place.

Travelers were now getting hungry and becoming cold, some were getting sick, and the storm continued to rage. Residents of Wellington were beginning to admit they had never experienced a storm of this duration and magnitude. Word was there was now 30 feet of snow at the summit. Unbelievably, later in the day, the weather got even worse. A warm, westerly wind, called by the locals, a Chinook, began blowing causing the temperature to rise just enough for the snow to turn to rain. This event sealed the fate of the doomed trains and their passengers, as well as some of the Wellington residents.

Meals were now limited to two per day. They were out of fresh meat, eggs, milk, and butter. Saturday morning's breakfast consisted of boiled potatoes and bacon.(19) But hunger and illness were no longer the primary concerns of the passengers. It was the fear of a gigantic snow slide that would certainly destroy the trains where they currently stood. They argued with the Great Northern officials to at least move the train back into the tunnel for safety reasons.

Photo courtesy University of Washington Special Collections division

Photo by A. Curtis

Entrance to west portal of Old Cascade tunnel at Wellington. According to official Great Northern telegrams, the passenger train was in tunnel for one night, but people became fearful of being trapped if an avalanche occurred and trapped them in the tunnel. The train was moved the next morning to the base of Windy Mountain

Despite the contradictions over the years as to whether or not this ever happened, an official Great Northern telegram from Superintendent O'Neill dated March 4, 1910, to H. A. Kennedy at the home office in St. Paul, Minnesota, should settle the matter. It also gives more descriptive details of the snow slide's devastation:

H. A. Kennedy,   **Wellington, March 4-6, 1910**
St. Paul

Snow slide at Wellington extended from west (This slide 6367 ft wide) end of depot to snow shed 2.1 third shed west, portion shed two east end gone out, shed 2.1 moved some and timbers bulged – depot not damaged. Motor shed, all motors, water tank, all trolly supports and wires gone, coal chute not damaged, but sand house gone – slide seemed to part at coal chute but took everything each side. Impossible to have placed train No. 25 wither in snow shed or tunnel, <u>train was in tunnel one night</u>* but passengers complained about being in tunnel and train moved out following morning. Train was moved to this site and placed just in the clear on No. 1 track, No. 27 on No. 2. When storm began, had 35 tons coal in chute and 2 ½ cars on track – soon as we found supply was getting low we killed all the engines not needed consisting of five and took what coal they had for snow machines. Weather so severe it was impossible to accomplish anything – slide east of shed 3.3 came down three times 1500 (feet) long, twenty to thirty five feet deep this point caused about all our trouble as we cleaned it three times and it is as bad as ever now. Have wired my office to give you names of all injured those recovered and missing.

                                        J.H. O'Neill (61)

*Author underline for emphasis

O'Neill does not state what night of the week that happened, but it is easily understandable why the passengers and crew members became nervous and anxious about being in the tunnel. Even though they thought it a good idea at the time (anyplace was better than at the base of Windy Mountain), they quickly realized that a slide could also come down there, covering the opening to the tunnel. In addition, it was even colder inside the tunnel, and to keep the heat on in the train would result in smoke and gas fumes that could easily render the victims unconscious or even kill them.

Another piece of evidence that the train was in the tunnel temporarily was confirmed by Edward W. Boles of Ontario, Canada, a passenger on the Spokane Local who survived the disaster, but his brother, Albert did not. Boles account appeared on page 11 of the Seattle Times, on March 4th. He was one of the members of the second party to hike out of Wellington to Scenic. He had been there only a few hours when he heard the story of the avalanche. Boles and some others immediately began the long hike back to Wellington. He was concerned about his brother, Albert who stayed behind.

Edward Boles, after locating his dead brother, gave his account to J.J. Underwood of the Seattle Times. The story was transmitted to Everett before the wires went down again.

STRONG CURRENT OF CRITICISM AT WELLINGTON

Everett – Thurs. March 3 - E. Boles, one of the passengers on GN train No. 25, swept to destruction at Wellington, said today that there is a strong undercurrent of criticism at Wellington because the coaches containing the sleeping passengers where left in what proved to be the most dangerous position possible to find. Boles says however that the train had been run into the Cascade Tunnel for safety, the very avalanche that swept so many to their deaths having been feared by experienced railroad men; but the women begged so hard for the train to remain in the open that it was run out of the tunnel where it could have remained in perfect safety.(72)

By midday, Saturday the 26th of February, the rotaries working west of Wellington were all stuck between numerous slides. Some were off the track, some were out of coal, and the workers gave up and hiked back to Wellington. The snowplows on the east side of the summit were in the same immobilized condition. Word of the failure to clear the tracks made its way to the passengers and crew. Edward Topping's note details what they heard, and the mixed emotions hope and despair he and the other's shared.

"Saturday, noon, still here, snowing hard, report this Am that there is six miles of uncleared track, some places 30 feet deep. They are working from Seattle toward us and we may get out tonight, tho I'm not believing anyone."
                                            -Ned Topping (91)

By now many of the stranded travelers were so agitated and fearful that they directly confronted O'Neill about what he was going to do regarding their safety. He told them the trains were in the safest part of the railroad yard at the base of Windy Mountain. It was a place where no snow slide had ever occurred before. There simply was nothing else that could be done until the storm let up. The superintendent had one other concern too.

Most of the snow shovelers were quitting. They were exhausted, hungry, had not yet been paid, and were (like everyone else) very nervous about their safety.

On Sunday, February 27th, the Wellington nightmare became more severe. It was no longer just the passengers, but everyone in town was talking about the probability of a monstrous avalanche. Windy Mountain and many other peaks surrounding Wellington, had been devastated by a large forest fire a few years earlier. Although it was true that no snow slide had ever taken place in the area that O'Neill had told the passengers the day before, there was no longer the huge forest of trees to help hold the build up of snow in place in the event the earth moved.

Very early that morning O'Neill entered telegrapher Basil Sherlock's office with a stack of messages to be sent immediately, but Sherlock had more bad news for the distressed superintendent. "Sorry," he told him, "the wires are down again. No messages coming in or going out."(19) Wellington was completely isolated from the outside world. O'Neill thought for a moment and the decided that someway, somehow, that he a some volunteers would hike to Scenic Hot Springs Hotel, four miles from Wellington as the crow flies, but nine miles following the rail route. He should be able to get his telegrams sent from there, and also find out how rescue efforts were coming along.

Moments after O'Neill left the office, Sherlock noted, "I saw a snow slide come down the mountain to the north, just west of the old switchback, in a place that they never had a snow slide before. It was the first snow slide I had ever seen and became alarmed. I told dispatcher Johnson about it and that I thought the trains were in a bad place." (96)

Dispatcher Johnson did not respond, but handed Sherlock a message that had arrived shortly before all the lines went down. It was from G. W. Turner, chief train dispatcher for the Great Northern at Everett, Washington. Regarding train No. 25 (the Spokane Local), it stated, "Use your best judgment and get your train into a place of safety." (61)

After reading the message, Sherlock set off to find Conductor J. L. Pettit, assigned to the No. 25 Spokane Local. At that time, Pettit was in a heated conversation with a number of his passengers in the Wellington depot. Sherlock found Pettit in a matter of minutes and described his discussion with the conductor:

Not wishing to get the passengers excited, I called Mr. Pettit away from them, giving him the message. Then I showed him where the slide on the mountain to the north had come down. We both walked down the track to the west and looked up the mountain to the south. Mr. Pettit said, "This is putting it right up to me, if I do not move the train and they have a slide, I will be to blame for it, and if I do move the train and they do not have a slide and I use up all the coal we have moving the train, and they have to cut wood to keep the train warm, I will be to blame for that." I suggested to Mr. Pettit they move the train back to just clear of the tunnel. The last rotary had died on the main track between Wellington and Scenic, there was no reason why we could not block the main track.(61)

While their discussion was going on, O'Neill had succeeded in organizing a hardy group of men who were willing to risk almost certain death hiking to Scenic Hot Springs Hotel, a journey of nearly ten miles and a drop in elevation of more than a thousand feet. Many of the train travelers and residents of Wellington pleaded with them not to go as the constant rumbling of the snow slides' horrible groaning continued to increase. They believed the expedition was hiking into what one of the passengers called, "the jaws of death." (66)

Nevertheless, O'Neill felt the risk had to be taken, as he was responsible for all the passengers and crew on both trains. After all, it was on his orders that all of them were now stranded in this nightmarish place. At nine o'clock that morning, Sunday, February 27th, O'Neill and his party left the besieged hamlet to try to make their way to Scenic. He was accompanied by G. W. Loveberry, a pioneer resident and horseman from Georgetown, then a suburb of Seattle, Jesse Wilder, a fireman with the Great Northern, a former member of the Washington State House of Representatives, L. C. Joseph of Colville, Washington, M. L. Horn of Wenatchee, Washington, J. Edward Rae of Spokane, and R. A. McLean of Leavenworth, Washington.

They quickly started their journey westward in the blinding snow, down the tracks toward snow shed 3.3 that stood 2,000 feet straight up the mountains above Scenic Hot Springs Hotel. The hikers had not gone far before they were made aware of how perilous their journey would prove to be. They first encountered a number of trainmen and linemen who were struggling to restore the telegraph wires from Wellington. At first, the railroad people thought the hikers had come to help them. When O'Neill told them of their plans to reach Scenic, he was told by the trainmen that he was crazy if he thought they could get to Scenic safely. The only way possible to reach the hotel would be to slide someway straight down the 2,000 foot embankment, and that would almost guarantee the death of all of them. They continued anyway.

After leaving the men repairing the communications lines, a gigantic segment of snow broke loose just above them with a deafening roar. They had still not reached the snow shed. It swept Jesse Wilder down the side of the mountain and out of sight of the terrified party. Believing the Wilder was killed outright, O'Neill and the others continued on, dodging fallen rocks and boulders, and barely escaping smaller slides until they finally reached snow shed 3.3, just above the hotel. The entrance to the shed was nearly completely sealed by snow nearly fifteen feet high. Slides were rapidly coming down all around them now as the men made their way into the snow shed. Fortunately there was enough of an opening near the top of the shed and just below the roof for them to crawl through. They quickly discovered a hole in the roof and climbed onto the top of the snow pack. As G. W. Loveberry later explained, "The top of the snow was not frozen hard and the prospect seemed like courting death if we slid to the canyon 2,000 feet below. But that was the only way, to my mind, and O'Neill agreed with me." (72)

At this point, they were all frozen with fear. At times, they could see below them the warm, inviting hotel through the snow, yet it seemed impossible to reach. But, they were also emotionally overwhelmed by the continuous sights and sounds of the slides all through the mountains. Regardless of the physical condition they would be in, when and if they arrived at the hotel, all of the men dived into the depths below. One way or another, they decided their nightmare would finally be over.

"We fell, rolled, slid and tumbled down the mountainside for nearly 2,000 feet," according to Loveberry. "Occasionally sinking a little way under the pack, running against tree tops and stump tops, but luckily landing in the creek bed, without a broken limb."(72)

All the members of the party collected themselves, finding it almost impossible to believe they had survived the fall. O'Neill, however, was thinking about the fate of Jesse Wilder. There might still be a chance he was alive. The superintendent said he would give $1,000 to anyone who would climb back up the slope to see if they could find Wilder. But J. W.

Merritt, a 6 foot, 2 inch tall, large muscular man looked O'Neill in the face and tersely told him what he could do with his offer. Looking back up the mountain, Merritt told O'Neill, "I'm a poor man, but I wouldn't try to get back up there for all the millions of Jim Hill's money, and if he gave me a week to do it!"(72)

They arrived at Scenic at about one o'clock in the afternoon and were beginning their walk to the hotel when Jesse Wilder, whom they had all given up for dead, appeared about one hundred yards away, walking down the creek bed, very much alive and apparently unharmed. They could not believe it and one of them mumbled, "It's a miracle."

Superintendent O'Neill immediately began to organize rescue parties, explaining what was happening at Wellington. He told everyone at Scenic of the horrendous conditions there and the needs of all the stranded people, passengers and residents alike. There was an urgency for food and every kind of necessity at Wellington. After describing the ordeal just up the mountain, O'Neill boarded the one rotary that was still working between Scenic and Corea, the next station stop east of Scenic.

Scenic Hot Springs Hotel

Photo courtesy Museum of History & Industry, Seattle

Photograph of original Scenic Hot Springs Hotel in 1908, taken from upper tracks of the Great Northern Railway. Here is where the parties that hiked out of Wellington slid 2,000 feet down to the hotel to get help.

The hotel where O'Neill and his companions had safely arrived was, at the time, one of this country's finest hot springs resorts. It had been open only about one year, as it had replaced the original Scenic Hot Springs Hotel that was built in 1904, but destroyed by fire in December 1908. It was the center of all activity in the town of Scenic (originally called Madison), one of the larger station stops for the Great Northern.

When the first hotel opened, it was nationally praised as one of the most unique institutions of its kind in the world. At the turn of the century, it certainly was one of the finest, upscale, and exclusive resorts anywhere. The three story, green and white structure was constructed in the midst of towering mountain peaks, nearly 3,000 feet above sea level. The beauty of the resort's setting was unquestionably the primary lure for people who wanted to get away for a vacation filled with the activities of those days. It's proximity to Puget Sound also made it ideal for people to spend merely a day or two for bathing in the natural sulfur hot springs.(94)

Indeed, it was the hot springs that brought people not only from Puget Sound, but from across the country and around the world. It was always a popular belief that the springs held healing properties that were good for just about anything that ailed a person.

Water from hot springs emerge naturally from the ground at a temperature that is at least several degrees above the ambient mean temperature.(20) Simply put, the temperature degree of the water is higher than the air temperature of its surroundings. These springs, such as the ones at Scenic, have been used for medicinal purposes since ancient times. The water percolates downward and comes into contact with hot rock and is heated by it. Places where this phenomenon occurs are in active volcanic regions, which certainly apply to the Cascade Mountains of Washington State. As the water heats and circulates underground, it often dissolves its host rocks, becoming highly mineralized. (13) This is what many people believe gives the springs its therapeutic powers.

Mr. J. V. Prosser knew all this and realized that a first-class hotel, situated in the beautiful Cascades, with the unique hot sulfur springs, would make him a very rich man. He would build his hotel there, and keeping with the social and political climate of those days, offer the facilities to only the elite, those of upper class standing. He said he would, "carve here in the wilderness, a spot where the weary may find rest, where the sick may get well, and where the nerve-strained person of the outer world may find the balm and coolness, in the whispering of the breeze and the murmuring of the waterfall, quietness and healing."(94)

Unlike the majority of hotels with these unique waters, Scenic Hot Springs was extremely exclusive. There was no public bar, gambling was absolutely prohibited, and people of "doubtful character"- in Prosser's mind – were simply barred from his establishment. The better element of society, in those days, and who would frequent the resort, hardly supported Mr. Prosser's restrictions and requirements. And it was not long after the hotel/resort opened that it became necessary to write months in advance to reserve accommodations.

Scenic Hot Springs Hotel itself was first rate, furnished in solid oak with rooms to accommodate 100 guests at a time. It was as modern a facility as it could be for its era and location. The building had electric lights, steam heat, call bells, and what many considered the best dining room service of any hotel in the Pacific Northwest. Besides the hot springs, Mr. Prosser's resort offered a beautiful gymnasium, billiards, lawn tennis, basketball, handball, croquette and other games of sport. During the year, it also periodically provided its guest with live entertainment. A visitor to Scenic Hot Springs could expect to pay $2.50 to $3.50 per day or $15.00 on up, per week.

In the early 1900's, a person traveling from Puget Sound to Scenic, would step from their Great Northern train, only 200 feet from the hotel entrance, into an entirely different climate, no matter what the season. It was a rarefied atmosphere which people of that era believed was a far better tonic, or bracer found on prescription shelves in their local drug store.(5) Vacationers would return home to eagerly tell their family and friends of the inspiring scenery, the trout stream that ran just behind the hotel, and the "balsam scented air, blown by the breath of glaciers."(72)

There were hiking trails through the thick, dense forest that surrounded the hotel. Many a city dweller took advantage of these beautiful, but at times, strenuous hikes. The most famous walkway from the hotel was through a crevice in the mountains behind the structure, which ended at an abandoned log cabin that once had belonged to some unknown mountaineer. It was said that on the walls of that crude hut, one could find engraved, the names of the most prominent citizens (political, social and business) in the Northwest.

Another one of the more popular strolls was called Surprise Falls, for an obvious reason. It was one of the shorter trails, extending only one mile from the hotel, formed by the wild animals that inhabited the hills around the resort. It twisted and wound its way under gigantic fir trees whose overhanging branches formed a sort of canopy so dense that the sun never got through to the ground. The trail was carpeted with pine needles, inches thick. But the beautiful stroll ended in a surprise when the unsuspecting hiker found himself or herself face to face with a sheet of water that roared and tumbled down over a rough faced cliff, a sheer drop of over one hundred feet.

For the bold and very daring, directly above this waterfall was a stiff mile climb up one of the steepest parts of the Cascades. Here was the foaming sulfur hot springs that burst out from beneath a gigantic rock, and was piped down the mountainside to the hotel a mile and a half away. (The staff kept the sulfur springs baths at the hotel at 130 degrees).(5) The climb to the origin of the springs was extremely difficult, and very few people made the attempt. Part of the way, it was necessary to hold onto ropes and wire cables to keep from falling down some gruesome gorge. But once one got there, the successful climber was rewarded with an indescribable and incredible view of the evergreen covered peaks and pinnacles, the valleys, lakes and streams of the majestic Cascades. From up there, hikers said the hotel looked like a dollhouse.

If that experience was not enough for the venturous climbers, they could still climb higher to a lake that Mr. Prosser and others afforded the best trout fishing anywhere in North America. It was said to be even better than the fishing at popular Deception Falls, one mile below the hotel.

Everyone agreed Scenic Hot Springs Hotel was a first-class operation in every way. One of the finest hot springs resorts in the world. As reported by the editor of the Seattle Mail & Standard of August 4, 1906, in an article called "AN IDEAL MOUNTAIN RESORT:"

Two days spent amid the delightful scenery of Scenic Hot Springs – and we did not go there for the hot springs either, but for the shade, the marvelous glory of the mountains and valley, the wonder of sunset skies, the thrilling music of murmuring pines and cedars and waterfalls – flashed by all too quickly as a panorama of beauty seen on swift passing trains, but we lived weeks in these few days. Scenic Hot Springs must be seen to be appreciated. (86a)

But that all came to a temporary end when on the evening of December 8, 1908, Scenic Hot Springs hotel caught fire and sadly burned to the ground. No one was killed and only one guest was injured, but the internationally acclaimed grand hotel of the Cascades was now gone, and almost everyone there lost all their personal belongings. At the time of the fire, the hotel building was valued at $50,000 with furnishings at nearly $35,000. Joseph V. Prosser was badly burned trying to save some of his valuables. He and everyone else were put aboard a Great Northern freight train and taken to Skykomish for hotel accommodations. (72)

The handsome three-story, green and white structure had vanished, but Prosser would rebuild the hotel the following year, this time designed as an enormous Swiss chalet. It was built on a scale that far exceeded the original mountain edifice. It would continue to offer all who came there, the same amenities and respites for which it became famous. The second and largest Scenic Hot Springs Hotel would last less than two decades. It was demolished by the Great Northern Railway in the mid 1920's to make was for the building of the New Cascade Tunnel. But before this took place, the hotel would play a major role in the avalanche disaster still to come.

Chapter 3:

Wellington: The Avalanche

Early in the evening, Sunday, February 27th, the telegraph wires were once again working at Wellington, but no one could tell for how long. Basil Sherlock immediately wired the dispatcher in Everett his prophetic concerns.

"If we get a Chinook wind, the whole town of Wellington is going to hell."

Sherlock's worst fears came true almost immediately after sending this message. The westerly winds did indeed pick up, and with them a rising temperature. The snow quickly turned to rain. But within a few hours, the Chinooks died down, the temperature fell, and the snows returned. The situation now at Wellington could not have been anymore dangerous. As the temperature fell below freezing, the rain that coated the twenty feet of snow that barely clung to Windy Mountain turned to ice, and was now rapidly being covered over by more snow, again falling at an estimated two inches per hour. It was another blizzard. The tracks were again obliterated from sight and the few laborers who stayed saw no reason to attempt to clear the rails. Twenty feet of packed snow, blanketed by a sheet of ice with new snow covering it, clinging to the side of a mountain with no forest to help keep it all in place, transformed Windy Mountain into the precipice of white death in the Cascades.

The few snowplows that remained at Wellington were no longer useful for anything, as Basil Sherlock states in his memoirs. "The coal situation was the key to the whole thing. All the snow fighting machinery had died on the main track for the lack of coal." Even with an adequate coal supply, the rotaries were rendered immobile by the relentless snowstorm. The final decision as to where the two trains and their passengers would remain (at the base of Windy Mountain) was now out of human hands. Nature had determined their fate.

Mrs. M. A. (Sarah) Covington's last letter, written from her stranded coach was addressed to her daughter back in Cleveland, Ohio. It is dated the 27th of February, 1910 and states:

"No one can tell anything about when we will get out. Some are in deadly fear that another landslide will come down on us. We can hardly see the tops of the mountains, they are so high. Six or eight men worked all day cleaning the snow from the roundhouse, the snow was higher than their heads…a man just came in who has been talking with a woman who has been here 17 years who told him that a land slide had never occurred here. I can't send this yet, you know, but will when the train goes."(96)

Sometime between 7 and 8 o'clock that evening, the telephone between Wellington and Scenic was temporarily restored. Trainmaster A. R. Blackburn hurried into Basil Sherlock's office and got in touch with Superintendent O'Neill at Scenic Hot Springs. He informed O'Neill how vehemently the passengers were complaining of their perilous situation. Some of them were threatening to leave the train and the town to make the dangerous hike to Scenic. Even if the tracks could be cleared, and that was a big if, and many of the shovelers had quit and walked through the 2 ½ mile tunnel back to Cascade Tunnel Station (they knew it was a losing battle and had still not been paid), the railroad would have to use what little coal was left to back the No. 25 closer to the tunnel. O'Neill was aware of the impossibility of moving the train(s). He told Blackburn to focus his energy on keeping the passengers as calm as possible and to prevent them from attempting the trek to Scenic. According to Sherlock, Blackburn failed to inform the superintendent of the slides that had been descending the mountainous slopes all day. As he described it, "Some of the slides broke off large trees [that remained] like pipe stems."

To his final days, Basil Sherlock always regretted not calling O'Neill back and telling him his thoughts on the whole precarious position they were all in. He was never one to mince words or never afraid to voice his opinions to anyone, whether they were his superiors or not. Sherlock later wrote:

"It appeared to me they were taking a chance, while I was not positive a slide would come where it did, to me it was apparent it could, and every operating rule book of every railroad in the country referred to SAFETY first, last, and always, while the most quoted rule in the book by all railroad men was 'In case of doubt, take the safe course.' "(96)

In Sherlock's mind, there could still be rounded up enough people in town to clear the track so as to at least back the Spokane Local away from the base of Windy Mountain. He was convinced that any jolt to the mountain would result in a horrible catastrophe, and in the current weather conditions, this could now happen at any moment. But the real reason, as far as he could ascertain, as to why the Great Northern people did not move the train, was coal. There simply wasn't much left. The little that remained was needed for the rotaries. The GN officials were still hoping the storm would let up any time and they could then clear the tracks in both directions so more coal could be brought to Wellington. "The coal issue was the key to the whole thing," said Sherlock. "Had we had coal, the snow machinery would have been able to keep working and the railroad opened, and possibly the passenger train would have been out of Wellington before March 1st." In this case, his observation was wrong. The immensity of the storm, the number and enormity of the avalanches, was simply too much for the railroad and its army of men and snow fighting equipment. Certainly there had been storms, bad storms in the winters before 1910, but this was one for the record books. Basil Sherlock could not have known that at the time.

Monday, February 28th, brought a number of small slides the once more brought down all the telegraph wires to once again isolate the hamlet. Considering everything that had been happening, or more precisely, what had not been happening, it was a fairly quiet day. Men were appearing at the portal of the tunnel after walking the 2 ½ miles from Cascade Tunnel Station and told the Wellington captives that they had heard rumors that the Great Northern was desperately trying to rent all the snow fighting machinery they could from other railroads, but were finding it nearly impossible as all the other lines were fighting their own battles with the blizzards raging throughout the other passes in the Cascades. At Wellington, the weather conditions on Monday changed almost every hour. It would snow for a while, then turn to rain, and then once more back to snow. All had been stranded on the summit for nearly a week now and still there was nothing to do but wait and hope.

One longtime resident of Wellington wandered into the telegraph office simply for conversation. After a bit of small talk, the topic turned to avalanches; after all, that was what was on everybody's mind. He explained the difference in slides to the telegrapher. There were sliding slides," he said, "and then there were rolling slides."

The way he described them was, "a sliding slide was when the snow would just start moving down a mountain, and nothing could stand against it. Only snow sheds built strong enough, embedded into the side of the mountain could withstand the slides while they passed over the top of the sheds. When the snow was wet and sticky, the limb of a tree, being weighted down with snow could give way, dropping the snow which would start to roll, picking up more snow as it rolled, the width spreading from both ends as it [continued] to roll."(18)

As the old timer continued his story, it reminded Sherlock of the first snowfall he had experienced at Wellington. That first storm dropped more than three feet of snow in the mountains before it turned to rain, which froze on top of the snow. He recalled that when a person walked anywhere on the mountainside, it seemed as if they were walking on cement, this ice on top of the snow was that thick and hard. The next snow continued to fall for days, leaving up to an additional fifteen feet of snow on top of the ice that blanketed the original three feet of snow. It seemed so unstable. As his friend continued his observations, Basil Sherlock looked out his office window at the mountains and no longer wondered if, but when the disaster would strike.

John Rogers, a real estate salesman from Seattle was among the passengers aboard the Spokane Local. Friends and relatives would describe Rogers' demeanor as cool, calm, and composed. His fellow travelers thought so too. But today, Rogers was rapidly losing his composure. What particularly unnerved him was how the surface of Windy Mountain had changed since they had arrived. He wondered if anyone else had remembered how the steep mountain looked only five days ago; how the tops of a few trees and some large stumps protruded sparsely through the snow. On this day, however, the mountain's appearance was terrifying to Rogers. It now looked as if an enormous, smooth, white blanket had been draped over it as there was no longer any sight of the trees and stumps. The amount of snow that had fallen over the past several days was enormous. How much more could the mountain hold, he wondered?

He was an active individual, who did not care for this isolation and nothing to do. He walked over to Bailets Hotel for some exercise, and after reaching the porch heard the now too familiar rumble of another slide. But this one was louder, and closer, a terrible roar. Turning to the northeast, he saw to his horror, a hillside give way, and gazed in awe of the hill's white cover simply rolling down its side. Then came the snapping and cracking sounds of what were left of the woods that still grew out of the hillside, but nearly buried beneath that white blanket. Rogers decided then and there he would get some other men together and follow O'Neill's party to Scenic. He succeeded in organizing a company of ten other fellows, four of whom were Great Northern employees, including Conductor J. L. Pettit. The eleven left Wellington for Scenic at about noon on Monday, the 28th of February.

They had not traveled far before they were confronted with the enormity and devastation of the blizzard. Incredible as it seemed, the conditions were worse than at Wellington. They found it almost impossible to follow the tracks of the railroad, as they were completely covered with snow. There were slides everywhere they looked, and hiking in these conditions required far more physical and mental stamina than they expected. It was now raining once again, and with each step they took, they sank either up to their knees or waists. Pettit was not sure he could make it to Scenic, and if he did, he was positive he could not make it back to the rescue effort that would be going on at Wellington. Not in these conditions anyway, he thought. Pettit gave instructions to the hikers of what to tell the people at Scenic Hot Springs Hotel, and then he turned to make his way back to the No. 25 Spokane Local at Wellington. He was met by many nervous, fretful, frightened, and nearly terrorized passengers. They had always liked Pettit, regarding him as the normally warm, pleasant person he was. Maybe they could convince him, now that O'Neill wasn't around, to somehow move the train eastward. Just enough to get it away from the base of the snow covered, steep peak that towered above them. Anyplace was safer than where they were now. Conductor Pettit simply replied with a haughty pose of exhaustion, "I'm not in charge, I have no authority."(48)

Just about all the track workers and shovelers had quit, and had taken their chances by hiking out of Wellington in both directions. The passengers were also angry and demanded a meeting as soon as possible with whatever Great Northern officials that were still left in town. They felt deserted by the railroad, and to some extent that may have been the case.

Forty-seven year old Edgar Lemman, an attorney from the town of Hunters, Washington spoke to Earl Longcoy, the nineteen year old secretary to J. H. O'Neill. It was a strange conversation as Lemman badgered the young railway official as to why they had not moved the train to a safer location. The lawyer went on to list how terrible the conditions were, in a sense answering his own question. All that Longcoy could do was listen. He too had no authority to do anything regarding their safety. Both men would be killed in the avalanche only hours away.

As darkness fell, everyone in town and aboard the trains were nerve-wracked by the constant flashes of lightning, which would eerily light up the snow-clad mountains that loomed all around them. It must have been a horrific sight, the total darkness, and then the illuminated sight (for only an instant) of the jagged peaks towering above. The jagged peaks that had held all of them prisoners for nearly one week. Then came the crack and pounding of thunder, and in the distance, the terrifying roar of slides. For many, this would be their last night alive, and for all the night was filled with great emotional turmoil and mental torture.

Later that evening, Basil Sherlock headed for his home. It was raining hard now and he was seriously considering where the safest places in town would be when the avalanche hit. Of course there was the tunnel, and as he looked around at the mountains, he decided that the Great Northern's bunkhouse, his own home, and any other structures on the eastern side of Wellington would be the mostly likely to survive the snow slide that was bound to come down at anytime.

It was just before 10 o'clock that night that Sherlock arrived at his house. He noticed that the snow on its roof was about a foot deep. Upon entering the house he told his wife that they would remain there until the snow started sliding off their roof, he would then "gather up what clothes they could carry and beat it for the tunnel."

Sherlock and his wife never got the chance to get to the tunnel. At 1: 45 on the morning of Tuesday, March 1, 1910, it happened! The entire side of Windy Mountain, towering two thousand feet above the town and trains, gave way and tens of thousands of tons of snow, boulders, trees, and other materials slammed into the No. 27 fast Mail and the No. 25 Spokane Local. The monstrous slide hit with such force that it tossed the trains high into the air, as if they were but toys, and then threw them down hundreds of feet into the ravine below Wellington. The avalanche tore open the cars as if a can opener had been used, hurling their occupants in all directions. There would be few survivors.

From the tremendous roar and earth movement, Sherlock knew immediately what had happened, he then heard somebody outside screaming, "Everyone up, the trains have gone." He and his wife headed for the bunkhouse, as he figured that was now the safest place in town. On his way, Sherlock stopped to wake up the electricians and engineers who were sleeping in their buildings. It was incredible, he thought, that anyone could possibly be asleep after what he had felt and heard. He also noticed while heading toward the bunkhouse, the lights coming on at Bailets Hotel and Fogg Brothers Restaurant. It was only a matter of minutes after the disaster that all those in that part of Wellington who had been spared by the avalanche, were awake. The scene of the destruction that had just happened put many of the residence in shock. Most were finding it hard to speak. The sound and sight of the avalanche was far more terrifying than they had imagined it would be.

Charles Andrews, Bob Miles, a gentleman named Flannery, and Sherlock huddled in a corner of the bunkhouse to quickly determine what should be done. It was obvious by the colossal size of the slide that everyone aboard the trains were all buried in the snow, as they saw through the night, nothing but one continuous blanket of white where the trains and some of the town's buildings once stood. Maybe some had survived, they thought. But how far was the wreckage scattered? How far down the ravine had the destruction carried everything? How deep in the snow were the victims buried? And could there possibly be any survivors? The four decided there was no more time to waste on these questions. Regardless of the conditions at what was left of Wellington, they had to begin right away to find the wreckage and hopefully some survivors.

Andrews knew there was a shovel over at the depot, which just missed being destroyed by the avalanche. He thought there possibly was another at Fogg Brothers. However, most of the tools they needed to rescue the victims were swept away in the avalanche too. The temperature was beginning to rise slowly, gradually turning the snow to rain. It was now nearly impossible for anybody to see anything or anyplace.

By now, others had joined Sherlock and his group. They determined time was of the essence and starting hiking toward the slide area. Sherlock was the last to leave the bunkhouse and called back to the women that the rescue party would bring back to them what survivors they discovered. The bunkhouse was made up of two large rooms with a smaller middle room, and the women began to arrange all of these rooms in order to accommodate whatever patients might be brought there.

As Basil Sherlock stepped outside, Trainmaster William Harrington showed up. He had gone down in the avalanche, he told Sherlock. Harrington was bleeding from the head and was very unsteady on his feet. Sherlock caught him before he fell and helped him into the bunkhouse. They had received their first casualty. He told Sherlock, "Don't go down there. Stay here and help take care of the injured." Watching the wives making up the beds as fast as possible, he realized they had no bandages, and they were certainly going to need plenty of them.

More residents were starting to come and go at the bunkhouse, creating confusion in their attempt to prepare for the injured that would be arriving at any time. Sherlock found a brakeman and instructed him to make his way to Bailets Hotel and bring back as much bleached cotton and bedding as he could carry. Not long after he left, the brakeman returned and informed Sherlock that Mr. Bailets has a gun and was walking up and down in a menacing manner in front of his hotel and store. He had told the brakeman that no one was getting anything from his establishment without money up front.

At that point, Basil Sherlock nearly lost his head, telling the brakeman to stay in there and assist in the bunkhouse. Sherlock started his journey through the rain to Bailets Hotel with the thought of "sticking the barrel of his (Bailets') gun down his throat and pulling the trigger."(96)

"My wife brought me back to my senses," he recalled, telling him not to do anything irrational. When he finally arrived at the hotel, Sherlock yelled at Bailets, asking him what was the matter with him anyway? Wasn't he aware of what had just happened and how horrendous the situation was? Bailets responded he was only trying to protect his property.

This response infuriated the telegrapher. "You're going to have a hell of a time doing it," he hollered at the innkeeper. "We're going to have another slide any minute, and your property, the depot, and Fogg Brothers will all be down in the canyon covered with snow, and when looking for you, I hope we don't find you."

Mr. Bailets changed the subject. Now he wanted to know if they planned to bring any of the injured to his hotel. Sherlock told him no, as his place was not safe. Just then, the door to Fogg Brothers opened and three or four men came running out and headed for the hotel. Bailets quickly locked the door and said nobody was getting anything from him until he was guaranteed it would be paid for. Basil assured him that the Great Northern would pay for everything. Bailets wasn't sure he could believe that. He handed Sherlock a piece of paper and told him to write down the names of every Great Northern official at Wellington. Bewildered by this behavior, Basil wrote the names of everyone he could remember, thinking that perhaps Bailets was in some form of shock and not thinking straight.

Mrs. Bailets finally appeared and, and being far more accommodating than her husband, gave Sherlock all the unbleached cotton and sheeting the hotel had available. He then spotted a number of raincoats hanging near the entrance and took them all to give to the men of the rescue party. He then ran back to the bunkhouse with the cotton and sheeting. The women immediately started tearing the material into bandages while Sherlock washed and bandaged Trainmaster Harrington's head. He saw that Harrington's injuries were more serious than either one had first thought. He helped him into a bed and told him to remain there.

Conductor Homer Purcell was the next survivor to arrive on his own. He was only half dressed. Purcell was in charge of rotary X-807, which had been stuck in a large snow slide just west of the town, near Windy Point. There was a telephone at snow shed 3.3 and somehow Purcell had made his way to it and contacted Irving Tegtmeier who was assigned to rotary X-801 currently at Alvin. Purcell told Tegtmeier that he and his crew were stuck and asked for help. He explained that if X-801 could make its way to the opposite side of the slide, perhaps the two rotaries, with extra shovelers, could break through and meet in the middle. They did break through the slide and both rotaries and their crews went back to Alvin where they coupled up and made their way to Wellington.(19) All of them were exhausted when they arrived at Wellington on the 24th of February. Most of them, including Purcell, were sleeping in the cars of the fast mail train when the avalanche hit. He and several others had been thrown clear of the wreckage and snow. The conductor had suffered a broken left arm and some lesser injuries. One of the wives bandaged it as best she could, and then made a tight sling to prevent any movement of his injured arm. Even with a broken arm, Purcell started rolling bandages as fast as he could. He knew from personal experience that there were survivors and that the bunkhouse would be transferred into a temporary hospital at anytime.

Sherlock, seeing that things were in order as best as could be expected, to receive and treat the victims to come, finally left for the disaster sight.

It was still almost impossible for him to believe that the entire side of Windy Mountain had given way. What he could see of the mountain in the darkness was a panorama of surrealism. At the base where once stood houses and other familiar buildings, plus the trains, all was a huge ugly white covering with pieces of debris scattered as far as he could see, sticking out from the snow.

The rescue efforts were already underway when Sherlock arrived at the scene. Somewhere the town's people had found more shovels and other tools and equipment to search for victims, alive or dead. Now that he was actually at the sight, once more the Great Northern telegrapher had to stop gather his thoughts and control his emotions. It was no longer surreal. It was very much real, and unnerving. He tried to put it all together in his mind. As unbelievable as it seemed, it was quickly apparent that the whole event was even more devastating than he thought. Standing there, he could see that another slide had come down after the monstrous avalanche. To make matters worse, the rain had started coming down even harder. The storm then knocked out what power was left, and the rescuers could only get their bearings from the few oil lamps they had and the constant flashes of lightening. Charles Andrews told Sherlock that he had witnessed a huge electrical bolt hit Windy Mountain and it appeared to him that was when the entire side of the mountain came cascading down onto the stalled trains. Andrews was an electric motorman for the Great Northern. He was in one of the small bunkhouses near Bailets Hotel when the avalanche occurred. He was not injured, but was not ashamed to tell Sherlock how the entire event terrified him.

Photo courtesy of University of Washington Special Collections Division

Photo by A. Curtis

What remained of Wellington after the avalanche disaster.

A Great Northern section worker and rotary conductor named Ira Clary, was one of the first rescuers at the seen. Some accounts in the local newspapers claim that he had been trying to sleep in the same car as Homer Purcell and he too was tossed from the wreckage and sustained only minor injuries. But his story given to Sherlock at the scene is a bit different. However, it does not detract from his account of the disaster, and is important to note.

He was in one of the bunkhouses and he and his companions ran outside to see what had happened after hearing the incredible roar of the mountain. "It was thundering when we ran out [of the bunkhouse]," he said to Sherlock. "The flashes were blinding and the thunder kept up an awful racket. We heard a faint moaning down the gulch, and made a break for it. There were only two or three little railroad lanterns for light. All around us we could hear trees snapping and other slides coming down. We did not know how big they were, but we stumbled and rolled down into the gulch where we could hear the cries."

"Some had grabbed up what axes there were when we first ran out[side], and then the lanterns showed a row of hands beckoning in every little hole and opening in the coaches. We started chopping between the outstretched hands and began to take them out."(96)

Clary continued his gruesome description. "We could hear the passengers crying for water and some were crying for nothing at all. We got some of them out alive, but some of them died before we could pull them out."(96)

Scenic Hot Springs

Sometime between 7 and 11 o'clock on the morning of the disaster, John Wentzel, a Great Northern section crewmember, staggered into the hotel at Scenic, completely exhausted and nearly in shock. Between gasps for breath, he told everybody there of the destruction of the trains at Wellington, and of the gigantic avalanche that had buried them and part of the town itself. "All whipped out," he uttered. "Nothing but smooth snow where the tracks were, and the trains were dumped into the canyon." Those who heard the news were stunned beyond belief. In fact, some were not sure if it was true, due to Wetzel's physical and mental condition.

Piece by piece, Wentzel was able to give them a more detailed account of what happened. The avalanche came without warning at about one o'clock in the morning. He was at Bailets Hotel when he heard something that sounded like a huge clap of thunder. But this time the earth shook and he ran outside just in time to see billows of snow and debris settling over the tracks where the trains had stood just minutes earlier.

Later, he saw men carrying women and children from some of the partly buried coaches. Some were moaning, but most appeared to be dead, Wentzel speculated. He had just finished telling his story to the stunned guests at the hotel, when the rotary carrying J. H. O'Neill arrived from Corea for more coal. Someone ran outside to tell the superintendent what had happened. He was staggered for a moment and all the color left his face. For a moment, it looked as if O'Neill himself would collapse. But he quickly regained his composure and ran to the hotel to get the story directly from Wentzel. After hearing everything that Wentzel could recall, O'Neill then telephoned the brakeman at Nippon, another station stop between Scenic and Wellington. From him, O'Neill gathered far more information about the tragedy in the hours after Wentzel left.

None of the rescue parties that O'Neill had organized at Scenic had left for Wellington. Their mission was now different. Food and other necessities were still needed, but now they would face the grim task of helping search and care for survivors. They would also need all the first aid materials they could gather before leaving. He worked feverishly with everyone to get the extra supplies needed for the victims. This would consume most of the day. When everything and everyone were ready to leave, O'Neill immediately went to the station house and sent the first known telegram to Everett, reporting as best he could of the avalanche that had just happened, then forwarded to the Great Northern offices in Minnesota. It was 12:45 A.M. on March 2, 1910, when J. H. O'Neill sent the following message to Superintendent J. M. Gruber and Assistant General Manager H. A. Kennedy in St. Paul:

> **The following from J. H. O'Neill, at 12:45 A.M. 3-2**
> **Mr. J. M. Gruber,**
> **Mr. H. A. Kennedy**

> **"Just received report from brakeman over phone at Nippon who had walked in from Wellington, said left there at 9 A.M. Rescue party had taken out twenty thought dead and ten injured. He left phone before I could get any particulars. Rescue train left Tonga at 4:00 P.M. and had two experienced mountain cruisers who will go over trail to Wellington. Special train with coroner Mr. Kimball and two assistants and undertaker, left Seattle 5:00 P.M. will be run as far east as possible. Five doctors and two nurses walking to Wellington now. Will endeavor to bring the money to Scenic Hotel. Weather Tonga west cloudy, west wind. Have report operator at Drury who advises slide 200 feet long, 50 feet deep demolished watchman's car just east of Drury, killed watchman Johnson. He also reports from curve east switch for half mile on a continuous slide 50 to 60 feet high and numerous other slides. From dam to Leavenworth it is one continuous slide 6 to 30 feet deep. Have no news of westbound rotary or relief train since they left Chiwaukum. Soon as brakeman who made report of west slope is located will try to get further particulars."**

From the content of the message, it seems apparent that Gruber and Kennedy had been notified earlier of the pending disaster. However, there are no telegrams dated earlier than this one, which are stored in the Great Northern Corporate papers at the Minnesota Historical Society.

Wellington: The Rescue

"Use that shovel and dig like hell if you think anybody's down there," Basil Sherlock told one of the rescuers. "And when you get tired, give your shovel to someone else, but keep shoveling."(96) It seemed almost meaningless, what they were all trying to do. It was so dark, and so many of the rescuers were still in shock. Still they had to do whatever they could. But the real rescue efforts would have to come at daybreak.

Just then, Sherlock heard someone yell that they had found somebody who was still alive but pinned in the slide. He ran to where he heard the rescuer's call for help and found John Gray, one of the Spokane Local passengers, lying in the snow with nothing on but a nightgown. He was buried to his waist in snow. Sherlock instructed Gray to put his arms around his neck and he would be able to pull him out. As soon as Sherlock tried to dislodge Gray, the victim let out a painful scream. One of his legs was broken. It was caught between two beams of what was left of one of the coaches. Sherlock and the unknown rescuer who had hollered for help, carefully dug away at the snow with their hands and somehow removed the beams from John Gray's broken leg.

Sherlock then got down on his hands and knees and with the assistance of the other rescuer, got Gray onto the telegrapher's back. Sherlock then climbed up the steep, frozen slope with Gray holding on to him around his neck. Exhausted, he made it to the now temporary hospital with the injured passenger. On the way to the bunkhouse, Gray kept asking about his wife and baby. At that time, Sherlock had no idea as to their fate. Gray was shivering from the cold and suffering from shock when they got inside the building. Two of the women took care to get Gray to a bed and quickly began constructing a splint for his leg. One of them said to Sherlock that some whiskey would help in cases such as Gray's. They were expecting (hopefully) more survivors. He headed for Fogg Brothers. Later, Anna Gray, John's wife and Varden Gray, their eighteen-month old son, would also be rescued from the wreckage, both with severe injuries.

It was now nearly three o'clock in the morning when Sherlock came out of the saloon carrying two bottles of whiskey for the makeshift hospital. He heard Mrs. Susan Bailets calling for him from the porch of the hotel. She told him that someone had left a little boy with a stick "running through his head" on one of her dining room tables. Sherlock ran to the hotel and was led to the boy by Mrs. Bailets. The first thing Basil Sherlock noticed was that the stick was varnished; it had to have come from the interior of one of the coaches.

It was a sickening sight. The piece of wood was about 2 ½ feet long, an inch wide, and about a half inch thick. It had pierced the skin of the boy's forehead, obviously scraping his skull. It had then weaved its way in and out of the skin, completely across the young victim's forehead. He appeared to be unconscious, but was rolling to and fro, uttering sounds that were undistinguishable.

Many thoughts were running through Sherlock's mind as he viewed this poor small victim. What could he and Mrs. Bailets do for the boy? And had any members of the two parties that left Wellington earlier, make it to Scenic? How any of the railroad workers who quit their jobs get anywhere? If so, were there any rescue parties on the way? When would they arrive? Did they know of the disaster and how unspeakably gruesome it was? He stopped his wondering when the child's uttering became louder. On the hotel's dining room table lay the most immediate matter. He turned to Mrs. Bailets and said, "the stick has to come out, or he'll end up with an infection, possibly blood poisoning. Can you get hold of a razor?" he asked. She ran into the store and quickly returned with a new razor. The blade needed to be disinfected. The hotel's cook came into the room, saw what needed to be done, and took the razor blade into the kitchen. There he had a large kettle of boiling water, and held the blade in the water until his fingers could stand it no longer.

In Basil Sherlock's own words, "I cut the stick out, being just as careful as I could to save the skin and flesh."(96a) Mrs. Bailets furnished a large blanket which Sherlock wrapped around the child. He then carried him to the bunkhouse. On his way, Sherlock decided that if the boy's parents did not survive the avalanche, he and his wife would adopt him.

There were no more beds that were not occupied when he got there, so Sherlock laid the young boy on the floor in a corner of a backroom. He then remembered that he had seen a child's bed, crated for shipment in the depot. He ran to get it. Arriving at the depot, Sherlock was surprised to find at least four injured people lying on the floor of his telegraph office.

He told those working there to get the injured out of the depot and to the bunkhouse as quickly as possible. Sherlock believed there was a very good chance that another slide could come down at any moment, sending the depot, Bailets Hotel, and Fogg Brothers Restaurant into the Tye River hundreds of feet below where Wellington stood. The few Great Northern employees at the depot who had not been injured, made boy scout seats with their hands and arms to carry those who could not walk to the bunkhouse. Sherlock carried William A. Duncan, a day coach porter on the Spokane Local, on his back into the bunkhouse, which had taken on the appearance of a full-blown hospital. He then went to check on the young boy, angry with himself for forgetting the bed he had gone to retrieve. Duncan died from numerous injuries shortly after being brought to the bunkhouse. He had endeared himself with all the passengers while stranded at Wellington, with his humor and singing. He even taught some of them how to dance.

It turned out that the little boy from whom Sherlock had extracted the large wooden splinter was seven year old Raymond Starrett. His mother, Mrs. Ida Starrett, was rescued after being buried in the snow for more than eleven hours, and was probably the last person taken from the wreckage alive. She was nearly frozen to death, and had suffered numerous injuries. Ida survived and raised her son to manhood.

Mrs. Starrett later recalled what it was like when the avalanche hit and her ordeal of being trapped under the slide. She said she was just about to fall asleep when the crash came. She had heard the thunderous road of the avalanche before it had hit her coach. The train was shaken terribly and thrown with a violence that no one could imagine unless they were on the train. "It seemed to be shot into the air and then checked by some obstacle. This gave a whirling motion and we seemed to roll with incredible speed far down into the valley," she told reporters in Seattle.

The impact of the slide shattered her coach, and she was hurled far from the wreckage. When the mass of snowy debris she was caught in finally came to a stop, Mrs. Starrett did not know the extent of her injuries, but was amazed to still be alive. If the search party could locate her in time, she might survive and be extracted from what she called, "that tomb of snow."

"I was held fast by timbers but could get my arms free. I lay a long time before any noise came to me, and I believe that was the most frightful period of all. Finally, I heard voices. I called and was answered. I was so deep in the snow though, that the rescuers could not locate me," Ida Starret explained.

She continued her remarkable story to the Seattle Times. "Ultimately, nearly 12 hours after the slide, the shovelers got near the place where I was held. I cried out to them, trying to direct them. I could tell by the sound of their shoveling that they were digging at the wrong place, and told them so. Then they moved nearer, and at last I could hear the shovels striking just above my face. I cried out a warning and they proceeded more carefully."(72)

One of the rescuers, in an attempt to locate her position in the slide, kept calling to her, asking her if she could see any light through the snow that covered her. Eventually, a glow of light did break through, and with extreme caution the shovelers brought Ida Starrett out from the slide. She immediately collapsed into the arms of two rescuers. They carried her to the bunkhouse where her son Raymond was. Sadly, however, her two other children, Lillian, age 9, and her 8-month old baby, Francis, did not survive the avalanche.

Years later, in the 1950's, Ruby El Hult located and interviewed Raymond Starrett for her book, NORTHWEST DISASTER. He was then the safety supervisor for Puget Sound Power & Light Company. At the time, Raymond's mother, Ida, was still alive, but confined to a wheelchair as a result of her injuries nearly fifty years earlier at Wellington. According to Ruby El Hult, Raymond was "a tall, handsome man, still bearing on his forehead a large scar received in the Wellington disaster."(19)

Ironically, Basil Sherlock's reminiscences of the Wellington disaster were sent to Ruby more than a year after her book was published. She filed away the 26-page letter and forgot about it as she was in the midst of writing another book. But the story of Sherlock and Starrett does not end there.

Shortly after her book, NORTHWEST DISASTER was published, Basil Sherlock obtained a copy in his home town of Willmar, Minnesota. Obviously the book was of great interest to him, and as he read it, he discovered the name of the seven year old boy whose life he had saved. It was now over fifty years since the tragedy, but with the help of Ruby El Hult, he finally located Raymond Starrett.[18]

His initial letter to Starrett is housed at the North Central Washington Museum in Wenatchee, Washington. The letter is reproduced here in its entirety, just as it was written, spelling errors and all.

April 4, 1960

Mr. Raymond Starrett,
Olympia, Wash.

Dear Raymond,
Am wondering if you would care to know how I met you, over fifty years ago.   Believe you were only a boy of seven years. If so, it will cost you a picture of yourself taken recently with your hat off. Perhaps you wish to forget it. For over fifty years I have. Twenty five of those years were spent working on the grave yard shift 12M to 8 A.M. and when the hands of the clock would point to 1:10 A.M. on March first, I would shut my eyes and see it all over again.

Last March first our news paper came out with a story in the way of a 50 year annivarsay of the avalanche at Wellington, Wsh. And since then, cannot get you out of my mind. Perhaps you will not remember me now. About March 3rd 1910 you knew me for I was in the temporary hospital and the nurse brought you in to where I was and said "Here is a young man that has been asking to see you for sometime." I was the one who removed the stick from your head.

Sincerely,

Basil Sherlock

On April 14th of 1960, Raymond Starrett responded to Sherlock with a four-page letter. It begins: "Sound familiar? Well, I should say it does. Greetings friend from out of the long past. I wish this 'Hello' could be with a good handshake. but guess this must do. Seems much like a dream. So glad you wrote." Starrett went on to tell Sherlock of his life during the half century after the avalanche. He sent his rescuer a picture of himself and asked for more information of the Wellington disaster, and for a picture of Sherlock.

The two men kept up a brief correspondence until Basil Sherlock died in the early 1960's. Records from Puget Sound Power & Light Company (now Puget Sound Energy) show that Raymond Starrett retired from the company after nearly forty years of service, and passed away on January 25, 1983 at the age of 80.(77) The two men never met personally except for those few days in the Cascades so very long ago.

The victims continued to arrive at the bunkhouse/hospital throughout the night. The least injured rambled in under their own power, but far more had to be carried in by the small party of rescuers. No one from Scenic had yet arrived. They kept the fire in the bunkhouse going in the one cast iron pot bellied stove they had. Blankets were kept against it to help keep them warm as possible so as to help "thaw out" the patients once they arrived. They were also administered a healthy dose of whiskey (courtesy of Mr. Bailets) to "help them thaw out from the inside." (66) Even the injured women did not hesitate to take their medicine. Women drinking hard alcohol was frowned upon in those days. But the whiskey was needed to settle nerves, as well as for the folk medicine belief that spirits from a bottle could very well prevent pneumonia.

Finally, a little past noon on March 1st, rescuers on snowshoes began arriving from Scenic. They were greeted with overwhelming exaltation from the exhausted people of Wellington. One of the first to arrive on the scene was a male nurse, J. L. Godby, who was employed at the Scenic Hot Springs Hotel when they got the news of the disaster. He went as fast as he could to the bunkhouse to begin supervising the almost impossible task of caring for all the victims who were already there with more still coming. He was amazed at how well all the women of the town were holding up under such unbelievable conditions. Godby told Sherlock that he had arrived with about fifty other rescuers lead by Engineer J. J. Dowling, but Superintendent O'Neill was not with them. According to Godby, as this was O'Neill's division, the superintendent believed he needed to take charge of the rescue train that would be bringing much needed help and supplies soon.

Godby also described to Sherlock, as best he could, how abominable were the conditions between Scenic and what was left of Wellington. The avalanche was far greater than anyone had imagined, he continue. Just about all the snow that covered Windy Mountain had come down the steep slope, and it was one solid, continuous slide from Windy Point, just above Scenic, all the way to Wellington.

A number of the men in the first rescue party to arrive with Godby, were the same men who had hiked out of Wellington only a day or two ago. What they witnessed upon their return was horrifying. Some of them needed time to gather themselves and regain their emotional bearings before they could be able to help search for victims. Others went to work immediately.

One person described the devastation upon arrival as though some gigantic knife had cut off nearly forty acres of snow from Windy Mountain.(36) The gash was in the mountain's side was enormous. It extended up the mountain more than one thousand feet, and now in the day light, everyone could see where the slide had broken away from the mountain, as the avalanche was huge in both depth and width.

Photo courtesy Museum of History & Industry, Seattle

The path of the massive avalanche at Wellington. Photo taken March 1, 1910.

Rescuers were now searching for bodies by following bloodstains across the snow. One of the searchers explained that just before he had left the scene, many men with shovels had been led by the blood trail, all the way down to Tye Creek, where many of the victims were incased under snow that was packed on top of them like cement. He explained that the bodies that were not mangled by the destruction of the cars, had been crushed beyond recognition by the enormous weight of the icy snow that had fallen upon them.(67)

Speculation among some of the searchers was that perhaps a number of train cars, or at least many bodies, had been tossed across to the other side of Tye Creek. Viewing the results of the intensity and magnitude of the avalanche, this was certainly a possibility. If this were so, and warmer weather brought on the melting of ice and snow, there was a danger of bodies dropping into the river and being carried away in the swift current.

The First Reports
Newspaper Articles and Great Northern Telegrams

By February 28th, it was widely discernable by the public in Seattle, Everett, and all Puget Sound, as well as those who lived east of the Cascades, in cities such as Wenatchee and Spokane, that something terrible was happening on Stevens Pass. Trains had not yet arrived, and were now many days overdue. Trains scheduled for departure were still at the stations. Great Northern officials had done a remarkable job in keeping the truth from the public. But the continued questioning by reporters was now rapidly intensifying. However, the fact must also be made that the railways' own people, on both sides of the mountains, had little knowledge of the dramatic events occurring on Stevens Pass. Those most in the know were the telegraphers, and Great Northern officials stranded the stormy locations near the summit.

It should be remembered that the Seattle Times had the only reporter on the scene. But J. J. Underwood, who was with the rescue party, could not file any dispatches due to the telegraph lines being down between Wellington to Scenic. The first piece of news to reach Puget Sound was fragmented, small on details, and many times incorrect. The source came from Scenic and the story told by John Wentzel. But it was enough information for the newspapers in Seattle to blaze headlines in all of their editions on March 2, 1910.

The front-page banner headline of the Seattle Times on March 2nd, pretty much prepared everyone for the incredible and contiuous stories that were to follow for the next several weeks. The Times was also aware of the beginning of coded Great Northern messages but could not obtain copies.

AVALANCHE
BURIES TRAIN AT WELLINGTON
TWO KILLED & SEVERAL INJURED
NO WORD AS TO OTHERS SAFETY
SNOW BURIES GREAT NORTHERN TRAIN

Everett, Tues. March 1 - The only message from Wellington regarding the avalanche was a code telegram to a Great Northern official received at 11:00 o'clock this morning.

RESCUE PARTIES RUSH TO SCENE!

Everett, Tues. March 1 – An avalanche descended this morning on the Great Northern westbound Spokane train, stalled with its 30 passengers near Wellington. The fate of the passengers is unknown. This train has been snowbound for a week. Besides the crew, it carried 30 men, women, and children.

Snowslides of the last two days have torn down the telegraph and telephone wires between here and Wellington and details of the accidents are unobtainable.

Fearing a catstrophe, the local officials of the Great Northern have hurried a special relief train to the scene. Every available physician in Everett and Snohomish joined the relief party. The rescue expedition will be forced to make a large part of the journey on snow shows as the track between here and Wellington is blocked in many places, and the army of workmen sent out when the first slides were reported have made little progress in removing the ten miles of snow blocking the line.

Hundreds of men from Everett and Snohomish volunteered to join the relief party.

It was nonstop and painstaking work getting to Wellington, from both the east side of the summit as well as the west. Two dispatches from telegrapher W. C. Watrous on behalf of J. H. O'Neill, sent to President Louis Hill and General Manager J. M. Gruber, clearly chronicle the conditions taking place on Stevens Pass. A more detailed account of the rescue efforts from Leavenworth on east is detailed later. But the two dispatches are worth reading.

SUPPLEMENT
CASCADE DIVN---Wellington----March 3rd
"Following from Supt. O'Neill at 2 P.M.

"At 10 A.M. rotaries located as follows:-X-808 headed east now colaing up at Scenic. Have a couple cars off track ahead of them but expect to work at noon and figure to reach Alvin tomorrow night Rotary X-801 headed west dead at Shed 3.3 Double rotary X-808 and 800 at Gaynor dead between switch, rotary X-807 demolished and down bank at Wellington. Rotary X-809 westbound last heard of them working on one side and making fair progress half mile west of Merritt. Was in slide 1800 ft long. They are trying to reach Gaynor to revive double rotary. NP rotary now leaving Seattle, Will be run direct to Skykomish clean out track to Scenic turn and doubled with X-808 On east slope were working 73 japs and Dalquists gang on west slope We are working 60 white men all foreighn laborers diserted. Sending 55 white men on No. 4 today. Last reports we had, they had recovered 28 bodies, they were covered in snow. The injured are in temporary Hospital in bunk house at Wellington. Have no reports of any snow shed caved in. Have just a wire to Wellington and will try and get full details at once.

Later"-News from Wellington: Found Condr. Petit, not yet found Blackburn or O'Neills clerk. Have found 35 so far, Figure there are about 25 more. Says have go out 26 alive, Details later
W.C.Watrous

SUPPLEMENT
DASCADE DIVN---Wellington---March 3rd, 1910
Following from Supt O'Neill at 2:38 P.M.

"Have recovered 29 bodies since accident, 24 injured being cared for here. All equipment total loss except trucks have force of sixty men searching for dead but account so much snow and cars being buried it is slow work. Figure we have 25 to 30 bodies yet to recover. Weather very bad and we are having some trouble keeping men. Rotary X-808 should be east of Alvin tonight it will take 10 days to open line between Alvin and Wellington. Snow is level with top of snow sheds and full of timber. Employing all men can get to assist clearing line, double rotary which are dead 2 miles west of here all full of water and ready

to do business soon as fuel reaches us. No slides where these machines stand. Intend packing coal from snow shed three.three to where machines stand in order to get them going. Have large slide east of Shed 3.3 which will keep rotaries busy for 36 hours.

W.C.Watrous

As the news of the disaster was received by Great Northern officials at St. Paul, and President Louis Hill in California, their worst fears were confirmed. The avalanche was bad…very bad. H. H. Parkhouse, secretary to President Hill received a Western Union cable from his boss late in the day on March 1st.

REDLANDS' CAL 2

H H PARKHOUSE

SECY TO PRES G N RY

STPAUL MINN

ARRIVED SAFELY THIS MORNING ALL WELL WIRE ME FULL PARTICULARS REPORTED BAD WRECK CASCADE DIVISION. LOUIS W HILL

Parkhouse wasn't sure after he received the message, how Hill had found out about the disaster. After all, he was just beginning a vacation in sunny California. But he knew his boss well enough that he had to provide him with as much information as quickly as possible, and there may not be time to confirm the accuracy of his accounts to Hill. He decided that all messages would be sent to the Great Northern president in code until they could determine how bad the incident at Wellington actually was. He also determined that the press and the public should be limited in their knowledge of the tragedy for as long as possible. Coded telegrams would be the safest way of transmitting this information. Parkhouse's first Western Union coded telegram to Louis Hill, in response to Mr. Hill's inquiry, informed him as best he could of the disaster, and is printed below, first in the coded form and then the translation.

St. Paul, Minn., March 2ⁿᵈ, 1910

To: Louis W. hill,
　　　　Care Casa Loma Hotel
　　　　Redlands, California
Message received. Adequate azure Wellington not caused canvasser Oliver cannonading soho. Number twenty five and fast mail held near Wellington chapman canvasser soho and while particulars

84

meager expandly despised. **Reuniting pensiveness have taken out unfair transept defrauder and till interchange. Counterpart apologue stenographer causes A sixteen and at least smiting tutor and error matutinals among traitor lair. Amuse penuriouslys outlive number twenty five myrtle overthrew lists interchange. Slide at Drury demolished watchman's car at that point and garishee deeming tripped Leavenworth six tripped traffic feet dense. This James monopolized we have had but account wire trouble cannot get full particulars.**

H.H. PARKHOUSE

Translation

Message received. Accident at Wellington not caused by wreck but slide. Number twenty five and fast mail held near Wellington caught by slide and while particulars meager evidently demolished. Rescue party have taken out twenty three dead and ten injured. Cook and stenographer Car A sixteen and at least six train and enginemen among those killed. All passengers on number twenty five more or less injured. Slide at Drury demolished watchman's car and killed watchman. Continuous slide for half a mile at that point and from dam to Leavenworth six to thirty feet deep. This worst mishap we have had but account wire trouble, cannot get full particulars.

Slowly over the next few days, the newspapers began printing articles of the disaster primarily based on stories told by people who had made it to Scenic Hot Springs. Most of them had left Wellington before the avalanche and the accuracy of the early reports are questionable. Nonetheless, the public was shouting for information, any information regarding the disaster. The Great Northern was not cooperating, so the newspapers reported anything they heard. The Wellington avalanche was of such magnitude that it was a front-page story across the country. "SLIDE BURIES TRAIN; 20 DEAD, 25 MISSING," read the page one headline in the New York Times on Wednesday, March 2, 1910.

Photo courtesy of Museum of History & Industry, Seattle

Wreckage of trains at Wellington on morning of March 1, 1910.

The New York Times would take the Great Northern Railway to task and question their responsibility in this matter in a scathing editorial a few days later. The Times wondered if this tragedy could have been avoided. It is reprinted later in this chapter.

The early morning edition of the Seattle Post Intelligencer of Wednesday, March 2, 1910 printed one of the first accounts by someone who had made it out of Wellington just before the avalanche. John Rogers, the real estate agent, gave his version of the conditions at Wellington on the night before the avalanche. He was returning home to Seattle from Soap Lake in Eastern Washington, where he was engaged in a major land negotiation. Rogers explained that to the best of his knowledge, the No. 25 Spokane Local had approximately 70 passengers aboard when they began the climb into the mountains.

The actual number of passengers aboard the ill-fated train has never been, and cannot possibly be determined. The reports ranged from as few as 30 to as many as 150. The Great Northern reached its "official" conclusion as to the amount of passengers by taking the names from the registers at Fogg Brothers and Bailets Hotel.(71) Whenever someone from the Spokane Local ate at one of these establishments, they would sign their name in a register so that the business would be properly compensated for the meals by the Great Northern. But it is very possible, indeed probable, that not everyone bothered to sign the register, and there were many aboard the train who were sick and a few who were invalid and did not bother to make the trek to Fogg Brothers or Bailets. Therefore, the accuracy of the railway's conclusion is highly questionable.

"At Wellington there are three tracks," Rogers explained. He described how the two trains were positioned, as well as the location of O'Neill's private car, the three General Electric motors (just recently arrived) that were used to pull the trains through the tunnel since it electrification, and two box cars. He believed that there were about sixteen to eighteen mail clerks on the No. 27 fast Mail train, and also sixteen track laborers who slept in that train or one of the box cars. Rogers' recollection of these track laborers will become important later on in piecing together just how many people were actually killed on the night of the avalanche.

It should also be kept in mind that Japanese laborers were kept away from passenger trains, and were normally assigned to box cars. This was the railway's policy in 1910. The fact that there were a number of Japanese laborers in the Cascades at the time of the disaster has already been established by Great Northern letters and telegrams already mentioned in this book. More will be printed in the following chapter.

The evening edition of the March 2nd Seattle Times, reported that relief trains from Seattle and Everett had already left for the disaster site. Hopefully, they would be able to get as far as Scenic. Then all those aboard, including the deputy coroners, undertakers, physicians, and nurses would have to hike the rest of the way to Wellington. On board the trains were dozens of rescue workers who had volunteered to pack in the food, medicines and other supplies that were needed. Four of these rescuers were from the Seattle City jail. They were given free lodging at the jailhouse, as they were unemployed at the time. This was a custom in Seattle in those days. There were nine of them to begin with, but upon reaching King Street Station, five backed out. The four others who did go on to make the trip and help with the rescue work, were all given paying jobs with the Great Northern, so grateful was the railroad for their help.(72)

Chapter 4:

The GN's "Jap Gang"

Jim Hill's dream of a large fleet of sailing ships some day crossing the Pacific Ocean, carrying on commercial trade with the Orient, continued to fascinate him. At first, Hill envisioned the enormous profits that could be made by the import of products and resources from the Far East such as Oriental teas and most importantly, Oriental silk. But another equation was added to his economic formula when it became apparent to him that the Orient, especially Japan, would also provide a huge market for cheap Japanese labor that could be brought to this country to work on his rail lines. There was always a continued need for railroad workers, and this need could be filled by taking advantage of the Japanese human resource market.

The foremost cause of the sudden shortage of railroad laborers was due to the 1881 Chinese Exclusion Act. It seemed to many native born Americans that the import of Chinese workers for the country's railroads was putting them out of work. Of course, the Chinese would work for very little money as opposed to what American workers demanded. As a result, a federal law was passed that refused entrance into this country by the Chinese to work on the railroads. This immediately caused a severe labor shortage for all the transcontinental railroads, as, despite the original objection of the Chinese getting all the railroad jobs, many Americans were still not willing to work the long, difficult hours, for the same pay received by the Chinese.

All the railroads were growing and suffering from the lack of laborers in the 1880's. And at this time, the Great Northern was growing and expanding the fastest; therefore the need for more workers wherever they could be found. The cost of transportation of the Japanese to this country would be minimal also to the Great Northern. Hill dispatched his friend and confidant, Captain James Griffith to Japan to negotiate with officials of the Nippon Yuzen Kaisha Steamship Steamship Company, an agreement to transport merchandise to this country. Griffith was successful, and the deal was, at this point, strictly legitimate.

On July 16, 1896, the Great Northern Railway and the Nippon Yuzen Kaisha Steamship Company executed a contract in St. Paul, Minnesota, establishing at the Port of Seattle, a connection for carrying freight and passengers between Japan, Hawaii, and Seattle.(39) In addition to silks, teas, spices, and other goods, what would become more important to the Great Northern, was the eventual transporting of Japanese laborers for construction and maintenance of the railroad. This unethical, but highly profitable part of the commercial relationship would not begin for another two years, but plans for transporting merchandise from Eastern Asia got underway immediately. In the following two decades, this enterprise (both legitimate and questionable) would grow into a major business partnership that involved one of Seattle's leading Japanese businessmen, and one of the city's most celebrated public figures.

In a telegram to Judge Thomas Burke dated July 17, 1896, W. W. Finley, representing the Great Northern Railway, proudly informed Judge Burke of the newly signed contract and the benefits it would bring to all involved in the venture.

St. Paul
July 17, 1896

Judge Thomas Burke
It gives me great pleasure to announce to you that Pre. Hill acting for the Great Northern and S. Iwanaga acting for the Nippon Yuzen Kabushiki Kaisha executed on the 16th instituted a contract between the two companies named for establishing at the Port of Seattle connections for carrying cargo parcels and passengers between the different ports of Hawaii, Japan, China, including Hong Kong and Formosa, Corea and Russia bordering on the Japan Sea; also the Philippine Group, the Straight settlements and the east generally served by the lines of the Nippon Yuzen Kabushiki Kaisha on the one hand points and places in the USA, the dominion of Canada and its Maritime provinces and the different ports of Europe on the other hand the first steamer will be put in service and on berth in Japan not later than the month of August. The importance of the contract to the City of Seattle and the Puget Sound cannot be over estimated. Shipping will begin August 1896.
W.W. Finley (61)

On August 31, 1896, the Nippon Yuzen Kaisha steamer "Miike Maru," sailed into Puget Sound and the Port of Seattle. It was a grand day for the growing city on Elliott Bay. Everyone took the day off, business was suspended, and just about the entire population of Seattle assembled on the bluffs overlooking Puget Sound to get the first view of the incoming ship. People speculated on how fast their city would now grow with this new trans-oceanic enterprise. Later that same day, all joined in a mammoth parade to celebrate the arrival of Seattle's first steamer in regular trans-Pacific service.(71) It was the birth of Seattle becoming a major world port city.

In order to enhance commerce with the Orient, James J. Hill organized the Great Northern Steamship Company in 1900, with a working capital of $6,000,000. He was not satisfied with the limitations placed on his endeavors by the size of the Nippon Yuzen Kaisha ships. The situation was hindering the growth of business between the Far East and the Pacific Northwest. "If the Oriental trade was to expand as it clearly should," Hill said in his book HIGHWAYS OF PROGRESS, published in 1910, "this arrangement (with other steamship lines) would not answer. The mechanism of transportation must be complete on sea as it already was on land. Somebody had to build ships that would carry at bottom figures. Most of the ships then on the Pacific were 2,500 to 7,000 tons."(41) Being impetuous as always, he immediately contracted for two steamships to be built, the "Minnesota," and the "Dakota." These two 28,000 ton steamships would be the largest in the world, and thereby keep shipping costs much lower. They would ply the Pacific between Seattle, Yokohama, and Hong Kong.

The following year, 1901, the Great Northern built its "Asiatic Dock" at Smith Cove in Seattle (today, it is Pier 88). A few years later, it would be occupied primarily by ships of the Nippon Yuzen Kaisha Company, and later, the two giants, the Minnesota and the Dakota of the Great Northern. This pier was constructed to eventually handle the importation of Japanese immigrants to work on the Great Northern Railway.

The arrival of the "Minnesota" and the "Dakota" at Smith Cove on Christmas Eve, 1904, brought an exciting Christmas to the residence and business people of Seattle. The two steamers, then the largest ocean carriers afloat, had attracted worldwide attention to the still small port city on Elliott Bay. The "Dakota" had a short life, however. It was wrecked in Japan in 1907. The "Minnesota" remained in service for the Great Northern until 1917, when it was sold for use in crossing the Atlantic in the European trade that developed after World War One.

Two years after the agreement between the Great Northern and Nippon Yuzen Kaisha, 1898, Charles Tetsuo Takahashi came to Seattle and founded the Oriental Trading Company. Using the ships of the Nippon Yuzen Kaisha Company, Takahashi's new business venture in Seattle would make him the largest labor contractor for railroads in the United States. Over the next twenty years, the Oriental Trading Company would supply thousands of Japanese workers for the Great Northern Railway.

C. T. Takahashi was born on November 1, 1874 at Gifu, Japan, the son of one of that country's richest landowners. He came to the United States in 1892 with the goal of starting a successful import-export business. Realizing his need for more business and English education, Takahashi entered the University of Puget Sound at Tacoma in 1894, and graduated three years later. After working briefly for the Japanese Consulate in Seattle, he met Yamaoka Ototaka, and together they pooled they resources to form the Oriental Trading Company located at 308 Jackson Street in Seattle.

Yamaoka was much older than Takahashi. A lawyer by profession, he had come to the United States many years before his young business associate. He was described as "an unusually splendid gentleman, a person of excellence, rare not only in Japanese-American society, but also in Japan."(39) Yamaoka, before coming to America, took an active part in a radical political group in the Prefecture of Shizuoka in Japan, and helped to plot the overthrow of the entire Japanese government. He was arrested and sent to prison for ten years for trying to assassinate several government officials. He was put to work in his country's coalmines. After being granted a general amnesty, Yamaoka made a fast trip to Seattle and before meeting his future business associate, began his new career by publishing the Seattle New Japan newspaper.

They made perfect business partners. Takahashi was the idea man. More outgoing and aggressive than Yamaoka, it was Takahashi who built the Oriental Trading Company and became its president, while Yamaoka, more reserved and studious, developed methods for implementing his partner's business schemes.

Late in 1898, the Oriental Trading Company was either approached by, or itself approached the Great Northern Railway, to procure for it an unlimited number of Japanese laborers for the railroad. The Great Northern, which had been completed to Puget Sound from St. Paul, only five years earlier, was now growing and prospering at an enormous pace. As a result, the railway was in desperate need of ever increasing numbers of workers all along its 2,000 mile line. The 1881 Chinese Exclusion Act caused a severe shortage of cheap labor for all the transcontinental railroads in this country, and the Great Northern was growing the quickest and needed the most workers.(44) The idea of importing Japanese workers was not original to the Great Northern. The practice actually began in 1891 when the Union Pacific contracted with a fellow named Tanaka Chushichi to supply it with the first thirty Japanese laborers to work on an American railroad. These workers soon gained the reputation for hard work and diligence, and it was not long before Japanese labor contractors became a thriving business, foremost of which would be the Oriental Trading Company with offices in Seattle and Spokane.

The legal representative in Seattle for Great Northern President James J. Hill was Judge Thomas Burke, one of the city's most influential and respected citizens. It was his office that administered the original contract between the Great Northern and the Oriental Trading Company. Burke's office also handled the manner of payment from the Great Northern to Takahashi for the Japanese laborers in its employ. After Burke's offices took its share of the money, known to both Hill and Burke and approved by both men, what pay the Japanese workers did receive from Takahashi's company was merely enough to keep them virtual prisoners of the Great Northern Railway and the Oriental Trading Company. Quite simply, they were left with next to nothing. In this way, they could not afford to leave their jobs with the railroad. As a vast majority of these workers were illegal aliens, where else could they go?

Thomas Burke was born in Clinton County, New York on December 22, 1848. His early years were marked by a struggle to gain a formal education. He did not come from a rich family, and his pursuit of knowledge was constantly interrupted by the need to work full time in order to survive and to amass enough money to continue his education.(64) His strong work ethic and tenacity eventually paid off when he graduated from the University of Michigan Law School.

Burke arrived in Seattle in 1875 and wasted no time in opening his law office. He was, like James Hill, a visionary. Everywhere he looked, he saw opportunities for growth and prosperity for the city and himself. The natural resources that surrounded Seattle and Puget Sound did not escape his eyesight, and looking over the bay towards the East, he also thought of his new home's location to the Orient. Seattle could and would prosper and thrive by the commercial trade with the Far East, more than any other city on the west coast of the United States. He made a mental note of this and thought all that was needed was a transcontinental railroad. Though Hill and Burke did not know each other yet, their thinking was on the same track.

Thomas Burke established the Seattle Chamber of Commerce, and when he heard that Jim Hill was going to build his Great Northern railway to the Puget Sound country, it was Burke who contacted the "empire builder" to explain the benefits of locating the railroad's terminus at Seattle.

Burke saw the Seattle-Great Northern relationship as the needed golden opportunity for his city to grow and prosper. He told Hill that what was good for Seattle, would be good for the Great Northern. Burke also lectured the members of the Seattle Chamber of Commerce the same thing. The more he talked with his associates, the more enthusiastic Burke became of the potential prosperity not far off. He explained to everyone in the business community that Seattle should be prepared to offer Hill anything he wanted in order to get the railway to choose Seattle as its western terminal. In his book, HE BUILT SEATTLE, author Robert Nesbit writes about how strongly Burke felt about the future of Seattle in partnership with Jim Hill.

"It would be a blunder if Seattle did not treat the Great Northern with the 'utmost liberality,' Burke wrote to his friend Daniel Gilman. He (Burke) set himself the task of saving Seattle from such a blunder."(64)

As mentioned, Burke and Hill thought along the same lines. The real opportunities that existed in trade with the Orient would not only help Seattle to become rich, but both of them would too. Burke, to give him his due, was probably more responsible for helping Seattle to become a world seaport than any other single person. But if it were not for Hill's decision to accept Burke's overtures to build his railroad to Seattle, Burke's dream may not have materialized. Burke's direct endeavors helped begin the trade and commerce between Seattle and the Far East. As a result, the Great Northern expanded and prospered, Jim Hill got richer, and Thomas Burke made some profits too.

Ironically, Judge Burke died on Friday, December 4, 1925, in New York City while addressing a meeting of the trustees of the Carnegie Foundation for International Peace. He had been a distinguished member of that organization for fifteen years. According to witnesses, Burke had just reached a point in his speech where he pleaded with his audience for a more friendly understanding and economic cooperation between the United States and Japan, when he suffered a massive heart attack and collapsed into the arms of Dr. Nicholas Murray Butler, the President of Columbia University. The physician who came to his aid said that death was instantaneous.(69)

Burke's wife was at the Roosevelt Hotel in New York City when her husband was stricken. Probably the first person in Seattle to hear of the judge's death was Dr. Henry Suzzallo, President of the University of Washington and close friend of Thomas Burke. He received the following telegram from a colleague who was at the meeting in New York when Burke died.

Judge Burke died instantly at 1:10 o'clock this afternoon in the midst of an eloquent speech at the semi-annual meeting at the Carnegie Endowment for International Peace.

He was speaking in his noblest vein for justice, mercy and fair dealings in our relations with the Oriental peoples, particularly the Japanese."(64)

One of Judge Burke's closest friends, C. T. Conover, a pioneer real estate tycoon in early Seattle, called Burke, "Seattle's first citizen." No doubt Burke exercised a great deal of power and influence in the development of Seattle. In the late 1800's and early 1900's, very little commerce in the city was carried on without the Judge's consent or involvement. He came to Seattle poor, living in the back room of his first law office. At his death at age 77, Burke was an independently wealthy man. In addition to his extremely successful law practice, he made a great deal of money in real estate. Thomas Burke is rightfully remembered as one of the prime contributors to the success of Seattle. Did his association with Charles T. Takahashi and the Oriental Trading Company add to his wealth? Of course. Was he directly involved, and if so, to what extent in the illegal importation of Japanese to work on the Great Northern? That question will probably never be completely answered. However a review of his personal papers helps put the matter in perspective. What is for certain is that Judge Burke knew of the practice, and did nothing to stop it.

Seattle certainly did benefit very rapidly from the new commercial trade with the Orient, and the wealth and growth of the city must be attributed to both Burke and Hill. As James Hill explained it in HIGHWAYS OF PROGRESS, "The market was opened, the opportunity accepted, our trade with the Orient no longer a dream, became a splendid fact as the statistic show. In the 10 years between 1893, when the Great Northern reached the coast, and 1903, the exports of the Puget Sound customs district increased $5,085,958 to $32,410,367 (or nearly 540%)."(41) This genuine enterprise most likely would never had occurred without the vision and collaboration of Hill and Burke

However, being an attorney, Thomas Burke also knew how to keep his name disassociated from the most profitable activity of the Oriental Trading Company. Burke's papers (housed in the archives of the University of Washington in Seattle) show that he and Takahashi knew each other very well, both personally and professionally. There are a number of letters from Takahashi to Burke dealing with contractual agreements with Japan and the Great Northern, as well as Christmas greetings that accompanied gifts to Judge Burke.

It was important for Burke, being an officer of the court, to do whatever was possible to remain convincingly 'unknowledgeable' of the illegal importation of Japanese laborers for the Great Northern. Of course he did know. He was Jim Hill's personal attorney in Seattle, and a friend of C. T. Takahashi, president of the Oriental Trading Company. Is it possible that at informal and formal dinner parties that he attended along with Takahashi, there were never any conversations between them of the illegal importation of Japanese laborers? It would have been interesting indeed, to know what was discussed at an informal dinner on board the SS Kaga Maru at 7:30 on the evening of Saturday, July 20, 1901 at the Great Northern dock at Smith Cove. Judge Burke was invited to that gathering by members of the Nippon Yusen Kaisha Company.(9) This invitation, and others can be viewed at the University of Washington's Suzallo Library, which houses the Thomas Burke papers.

There are other pieces of tangible evidence that Burke was aware of, and accepted the practice of, how Japanese laborers were being brought to this country. A typical letter from the Great Northern Railway Line Treasurer's Office to Thomas Burke explained the payments for this practice in detail. The following was written by F. A. Davis of the Great Northern in St. Paul to Thomas Burke on August 8, 1900.

Mr. Thom. Burke
      Attorney, Seattle, Wash.
Dear sir-
    Enclosed please see draft #12135 for $10,596.95 on Montana Bank, Helena, Mont. and draft #7371 for $10,000.00 on Washington National Bank, Seattle, favor of F. A. Davis, paymaster, made payable to you.

    This completes payment on account Japanese Laborers for month of June 1900.

    I send you to-day by Great Northern Express a package containing receipts for amounts as shown on statement sent Mr. Campbell July 21ˢᵗ. He signed these receipts and returned them to me for former months, but June being divided, a portion of the amounts going to him and balance to you. I do not know if you would be willing to sign all of them. If not, I presume some one in office of the Oriental Trading Co., to whom I think the statement is given, would sign them.

    It is necessary that these receipts be signed and sent to me that I may be able to show on each separate payroll, and also that I may get credit for payment of same.

    Trusting that you may be able to return receipts to me without delay, I am,

                   Yours truly,
                   F. A. Davis
                   Paymaster (61)

On February 16, 1899, Takahashi and his partner, Yamaoka, agreed to provide all the Japanese workers that the Great Northern would require. These Japanese workers in the Cascades were to be paid $1.05 per day for 10 hours of work each day. But they would never receive this amount, nor would any of the laborers in the years to come. In 1900, the Oriental Trading Company provided the Great Northern with over 2,500 Japanese laborers. The following is the contract by which the Oriental Trading Company agreed to supply the first 2,500 railroad workers.

Vice President B.T. Downs
Great Northern Railroad Company
Greetings:

According to the conditions stated below, the Oriental Trading Company shall supply the Great Northern Railroad, Japanese workers to act as extra laborers, cleaning workers, coal porters, etc., during the year 1900.

The above named company shall supply first-class Japanese workers as they are needed to the railroad company east of Blackfoot in the state Montana, at a rate of $1.10 for each 10-hour day's work, and to Blackfoot and the area west of it at a rate of $1.05 for a 10-hour day's work.

The above named company is expected to supply janitorial and dining hall personnel, and it is also expected to supply a secretary or interpreter to each work group. Their wages shall all be paid by the railroad company.

When there is need for a Japanese labor supervisor, he shall be transported from Seattle to the place of work by train at no charge.

All necessary goods belonging to the supplied workers shall be transported from Seattle to the place of work free of charge.

At the time that work is completed, or when workers are transferred to another place of work, or in cases of illness, the workers shall be transported by train at no charge to Seattle or the station closest to their destination. The railroad company shall also supply the immigrants with tents or housing needed. In addition, it shall deliver each immigrants work schedule by the third day of every month.

The Oriental Trading Company shall supply all necessary bedding, kitchen utensils, and other household equipment.

According to the conditions stated above, the Oriental Trading Company shall supply 2,500 Japanese workers during the year 1900.

In order to guarantee the wages of immigrants supplied under this contract, the above named company will deposit a public securities bond with the American Bonding & Trust Company in the city of Baltimore.

The above named company agrees to the conditions stipulated above and to the workers concerned for a period of four years.

> Yours truly.
> C.T. Takahashi
> Oriental Trading Company (39)

The Great Northern's response follows:

> **10 January, 1900**

Oriental Trading Company
Messrs:
In regard to the letter we have received concerning your supplying the Western Division of the Great Northern Railroad Company with Japanese workers during the year 1900, we agree to put this contract into effect immediately. The sum of 5,000 dollars shall be deposited for this purpose of supplying at least 2,500 men to the Western Division during the present year. In addition, we will prepare public documents for the depository, Moe L. Campbell. The said documents shall insure payment to the Japanese workers of the wages stipulated in this contract. A copy shall be furnished to each Japanese labor party, which will give notice that the company is responsible for any errors with regard to wages that are brought to its attention during the 90-day period from the end of the month.

> Yours truly,
> B.T. Downs

> **V.P., Great Northern Railroad** (39)

Takahashi and the Oriental Trading Company immediately went to work to provide these laborers. Takahashi contracted with the Morioka Company in Tokyo for their assistance in procuring as many men as possible, as quickly as possible. The Morioka Company was one of Japan's largest and most successful immigration companies. It took no time at all to round up the 2,500 laborers that were needed to be brought to the United States to work for the Great Northern Railway Company as the following two Great Northern Railway Line telegrams to Thomas Burke show.

St. Paul, Minn. Aug 23d 1900

Thos. Burke

Dear Sir, Enclosed please see Dft #8267 for $19979.40 on First National Bank, Great Falls, Mont, and Dft #7470 for $17973.10 on Washington National Bank, Seattle, Wash, payable to your order on account Japanese Laborers for July, 1900 for Kalispell Div. And Cascade Div. Respectively. The total amount to be sent you as per statement herewith is $68779.95. Dfts. Enclosed amount to $37952.50 leaving balance to follow of $30826.55. The receipts will be sent you in a day or so.

Yours Truly,
[signed] FA Davis (9)

St. Paul, Minn. Aug 30th 1900

Thos. Burke Atty.

Dear sir, Enclosed please see Dft. #7486 for $7000.00 on Washington National Bank Seattle, and Dft. #9776 for $5000.00 on Puget Sound Bational Bank Seattle, Dft. #12271 for $4982.20 on Montana National Bank Helena, Dft. #8296 for $13844.35 on First National Bank Great Falls, making Total $30826.55 which with $37952.50 sent you 23rd completes the July payment for Japanese laborers as per Statement showing Total of $68779.05.

I send you by Great Northern Express to day receipts for amount as above, kindly return as soon as practicable, Obliging
Yours Truly,
[signed] FA Davis (9)

The manner in which these transactions took place was cleverly set up so as to make it nearly impossible for any outside party to follow the money trail, and to maintain the reputation of certain businessmen in Seattle and St. Paul. When the operation of bringing the Japanese laborers into this country began, the money to fund it was placed in trust with two financial institutions in Baltimore, Maryland. At the time, the 'Great Northern Railway Line,' consisted of the Great Northern Railway, the Duluth, Watertown & Pacific Railway, the Eastern Railway of Minnesota, the Montana Central Railway, and the Willmar & Sioux Falls Railway.

The latter was used to help cover up the way the payments to the workers from Japan were handled.

The initial contract for depositing the currency for payments to laborers reads in part: "C.T. Takahashi, O. Yamoaka, and M. Tsukuno, doing business in Seattle as the Oriental Trading Company and United States Fidelity & Guarantee Company, a corporation duly organized and existing under and by virtue of the laws of the state of Maryland, office in Baltimore, as surety, are held and firmly bound unto the Willmar & Sioux Railway Company of Minnesota, a corporation in the penal sum of $10,000 to payment of which sum to the said Willmar & Sioux RR CO., its successors and assigns, we hereby jointly bind ourselves. Sealed and dated 29th of August 1900. (9) This document goes to say that the Oriental Trading Company has obligated to furnish 500 [more] Japanese laborers during the balance of 1900. Laborers were to be paid $1.10 per day for 10 hours work.

The checks for the laborers were to be made payable to the Puget Sound National Bank of Seattle. However, the funds were to be disbursed only upon checks drawn by the Oriental Trading Company and countersigned by H. L. Sizer, and agent for the Willmar & Sioux Falls Railway. The checks would be drawn in favor of the laborers according to the list and book furnished by the W&SF Railway, or its agent, and the balance of the funds, after all the claims were paid, were given to the principal obligor, that being the Oriental Trading Company. This contract was signed by both Yamoaka and Tsukuno.

There was one other, and very similar labor contract agreed to later that same year by the same railroad, the W&SF, but with the American Bonding & Trust Company of Baltimore.

It would take some years, but eventually the Seattle Star work break the story of just how these monies were distributed and just how little the Japanese workers received. More results of research and investigation into this matter, as well as the Seattle Star article are presented later in this chapter.

In later years, however, as demand for more and more laborers grew, it became much more difficult to 'recruit' the number of workers needed by the railroads; both the Great Northern and Northern Pacific. There just were no longer available, the number of men to bring back to the United

States for work on the railroads. The supply of laborers had been rapidly depleted. Representatives of the Morioka would find it difficult to explain this to Takahashi, who would find it inconvenient to tell Burke, who had no desire to inform Jim Hill that there was now a shortage of laborers coming from the Orient. Knowing Hill as well as Burke did, he knew the 'empire builder' would respond in his traditional way to such problems. Do whatever was necessary to get the needed workers over here as quickly as possible.

So representatives of the Oriental Trading Company, sailing on ships of the Nippon Yuzen Kaisha Steamship Company, would make the vessels stop in the Hawaiian Islands on their way to America, to see if there were any men wanting to travel to the United States to work on the railroads. In one instance in 1905, the 'Olympia-Go' stopped at Honolulu and representatives of the Oriental Trading Company somehow pulled away about 600 Japanese pineapple and sugar cane farm workers, put them on the steamer, and transported them to Seattle. Whether they were forced on board, or coerced to sail with promises of a better life working on American railroads, is not known.(39)

But even this practice was still not getting the job done. The railroads were growing as the country expanded. Jim Hill's prize, the Great Northern, was growing the fastest and becoming one of the richest. There was still a great need for more workers and hill decided upon a more direct and respectable approach. He wrote directly to Minister Takahira Kogoro of the Japanese government the following letter dated March 6, 1906:

"I have heard that in Japan at this time many people are troubled by a lack of food. If this is true, it occurred to me that at least 3,000 to 5,000 of them could find permanent employment with the Northern Pacific or the Great Northern Railroad. If the Japanese government has no objection to these people's traveling to the United States of America, I think it would be of value to advertise in Japan that the opportunity for permanent employment with these two railroad companies exists for the number of people I mentioned.

Please inform me whether or not the Japanese Imperial Government is inclined to allow these people to travel to this country."(40)

Meanwhile, as Hill was pursuing direct dealings with the Japanese government, Ototaka Yamaoka of the Oriental Trading Company was in Japan using another one of his own methods for obtaining laborers for the Hill lines. He very successfully deceived government officials with a flood of passports that were nearly perfect forgeries. They were so good they became known as the 'Yamaoka passports.'(45) Using these false documents, he was able to send hundreds more to America aboard the trusty steamships of the Nippon Yuzen Kaisha Company. And again, Yamaoka promised these men that there was steady employment and good wages waiting for them across the Pacific.

In addition to supplying the Great Northern and other railroads with an adequate number of Japanese workers, labor contractors, (ie) The Oriental Trading Company, needed to get their newly acquired workers past the Immigration offices. This would not, at first, be easy. For one reason, a large percentage of Japanese would not be able to pass their physical examination. The primary reason was that so many had trachoma, a serious eye disease that became common in Japan around 1895, following the Sino-Japanese War. The solution to this problem of getting the laborers into the United States was handled by the steamship companies, simply by paying off the doctors, both in Japan just before departure, and in the United States upon arrival. According to an article in the October, 1906 issue of AMERICA-BOUND MAGAZINE:

"...illegitimate ties existed between the American examining doctors and the steamship companies. Success or failure in the eye exam was not decided on the basis of medical science. Instead, the figures were adjusted to agree with the number of passengers a given ship could hold. Success or failure was subject to the convenience of the Oriental, Pacific, and East-West Steamship Companies."

Without a doubt, there was complicity among quarantine doctors, immigration officials, lodging houses, and doctors in private practice. In any case, it was the aspiring immigrants who suffered. Many travelers had do deal with corruption in order to pass their eye exam (as mentioned earlier) before they boarded their ship. Once on board, they spent their time pouring medicine into their eyes in preparation for their second eye exam when they reach the United States. Upon arrival, they were fleeced of what little money they had left by the corrupt quarantine doctors and innkeepers.

It was rumored that San Francisco was very strict about disembarkation of Japanese immigrants there, and Seattle was relatively lenient. In a letter dated April 14, 1900, the Japanese Consulate in Seattle, Narita Goro wrote to Japanese Foreign Minister Aoki Shuzo in Japan explaining why it was much easier for immigrants to enter the Port of Seattle. Seattle and Tacoma immigration officials anonymously worked through interpreters to levy a secret 'head tax' of $1.00 per immigrant. Because of this added fee, not a single Japanese had been refused permission to land at Puget Sound since Narita took office in July of 1899.(39)

There were also many instances where the immigrant, hoping for a new start in life in America, ended up being depleted of all his money upon arrival in the United States. If he wanted to remain in this country and go to work for the railroad, he was just about guaranteed to pass his physical examination at the cost of how much money he had on his person. But that was when his troubles really began. The Japanese immigrant had left himself at the mercy too many unscrupulous people. They would take from him, which was not much, everything he brought to this country, leaving him completely destitute and at the mercy of the Japanese Labor Contractors.

As far back as the early 1900's Seattle, as well as other west coast ports, had its own immigration detention center, built especially to house Japanese until they were ready to go to work for the railroads. There were a few Japanese who were fortunate enough to find work in other areas, but by and far most of the immigrants were held in what was officially called 'immigrant halls' until the railroad called them to work.

Seattle's own immigration detention center stood next to the U. S. Immigration Bureau offices, about 600 yards from the wharf where ships from the Far East made port. It housed about 100 Japanese at a time, mostly men, but some women. The rooms the men and women stayed in were separated from each other. Even husbands and wives were forbidden to share a common room. Visits and conversations were strictly limited, and many times simply restricted. Heavy wire screens covered every window of the detention facility in order to prevent escapes. While they were detained, the immigrants were allowed to receive articles such as books, clothing, and some types of foods from friends and relatives living in Seattle. Of course, all these goods had to pass an official inspection before any of them were given to the detainee. There were times set aside for them to meet with visitors in a separate interview room, and letters they wrote to family and friends on the outside, were opened, read, and if necessary, censored by immigration officials.

To add insult to injury, these 'prisoners' were charged for being housed at the detention center. The cost of food was set at 45 cents per day and was paid by the ship's company that brought them to Seattle. However, when the ship set sail back to the Orient, the immigrants themselves had to pay the cost out of whatever was left of their meager savings they had brought with them. Many thought they would recoup their money once they finally went to work for the Great Northern or Northern Pacific. However, this simply was not the case.

In addition to the official immigration detention centers, there were also Japanese-managed inns. These held mostly illegal immigrants brought to America by the labor contractors for the railroads. These Japanese-managed inns disguised themselves as primarily temporary employment agencies, but they were, in fact, 'fronts' for labor contractors such as the Oriental Trading Company. This was important as these companies needed to maintain their public image as strictly importers of fine silks, Oriental teas, Eastern art, and general merchandise from Asia. (39)

The Japanese workers brought in by the Great Northern through the efforts of the Oriental Trading Company would never see a fraction of the money mentioned in the 1899 contract between the two businesses. Not only this, they would be held as virtual prisoners of the railroad and the labor contractor, with practically no means of escaping. It was a very clever and well thought out plan by the Oriental Trading Company and the Great Northern. They made it impossible for any of the workers to quit their jobs, except from perhaps an untimely death due to some unexpected accident while on the job. These Japanese laborers were often assigned the toughest and most dangerous of all the jobs along the railway's line.

In Kazuo Ito's book, ISSIE, are reported personal accounts by Japanese laborers that vividly describe the conditions of their employment with the Great Northern and other railroads.

Uhachi Tamesa recollected his helping work on the construction of the first Cascade Tunnel on Stevens Pass. "Soon after I joined a Great Northern gang which was working near a tunnel on the other side of the Cascade Mountains. Our job was to change the rails and ties inside the tunnel. Six of us in two rows lifted the 40-foot rail, using levers. We slept in double-decker bunks in a freight car, in the center of which was a coal stove.

Breakfast was bread, butter, and coffee. For lunch, bread, butter, and water. For dinner we had rice, pickled radish and fish, and vegetables boiled with soy sauce. We also had Japanese tea."(44)

Yoshiichi Tanaka also recalled his experiences of life working for the Great Northern. "I worked gangs and sections on the Great Northern from 1912 to 1918," he remembered. "The place was the Cascade division about 120 miles between Seattle and Leavenworth. The four towns and villages along the way, Nippon, Corea, Alpine, and Tye (the new name given Wellington), were abandoned because a new tunnel was opened and the trains no longer went through them. Consequently their names disappeared. The area where they had been was one of the most perilous places in the Northwest. The town of Nippon had been named to commemorate a Japanese engineer who had helped in the construction there, but whose [full] name is unknown. This Nippon village contained a sawmill and 5 or 6 houses in 1913 or 1914, but I heard the express had never stopped there. Most of the workmen were single."(44)

Mr. Tanaka reflected on other Japanese laborer's experiences and treatment by the Great Northern. "We laid new tracks, changed ties, did leveling and adjusting, and took care of emergencies. Even if it was midnight in the coldest part of winter, if there was an emergency we had to rush to the scene and make temporary repair. Lodging facilities were awfully poor. Twp rows of beds made of boards were run along the inside walls of old freight cars. Instead of mattresses, we spread straw on the boards. Innumerable bedbugs marched all over us."(44)

Photo courtesy of Minnesota historical Society

The Great Northern station stop at Nippon taken in the early 1900's.

Yes, there were many Japanese laborers in the Cascades in the early part of the 20th century. Just how many at any one time is impossible to determine. But at times, especially in the winter, it certainly numbered in the thousands.

Even today, the Burlington Northern Santa Fe Railroad (the current name of the Great Northern and Northern Pacific railroads) remains sensitive on this issue. When asked if the Great Northern ever employed any Japanese laborers in the Cascades and Pacific Northwest, the official answer from the railroad's Public Relations Department provided to the author was "perhaps, but mainly Scandinavians and Italians."(8)

James Wolverton, who retired from the Great Northern Railway in 1962 recalled, "I worked with my dad in 1913 with a gang of 110 Japanese relaying track in Northern Idaho. And there were always several gangs [Japanese] of between 45 and 50 at Tye, formally Wellington. They were 'surfacing' gangs."(98) Wolverton also mentioned that there were a number of Greeks and Italians, but they were far outnumbered by Japanese.

Probably it was the Seattle Star daily newspaper that best explained the inhumane conditions these workers were kept in. They were practically slaves of the railroad. The front-page article of Tuesday, February 17, 1910 is here reprinted in its entirety. The major article was also important enough to the Great Northern, as Louis Hill, the railroad's vice president requested a copy which was sent to him by Al G. Ray, a representative of the railway in Seattle.

FOUR THOUSAND JAPS HELD IN SLAVERY ON HILL ROADS

Four thousand Jap laborers are held in practical slavery on the Hill roads, working between Seattle and St. Paul. Their great master is the Oriental Trading Company of Seattle, which makes a quarter of a million dollars a year off them

When the Jap laborer lands in this country, he is steered into the offices of the Trading Company - if the arrangement is not made before he leaves Japan - and enters into the contract which binds his as the personal property of the labor firm. For the Trading Company has a contract with the Hill roads to supply labor. As much as the railroad needs. The Trading Company gets a generous rake off from each man, while the laborers themselves, ignorant, helpless, unable to speak English, think themselves fortunate to get a job.

GET $1.35 A DAY

The men go to work for $1.35 a day. But out of this, the Trading Company gets 15 cents a day for getting them the job. Also it supplies the provisions, at fat profit, as the railroads carry the goods for nothing and they charge the men at an advance of what they could buy them in the neighborhood.

Out of this comes also 50 cents, hospital fees every month, and a dollar a month which the Trading Company credits – no one knows why – to "office expenses."

Something like $29.70 a month for the men – a quarter of a million every year to the company - this is the Jap captains of industry have

learned to capitalize the profits of the working men. Not much different from the United States, is it? Except that it's a little cruder, a little less diplomatic. The American workman can persuade himself that he is a free agent, able to work when and where he likes.

HILL THE BOSS

J.J. Hill, the big boss, C.T. Takahashi, president of the Oriental Trading Company, the immediate active boss, with hordes of smaller bosses known as overseers or bookmen, scattered along the Hill lines - these are the men in authority in the United States, as the Japanese laborer learns when he strikes the northwest.

The branch overseers are over the bookmen. They watch to see that the Trading Company gets all the profits it thinks it deserves. Any one who can get a dozen laborers together can be made a bookman.

The bookmen exact from each of the men under their control from 5 to 10 per cent of their wages. In case of sickness or accident on the part of some of the gang, the bookman in league with the section foreman, does not report the shortage to the central office, but lets the rest of the laborers do the entire work, then he draws the wages in the name of the disabled workman and divides it with the foreman.

WHAT THE COMPANY GETS

15 cents a day from each of the 4,000 men, $15,000 a month.
Profit from provisions, $3,900 per month.
Hospital fees, $2,000 per month.
For "office expenses," $4,000 per month.
Total for company, $25,000 per month.

WHAT THE MEN GET

$1.35 a day minus 15 cents a day for the company, minus a dollar a month for "office expenses," minus 50 cents a month hospital fee, minus cost of groceries and foreman's petty graft.
Total for men, at the most $29.70 [per month]. (71)

"The Boss System," as it was called in the early 1900's, was cleverly constructed in a way to shield most of the big-time businessmen from any provable, legal connection as to what was really happening to these immigrant laborers for the Great Northern. In fairness, it should be pointed out that it was not only the Great Northern that was the culprit in this enterprise. The Northern Pacific, one of Jim Hill's railroads, and the Union Pacific were also getting a bulk of their workmen in the same way.

As soon as the Japanese worker was sent to his new job with the Great Northern, he never worked in direct communication with his employer. He worked through the Japanese 'boss.' In addition to helping keep the hands clean of such men as James J. Hill, Thomas Burke, and Charles Takahashi, this system made it easy for the 'bosses' to exploit their fellow workers, and to concentrate power and money into their hands also.

The 'boss system' probably came about because almost all of the Japanese immigrants had no choice but to rely completely on a middleman. He was unable to speak English as the Seattle Star pointed out, which was bad for him, but good for the middleman. In short, the Japanese railroad worker was without any honest guidance in this strange, new country. He could not communicate with his employer if he had any questions or complaints regarding his working conditions. Unlike European immigrants that came to work for the railroads, these Japanese came primarily from farming villages, many times against their will as has been seen. They had no working experience in an industrial, contract society. Their understanding of the labor situation they were now a victim of, was limited or nonexistent.

This is where the 'bosses' came in. They quickly took advantage of the immigrant's ignorance of the new culture and their difficulty communicating, leaving the 'boss' to take control of his life. The 'bosses,' like those who worked for the Oriental Trading Company, in reality owned the immigrant. These 'bosses' were also the upfront people who operated the Japanese-managed inns, or as they were called by the immigrants, "Hanba," meaning meal house. Here the worker was furnished one square meal a day, and slept in the only clothes he owned on a mattress spread out on the floor. Interestingly, the manner in which these laborers were treated at the "Hanba," was limited to just the Japanese. Immigrants from Europe and elsewhere were not subjected to this treatment when they arrived in America, while waiting to be assigned work on the railroads.

Almost all the 'bosses' took advantage of the wages that would eventually be paid to the Japanese workers under their control. Although the following account does not precisely agree with the Seattle Star article, it offers more proof of the actual mistreatment received by the immigrants.

In his account of the "Boss System," researcher Tsurutani Hisashi wrote in the Japanese Times, published in Tokyo in 1977:

They (the bosses) had the workers pay $1 per month as "office fees." If we take the Oriental Trading Company of 1910 as an example, the boss contracted with his workers to pay him 5 cents a day as a commission, and also took 50 cents a month for hospital fees. Since, according to Fujioka Shiro's "Traces of a Journey," at its peak, the Oriental Trading Company embraced 6,000 workers and its lowest point, there were no less than 3,000...even if we use a conservative figure of $2 a month as the boss's rake-off, it amounts to an enormous sum. Beyond this, beginning with their income from the boarding house room-and-board charges (about 50 cents a day in 1897), the bosses devised a number of schemes to fleece the workers of their wages, including selling them expensive clothing and food, or opening gambling halls and bringing in prostitutes on payday. It was said the bosses lived like kings.(39)

If the 'bosses' lived like kings, the actual owners of the Trading Companies lived even better. Certainly this is true concerning C. T. Takahashi. He could be seen driving around Seattle in his big black touring car as far back as 1912. He was fond of giving large and elaborate parties, and always found time for entertainment and recreation. To the average citizen of the city, Takahashi was a pillar of the Japanese Community. He was the President of the Oriental American Bank, President of the Oriental Trading Company ("importers of fine oriental silks and teas"), a member of the Seattle Chamber of Commerce (founded by Judge Thomas Burke), and a member of the Japanese Commercial Club of Seattle. He lived on Seattle's fashionable First Hill at 907 Fir Street, about one mile from his friend, Thomas Burke, who resided at 1004 Boylston Avenue.(76a)

A letter from B. T. Downs of the Great Northern Railway, to his assistant H. A. Kennedy makes mention of Mr. Takahashi and the railroad's knowledge of what was happening to the Japanese immigrants.

GREAT NORTHERN RAILWAY COMPANY
OFFICE OF GENERAL SUPERINTENDENT

Spokane, Feb. 16th., 1910

Mr. H. A. Kennedy,
    Assistant General Manager,
        St. Paul, Minn.

Dear Sir:

    Referring to your letter of February 9th., to Mr. Taylor and our several telegrams, concerning rates of pay for Japanese labor, I have found that Mr.Takahashi has instructed his men, in accordance with contract, which he understood from the conversation with both yourself and Mr. Gruber, would go into effect Jan. 1st.

    Mr. Takahashi has had considerable trouble in holding some of the men, such as those employed at Coal Chutes, roundhouses and on the Mechanical rolls and explained that any different arrangement, would cause him no end of embarrassment, as he has been accuse by the men of endeavoring to pocket the difference between the rates in effect as he supposed and those mentioned in contract. Under these conditions, I authorize the payment of all laborers, in accordance with contract rate and on Kalispell Division, deductions will be made from pay of track men on February rolls. The total rolls will show a less amount expended under contract, than under the arrangement that was in effect.

                  Yours truly,
                  B.T. Downs
                  General Superintendent

Takahashi was so popular and well regarded that the magazine TOWN CRIER in its July 20, 1912 issue, referred to C. T. Takahashi as "a fine representative of an enterprising race and an important factor in the business and social life of the city of his home."[92] All very true, but with one exception. The bulk of his wealth was gained at the expense of his fellow Japanese. The people of his own race that he helped bring to this country, most of the time illegally, only to forfeit whatever they had, with the false hope of making a better life in America working on the railroads.

Takahashi's career was not without public controversy, however. For example, at the time of the Wellington avalanche disaster, Takahashi practically destroyed the Japanese Association of the State of Washington.

This was a corporation of Japanese businessmen in Seattle that was formed to promote trade between the Pacific Northwest and Japan.

On February 26, 1910, the Japanese Association of Washington held its annual meeting with the primary purpose of electing its officer for the coming year. It was a tumultuous meeting. By midnight, only the president had been elected, it was none other than Charles T. Takahashi himself. The contest for the presidency was very close, he won by only four votes.

On March 1, 1910, Takahashi had appointed two trustees to help him run the Association. He had no authority to do this on his own, according to members. They charged him with using "dictatorial methods" that could lead to the collapse of the Japanese Association. Trustees had to be a stockholder in the corporation, and the two men appointed by Takahashi, without the consent of the Board of directors, were not stockholders.(72)

The next meeting, held on the evening of March 4, 1910, rapidly deteriorated into uncontrollable anger. It became so chaotic that it almost led to physical violence when some of Takahashi's opponents alleged that he had been fraudulently elected to his position. Many members were calling for him to resign immediately. But Takahashi had more allies than he had enemies, and retained his presidency of the Association. He told the Seattle Times on March 6, 1910 that there was some dissatisfaction currently within the Japanese Association, but he was sure the matters would be properly addressed and settled quickly without any difficulties at the next meeting. They were and he stayed on as president and his two newly appointed trustees remained also.

Charles T. Takahashi, as did his friend and business acquaintance, Thomas Burke, died in New York City. He had fallen victim to what was called "Spanish influenza," and died on Sunday, January 11, 1920, almost six years prior to Burke's death. He had left Seattle for New York City a month earlier. Takahashi had spent most of the year 1919 in Japan helping to further the development in shipping between that country and the Port of Seattle.

It was claimed that he was on the threshold of the largest commercial venture in his life. By now, Takahashi's interests were more in farming (he held financial interests in some of the largest wheat farms in Washington and Idaho), as the need for immigrant railroad laborers was now dwindling. He had also gone into the exportation of steel for the railroads and ship building industries in Japan. At the time of his death at age 45, the Japanese North American Times referred to him as "the most widely known Japanese resident" of the United States.

Takahashi no doubt originally made the bulk of his fortune in the illegal importation of railroad workers. And as detailed earlier, another and even more prominent man, who at the very lease knew what was going on, and possibly could have stopped it, was Judge Thomas Burke. After all, he was an officer of the court, an attorney sworn to uphold the laws of the United States of America. Instead, he knowingly condoned the practice of the Labor Contractors.

But in all fairness to them both, it must be remembered that these two men, especially in their later years, did more to create and expand the bold endeavor of trade with the Far East than just about any other entrepreneurs in this country. Their vision and enthusiasm helped begin the enormous and successful commercial trade from which the United States continues to benefit. Probably the most revealing of their hopes and dreams for future personal and economic ties between America and Asia, is contained in a letter to Burke from Takahashi. The reference is to Burke's efforts in allowing Japanese to own property in the Northwest.

February 13, 1917

My dear Judge Burke,
    I want to thank you for your efforts in the matter concerning which I wired you while you were in Washington. The state legislature of Idaho has declined to pass the bill with reference to alien Japanese ownership of land. I gather from the newspaper reports and your telegram that the action of the legislature was largely due to the influences which you set at motion in Washington. I believe this was a most timely act for in this day and age there are particular reasons why the relationship between this country and Japan should remain undisturbed. I want to say to you personally that I feel highly pleased that the Pacific Northwest has so many loyal, broadminded men who can see these problems in the right light and it is largely owing to their attitude, of which you are a leader, that the immense trade has grown up between this country and Japan.

    I have taken great pleasure in giving to the Japanese Consul the facts about this matter and your large share in the result. He has

cabled this to the foreign Department of the Japanese government, and your name is inseparably identified with this public spirited and wholesome action. When I speak of my personal satisfaction with the efforts you have put forth, I am voicing also the very keen appreciation of the Japanese people generally upon this point.

> Yours Very Truly,
> **C.T. Takahashi** (9)

The Japanese railroad workers, in later years, spoke proudly of the years 1905 and 1906 as their high point in building and maintaining American Railroads. In addition to the Great Northern and Northern Pacific, the Union Pacific and Southern Pacific employed a great number of these immigrants. Because a law was passed in 1907, prohibiting the transfer from Hawaii to the mainland, any more Japanese, one supply route was cut off for the railroads and the number of workers declined. Times were changing.

Many changed jobs in later years since railroad work was becoming more seasonable and unstable. Farm work, which lasted most of the year, provided them with a more stable and regular income. As 'Issie' railroad workers began to reach old age, they either retired or returned to Japan. Since most of the Japanese workers disliked the heavy labor and isolation of railroad work, and with the passing of new protection laws, they were now more free to go their own way. This led to a rapid decrease in railroad Japanese laborers in America. As a result, the once thriving business of contracting for workers on the railroads, was hit hard. Many of the 'bosses' who had boasted to friends and associates of their living standards that rivaled prince's, ended their lives in financial misery.

According to the Los Angeles Japanese Daily News, the number of Japanese immigrant laborers for the nation's railroads fell to 10,000 in 1909, and by the early 1930's, the number had dwindled to about 2,000. Ironically, although by the 1930's, many Japanese laborers were professionally trained and well established in all forms of railroad work, when war broke out between Japan and the United States in 1941, the Western Defense Command issued a 'dismissal order' because railway transportation facilities had great military importance. The railroads dismissed all their ethnic Japanese workers immediately.

Chapter 5:

Rescue Efforts East of Wellington

Help was also being sent from the east via a relief train from Wenatchee. J. C. Devery, the Assistant Superintendent of the Cascade Division was in charge of keeping the tracks cleared and eventually the rescue operation needed at Wellington. It was slow going and at times impossible to break through the numerous snow slides east of Leavenworth. The situation was not that much better on the eastside of the summit. One slide was estimated at 200 feet in length and 50 feet deep, near the station stop of Drury, six miles east of Leavenworth. The slide destroyed one railroad car and killing one employee. Early that last week in February, Devery made the first of many attempts to get to the summit. The first work train got only four miles from town before a number of cars were derailed due to the heavy snow on the tracks. Trying to make its way back to Leavenworth, the rest of the train and its two engines derailed. Devery, despite a bad leg, and his crew had to walk back to town.

This event took place at Tumwater Canyon, another perilous section along the Great Northern's Stevens Pass route. The canyon was also a treacherous journey during the winter. It was dug out of the hills of the Leavenworth "West mile-board and for nine miles, twisted its way around the mountains, while the Wenatchee River wound through it, coursing the nearby tracks. The sides of the gorge were so steep that in late winter, when snow started to melt during the warm hours between 11:00 am and 7:00 pm, slides were liable to crash down on the track. After sundown, when the air grew chilly, Tumwater Canyon was again safe for traffic."(10a)

Much of the information that follows, regarding the events on the eastside of the Cascades, are the recollections of Great Northern Engineer John P. Brady who was there at the time. He told his story to the editor of RAILROAD MAGAZINE, Freeman Hubbard in 1946.

A few days later, Assistant Superintendent Devery decided to make another attempt at clearing the rails westward. According to Brady, who was along for this journey, "When we reached the slide, we stopped to look it over. The snow was wet and heavy, and I didn't think we could do much with it. However, Devery wanted to try, so we backed up and took a run for it. When we stopped, we were about an engine length into the snow, and the #1920 – the heavier engine – was off the track, headed for the river. The section men with us earned their ride. They dug out the #1920, rerailed her without much trouble, as we all hauled her over the heavy snows. By this time Devery had decided to give up the attempt, so we ran back into Leavenworth, and tied up about 6:00 pm."(10a)

Word came from Great Falls, Montana that another rotary snowplow should reach Leavenworth by February 27th. As soon as it arrived, the rescuers would be ready to hook up to it with a pusher engine and a caboose for the men to sleep in. They left Leavenworth again the evening of the 27th. As they entered Tumwater Canyon, they ran into a number of small slides, none of which posed any difficulties. But on the morning of February 28th, they ran into another unforeseen problem. This time it was not caused by nature. The rotary pusher engine had run out of water. Engineer Brady and the rest of the crew were stuck again. They were several miles from the next station stop at Merrit, which had a water tank, but it helped that the tracks were on level ground for those few miles. A little innovative thinking and a lot of muscle, they got to Merrit as John Brady explained. "The rotary had a foot of water…there was nothing to do except melt the snow. We shoveled away till the tank was pretty well filled. Then we placed a tie across the rails and managed to back the rear truck of the tank up onto the tie. Tilting it sent the water forward. When we got inside the tank, we piled snow up around the tank valves and started the thaw-out hose working. Enough snow melted so that we finally succeeded in getting started and reached Merrit tank shortly before noon."(10a)

They were at Merrit for approximately one hour and began the eleven-mile journey up the 2 per cent grade to Cascade Tunnel Station. This leg of the trip proved very slow going. By 7:00 P.M. they had only managed to make one-mile after leaving Merrit. They went back and spent the night there. Early the next morning, March 1st, the rescue party which included, besides Brady, fireman Ralph Helfreitch, and engineers John Maryott and Harry Geerds, was awake and helping the night crew get the rescue train ready for its next attempt at getting to Wellington. The Great Northern kept several cars filled with coal for emergencies at Merrit. The train and its crew was finally ready to leave about 10:00 A.M. when Superintendent Devery, along with general Master Mechanic Kelly (for the Cascade Division), ran up to them from the telegraph office. The lines were still down at Wellington, he told everyone, but they had received word from Spokane that a giant avalanche had occurred at Wellington earlier that morning. Wellington was only fifteen miles to the west. It sounded very bad and they were more anxious than ever to get there. But Devery also informed them that there was another message reporting a rotary and a pusher engine were stalled at Gaynor, the next station stop four miles west of Merrit. He didn't know for sure if they were off the tracks or out of coal and water. He only knew that the crews had abandon the engines and hiked back to Wellington.

By 7:00 P.M. that evening, they had progressed only one half mile, due to more motor trouble. The entire day of March 2, 1910 was spent plowing through heavier, deeper, and wider slides. Again they were able to travel only another half mile. It was unbelievable. They had left Merrit two days earlier and it was still three miles away; Wellington, twelve miles. It is important to note that each night, they would have to back down to Merrit for more coal and water for the train, and so the men could eat.

On March 2nd, word came from Spokane that the General Manager of the Great Northern, J. M. Gruber and his assistant, George Emerson had arrived from St. Paul and were waiting for word when the tracks would be cleared for them to get to Wellington. While waiting in Spokane, Gruber began organizing two large relief trains. That same day, the rescuers, working so desperately to get to Wellington from Merrit, succeeded in clearing close to one more mile before having to return to Merrit. The next day's work March 3rd, brought them within a short distance of Gaynor and the two dead engines that still blocked the track. Engineer John Brady remembered, "That night, while we backed up to Merrit, we were more hopeful. The storm was broken and we were having fair weather to work in. Devery ordered the night crews out to see if they couldn't get the stalled engines off the main, in case the special from Spokane should arrive at Merrit early in the morning. However, after working until ten o'clock the night crew returned to report that the left-quarter shaft on the rotary had broken and the machine was out of commission. We tied up then, planning to start the crippled plow east to Spokane the next day."(10a)

The two trains with General Manager Gruber arrived late in the afternoon of March 4th. One train came complete with all the necessary equipment for clearing rails, machinery to get derailed engines back on track, a dining car, and enough cars to accommodate the nearly 250 laborers that Gruber had managed to recruit. The second train was made up of cars of coal, food and medical supplies, and a carload of dynamite for blasting the sides of mountains to help with avalanche control. That evening, Gruber sent the first of his many telegrams from the Cascades to

Louis Hill (son of James Hill), president of the Great Northern. Though at times difficult to read, the Great Northern telegrams add considerable information as to the trials and tribulations of all those on Stevens Pass.

8pm
Merrit Mar 4
L.W. Hill

Reached Leavenworth 10am and came far as Gaynor where Mr. Kelly had resurrected dead rotary by packing coal about ¼ mile by men over snow drifts they worked east and got through all drifts to where their west bound rotary broke down about midnight last night. Track now open from Gaynor to 1¼ miles east of Chiwaukum. Between there and Leavenworth about ten to twelve hours work with one rotary. Machine here will reach those slides about eleven PM and work at them all night rotary being double crewed...200 kegs powder reach Leavenworth six am fifth to loosen up hard slides and those filled with timber. Understand slides between Gaynor and Berne are almost continuous and full trees...powder will materially help in such slides from Berne to Tunnel...Expect rotary from Kalispell reach Leavenworth about noon fifth which will have for relief in case any break down...have 250 men between Lvnworth and Gaynor about 60 of them citizens from Lvnworth who volunteered their services...100 more reach Lvnworth in am and will be all we can use...will go to Tunnel tomorrow and try and estimate probable time we can have line open that far but will depend great deal on how much timber is encountered. Mr. Emerson go with me.

J M Gruber

The citizens of Leavenworth had held a town meeting in the Opera House on the evening of March 3rd to organize relief help for the Wellington disaster. These are the volunteers Gruber referred to in his telegram. Berne (referred to in Gruber's same telegram) was the last station stop before Cascade Tunnel Station. Here the rescuers and supply trains ran into a slide 800 feet long and nearly 50 feet deep covering the tracks. The men were kept busy night and day shoveling the snow from the rails. Another telegram from Gruber to Louis Hill explained the difficulties at Berne. It also described the early use of dynamite for avalanche control.

10pm Berne   March 7-8
L.W. Hill,
I.J. Swan, St. Paul

   As near as I can judge would say that slide we are now in should
be opened by noon to two o'clock tomorrow. Rotary moved about 150
feet today but did a great deal of shooting with powder. Necessary in
order to get snow moved away where rotary could work to put in two
shots at right angles to the track and then account of very high cuts
had to put in some back shots on the high side to loosen the overhang.
Will have one powder gang shooting until midnight tonight if the
trench that was dug down by the hand shovelers to about fourteen foot
depth, height of the rotary so as to loosen up the snow when the rotary
reached it...the only other slide to Wellington to any consequence is
at west switch at Berne and think we can go through that in two or
three hours. No outward appearance of trees in it while a very large
number have been encountered in the present slide. Rotary is holding
up first class have had no breakdown or delays from it. Working
cautiously to avoid it as it is the only large one we have. Others on the
east side will not cut large enough swath and will not throw snow over
the height the present one does and would necessitate shoveling a good
deal more of the snow.

J. M. Gruber

   On March 10th, the party broke through to Cascade Tunnel Station. They
found the town almost completely destroyed. Engineer Brady described
what they saw. "We reached Cascade Tunnel, finding the company
buildings and water-tank there completely demolished, and the wreckage
of the large dormitory, eating house, section house, ten employees' cottages
and two stand-pipes strewn down the mountain side. It seemed a miracle
that no one had lost his life, though a number of company employees were
badly injured. The people had fled through the tunnel to Wellington. We
plowed out the main-line and both passing tracks, then dropped into the
two mile tunnel. When we exited at the west portal at Wellington – the
sun was shining and it was a fine spring afternoon. But we looked upon
a scene of a terrible catastrophe; the avalanche had struck at 2:00 am on
March 1st, while we had been sleeping peacefully at Merrit."(10a)

Wellington, The Rescue Continues

March 2nd and 3rd finally brought the many needed doctors, nurses, coroners, and rescuers to the cataclysm in the Cascades. Help from both sides of Wellington were now flocking in, primarily from the west. J. H. O'Neill was there, taking charge of the entire recovery effort. The destruction was beyond his imagination. From what he saw, he was amazed that there were any survivors.

Photo courtesy Museum of History & Industry, Seattle

Wreckage and debris of passenger coaches just after Wellington avalanche.

The Sheriff of Wenatchee, Ed Ferguson had hiked in through the tunnel from the east, along with five or six other rescuers from Peshastin (a station stop near Leavenworth), where only days earlier the Great Northern had suffered another mishap. On Tuesday morning, February 22nd, a GN Fast Mail train, a freight train, and passenger train No. 2, were all three involved in a collision that had nothing to do with all the snow slides. As the westbound Fast Mail approached the Peshastin depot, the freight train was expected to take a sidetrack. However, control of the freight train was lost when its air brakes failed and stayed on the same track that the No. 2 passenger train was on. A brakeman, seeing the inevitable collision between the freight train and the No. 2, threw a switch that sent the freight train colliding into the Fast Mail train, and avoiding hitting the passenger train. The collision wrecked the tender of the Fast

Mail engine, and smashing two box- cars of the freight train. But the No. 2 passenger train did not escape the wreck completely. Its baggage car was smashed inward from heavy debris of one of the other trains. There were a number of injuries to passengers and crew aboard all three trains, but no fatalities. Just a lot of damaged rolling stock.(67) All train movement at Peshastin was delayed for eight hours.

Sheriff Ferguson said the sight of what was left of Wellington was beyond description. Shortly after he got involved with the actual rescue work, the sight became gruesome. What his eyes first gazed on was a completely severed body. He then noticed bodies "packed like sardines" in about a 20-foot square radius.(74)

Most of the survivors had been thrown clear of the wreckage and laid on top of the snow, or were buried just a few feet under the white powder. Searchers at times would simply stand and listen to hear any voices coming from under the snow. When they heard anything, they would take off in that direction and began digging. Some of the rescuers reported the eerie sight of seeing the smooth, white blanket begin to move in spots. A hand would appear, and then another. They immediately rushed to the poor victim who was trying to dig their way out of their frozen tomb.

It had been more than a day and a half since the avalanche. O'Neill and the other rescuers were aware of the fact that the chance of finding any more victims alive was just about lost. The work would now be that of recovering the dead. O'Neill asked for a count of how many survivors there were in the temporary hospital. And could anyone give him an estimate of how many bodies were still buried in the ravine? He needed to report to Everett and St. Paul just how bad the situation was. He was also concerned about the now constant rain that was falling. The temperature was slowly climbing, bringing about the chance of another avalanche to come down on the rest of Wellington and all the surviving victims and rescue people. He figured there were approximately one hundred men with picks, shovels, axes, crowbars, working themselves to exhaustion. It was comforting to know that more were on the way, but how long would it be before they arrived?

Photo courtesy of Museum of History & Industry, Seattle

Photo of a twisted rotary snowplow and possible locomotive. A group of rescuers can be seen in background, standing on a hillside.

As O'Neill stood on top of they slide, watching the rescue effort, Basil Sherlock walked up to his with a piece of paper in his hand. Maybe this was the body count of the survivors and the dead that he was waiting for. Before Sherlock handed him the paper, O'Neill asked what did he think of the idea of using Alaskan snow sleds to remove the dead from Wellington? From now on, the rescue effort would primarily be concerned with recovering the dead, and O'Neill wanted Sherlock's thoughts on what he believed would be the most effective and efficient way to do this. He also explained to Basil that it would take three men per sled to get them to Scenic. One to lead and steer the sled, while two more, with ropes attached, would have to hold the sled back from running away with its cargo. Sherlock agreed.

Then O'Neill began talking about his private secretary who had gone down in the slide. Earl Longcoy was only 19 years old, and loved his job with the Great Northern. O'Neill saw a bright future for the enthusiastic young man. He lived in Everett and was awaiting the arrival of his widowed mother from Green Bay, Wisconsin. O'Neill knew that Longcoy's mother was currently on a train heading for Washington. He was sickened by the fact that he had no way of locating her before she would arrive to find out the terrible fate of her young son.

The Superintendent then asked what the paper was in Sherlock's hand. Without saying anything, the telegrapher handed it to his boss. It was his resignation. "You're not going to quit now?" O'Neill protested. Sherlock told him that he would stay on until properly relieved. "How could anyone not see this disaster coming? Why were the trains allowed to stay where they were? All this death might have been prevented." This is what Sherlock told the Superintendent. O'Neill did not answer. He simply handed back Sherlock's resignation.

After a few moments of silent contemplation, O'Neill said, "You don't want to quit. When you're relieved, take a vacation for a while and go back east, then when you return, you'll want to stay on."

Sherlock told him that he and his wife were leaving, and wanted to go somewhere, anywhere there was no snow. O'Neill responded, "I'll get a man up here to relieve you. When he shows up, think this over and let me know." (96a) The two men parted and O'Neill went to the telegrapher office, got the information he was seeking regarding the number of casualties, and filed his first dispatch to Everett from the Wellington disaster.

Wellington - 3-2-10 Following is report of hurt in accident at Wellington: Engineers Osborne, Martin, Carroll, Jarginson, fireman Gilman, Bennington, Jinks, Mauk. Engineer D. Tegtmor, Fireman S.A. Bates, J.D. Kurdee badly injured. Fred Nelson slightly injured. Conductor M.O. White, slightly injured. Porter A. Smith, L. Anderson slightly hurt. Mail clerk A.B. Hursell, slightly hurt. Up to six P.M. have recovered 23 dead bodies, 25 still missing. 15 alive, will get names of all passengers injured and missing in A.M. (61)

Many of those named were misspelled, some of them later died from their injuries, and some names do not appear at all on the official list of injured or killed workers distributed by the Great Northern.

Most of the men had been dug out of their snowy encasement by a rescue crew who followed the sounds of their tapping that they made from the end of their mail car. The car was broken in half by the force of the avalanche. It took nearly seven hours of laborious digging to rescue the trapped train workers, but the rescuer's efforts saved a number of lives.

The gruesome sight that Sheriff Ferguson first viewed, was now being seen by more and more of the rescuers. One crew stumbled upon an enormous log that had been snapped like a toothpick by the overwhelming strength of the avalanche. Underneath the huge log, they discovered six badly mangled and crushed bodies. Some were so badly disfigured they could not be identified.

One rescuer staggered up the hillside gasping how he had come across the body of a man embedded in the side of a huge evergreen tree. He was held there by a portion of railroad track wrapped around the truck of the tree. The rescuer then became physically ill after telling the grisly details. Another searcher entered the bunkhouse to tell of finding the severed hand of a woman with a ring on one finger that had the initials C.O. engraved on it. This discovery led them all to believe it must be that of Catherine O'Reilly, a 26-year old nurse from Sacred Heart Hospital in Spokane.

The horrifying tales continued as more of the volunteers helping in the search returned up the hillside for much needed physical and emotional relief. There were some who maintained and appetite and needed nourishment. They were all convinced that if anyone else were alive in the snowy mass, it would be a miracle. It was another nightmarish night. The sight of the rescue parties tramping around the top of the enormous avalanche at night, walking on top of the graves of who knew how many victims, painted an eerie and unnerving portrait in the minds of everyone at Wellington. To those who stood on the porch at Bailets Hotel or Fogg Brothers Restaurant, the searchers could be seen by the dim light of their lanterns and the occasional flash of lightening.

Meanwhile in the bunkhouse, those passengers and crew members who had survived the slide began telling what it was like on the trains when the avalanche hit. Ray Forsyth, a Great Northern section worker was sleeping in one of the passenger cars of the Spokane Local when the car was suddenly and violently shaken by the force of the slide. Earlier that evening, he had feared for his safety while trying to get some sleep in one of the railroad's smaller houses for its workers. Finding sleep impossible, he made his way to the No. 25 that fateful night. He was in a car with several women and quite a number of children. In telling his experience, Forsyth said that, "it seemed as if the car was lifted bodily from the track and was held poised in midair. Suddenly, it [the car] toppled over the edge and rolled down the steep embankment. Instantly the air was filled with the shrieks of the injured. A fearful storm was raging. A high wind was blowing and there was a spectacular electrical display.(69) He also told of how the survivors of his car were helped by others who could only see what they were doing by the flare of the lightening, "which was almost incessant."

Henry H. White, a salesman for the American Paper Company, who recently moved from Minneapolis and currently lived at 510 Broadway in Seattle, was in the bunkhouse-hospital, suffering from serious chest injuries. He told those around him of what it was like when the avalanche hit his car. "Things happened so fast that it is hard to remember what took place. I heard a crash like thunder, then I felt myself going through a window or the roof." White went on to describe what he then saw after being thrown from the train. "Crawford, another survivor, followed as though shot from a catapult. Brakeman Ross Phillips climbed through a hole without his nightshirt. Crawford told me to keep cool till the snow stopped moving. There was a heavy wet snow and a strong wind blowing at the time." (72)

White told how he helped to dig out of the debris, Porter Lucius Anderson who was aboard the sleeping car named, "Winnipeg." Someone then handed him two blankets, one of which he used to wrap around Anderson's bare feet, and the other he gave to Brakeman Ross, who was nearly naked. White then went on to tell of the disturbing sounds of people moaning and crying all along the slide area. White could do no more, as he was badly injured himself. A rescuer helped him and the rest up the hill to the makeshift hospital in the bunkhouse.

But who was Crawford? Obviously Henry White knew him. However, the 'official' Great Northern list of those who survived, died, or were never found, mentions no one by the first or last name of Crawford.

On March 7, 1910, a Great Northern telegrapher by the last name of Britton arrived at Wellington with a letter dated March 5th, from telegrapher Flannery, reading:

Bearer, Mr. Britton is to go to work as telegrapher at Wellington. I understand Sherlock does not want to stay, if he has not changed his mind, you may use Britton to relieve him, otherwise use him to relieve Avery. Let me know when and what position Britton takes over. [signed] **G. W. Turner** (96a)

Britton took over for Basil Sherlock on the same day he arrived, but Sherlock did not leave immediately. He and his wife felt the need to stay with the people in the makeshift hospital at the bunkhouse. At one time, there were as many as fifty victims there, but the number had dwindled to ten, when the first relief rain arrived from the East. Mr. And Mrs. Sherlock stayed at Wellington until his paycheck arrived by train on March 15th. They then left the scene of the "white death" as he called it on the 18th of March 1910.

In his reminiscences, Sherlock recalled a number of tales of heroism and tragedy. In his own words he reflected, "Since March 2nd, there were dead bodies laying all over the floor of the depot, just far enough apart so that the telegraphers could step over them to go back and forth to their instruments. The undertakers were working in the freight room."(96)

On March 8th, what must have been a very emotional moment for Basil, took place in the bunkhouse. A nurse came over to him saying, "Here is a young man who has been asking to see you for some time." (Sherlock recalled these same words decades later in his letter to Raymond Starrett, printed earlier in this book). It was little Raymond Starrett, the seven year old whose forehead had embedded in it the piece of wood that Sherlock had successfully removed on the dining room table at Bailets Hotel. Sherlock recalled, "I got up and looked at him, he smiled and I smiled back, then we shook hands. I could not talk, for I had seen his two sisters and grandfather (Mr. William May, laying dead on top of the snow."(96)

May 25, 1910, while Sherlock was working for the Chicago Great Western Railroad, at Byron, Illinois, he received a letter from the Great Northern Railway. It was from Vice President and General Manager J. M. Gruber. The letter was sent to him at Wellington and was forwarded to him at Byron. It reads as follows:

GREAT NORTHERN RAILWAY
General Manager's Office
St. Paul, Minn. May 8, 1910

Mr. B.J. Sherlock
    Wellington, Wash.
Dear sir:
    I wish to express for the Railroad Company, it's sincere appreciation for the meritorious service rendered by you, in connection

with the catastrophe which occurred at Wellington, in our Cascade mountains, morning of March 1st, 1910, caused by an avalanche of snow coming down the mountains, carrying to destruction our Mail train #27 and the passenger train #25, causing the loss of a great many lives, as well as injuries to passengers and employees.

I also enclose check for two hundred dollars, and shall be glad if you will sign and return the enclosed voucher.

Yours very truly,
[signed] J.M. Gruber (96a)

This was very much out of the ordinary for the Great Northern to do. The company had a policy at that time to say very little when all was going well with its operations, and to say nothing at all when anything went wrong!

Sherlock's final thoughts are worth noting too. He talked about how something so terrible that happened at Wellington, could not happen fifty years later. With new and better forms of communication, and modern methods of disaster relief, the stranded people could have been removed from Wellington before the avalanche.

"Most of the dead were smothered in snow," Sherlock contended. "Some were forty feet below the surface of the snow. Over a mile square [the size of the area that covered the wreckage], **where the slide ended, there was nothing in sight but snow. Personally, I think that, it is remarkable, although it was only few, that** [some] **were recovered as they were."**

Basil Sherlock
Willmar, Minnesota
March 31, 1960 (96a)

In fact, Sherlock's thoughts of new and better forms of communication had already been discussed only ten days after the Wellington disaster. The following letter from President Louis Hill explains:

Redlands, Cal., March 10th, 1910.
Mr. J. M. Gruber,
General Manager, St. Paul, Minn.
Sear Sir:
In connection with attached, I wish you would have Mr. Little figure on question of practicability of installing wireless, say,

Wellington to Skykomish and Leavenworth. My impression is that the outfit would not cost us to exceed $5,000.00 and when snow troubles break our telegraph line we could resort to the wireless for emergency and limited use. Understand when snow is on the ground wireless is very good. Also understand static conditions better in moist climates, which would be favorable in this locality.

Yours truly,
[signed] **Louis Hill**
President (40)

The First Reporter on the Scene

On the front page of the Seattle Times of Thursday, March 3, 1910, appeared the following banner headline set in the largest type the paper had:

118 VICTIMS

It was one of the first dispatches from J. J. Underwood, a staff reporter for the Times, and at the time, the only newspaper reporter on the scene. The story is important as it was written by a professional journalist who was actually at Wellington. He was an eyewitness to the results of the disaster and the first reporter to talk with and interview the people who were there when the slide happened. Underwood's reports were considered the most accurate (even by the Great Northern) of all the newspapers that eventually got reporters to the scene. His story follows:

Wellington, Thurs., March 3 – The scenes here are indescribably awful. Seven bodies were recovered during the night, and seven more today, making the total number recovered to date thirty-five.

The Great Northern's list of dead and missing - and the missing must also be counted as dead – now total eighty-eight. Add to this number the 30 laborers who were also swept down into the canyon, concerning whom the railroad's list says no word, and the appalling death roll has apparently reached its completion with 118 wiped out.

Two of the seven were electricians who were sleeping in a cabin at the edge of Wellington. The cabin was carried 300 feet down the gorge.

No hope is entertained by anyone here that any of the missing are alive.

Of the sixty-five or more bodies still in the terrible tangle of snow, ice, trees, and wreckage, probably fifty will have to be left for weeks, perhaps months.

It is freely predicted by many of the workers that the bodies not recovered must be left to summer.

Superintendent J. H. O'Neill says the slide was caused by a terrific electric storm. He expects to open the road by April 1. The men sleeping in his private car were all killed. The icebox was the only part of the car found.

The car in which Mrs. Covington slept has been found and one body taken out.

Three slides have occurred between here and Scenic during the last 2 days.

Wreckage is strewn over a half square mile. All that can be seen is portions of timber sticking up through the snow. One hundred and fifty men are digging for bodies. The climb up the hill between Scenic and Wellington is not unattended with danger. If the rain continues there will be more slides. If it freezes, the people here will encounter difficulties in getting out. Preparations are being made to send bodies to Scenic on toboggans.

A number of dagoes immediately after the accident commenced robbing the bodies. They were driven off by railroad authorities before the deputy sheriffs arrived. Dr. H.K. Stockwell, of Stevens hospital in Monroe, is in charge of the 17 patients there. Mrs. Toddhunter, a trained nurse who has reached here from Scenic, arrived after noon, in overalls and gumshoes. She was in an exhausted condition, but has recovered and is now working. Two women from Hot Springs are assisting. Meat was brought in by the railroad company's guides this morning.

Temporarily, a line has been strung over the snow between here and Scenic, but reported small snow slides may put it down at any moment.

Thirty-one bodies are packed like sardines in the small structure in the rear of the telegraph office. They will be taken to Scenic for burial as soon as possible.

Mrs. Covington's body has just been recovered.

Division superintendent J.H. O'Neill says that all the fuel had been exhausted when the accident happened.

Underwood's first report from Wellington is interesting in a number of ways. It certainly helps to understand what was happening at the summit and how the terrible scene appeared to those who were the first to arrive. But perhaps the most intriguing of all is his mention of the "30 laborers who were swept down into the canyon…concerning whom the railroad's list says no word." Could these laborers been Japanese, assigned to the rotary snowplows? It was not unlike the Great Northern to deny any responsibility if anything like this did happen. And more likely than not, the railroad would simply refuse to acknowledge the incident even happened at all. Remember what the longtime residents of Wellington had told Basil Sherlock as to how the grounds all across the area , housed the unmarked graves of the many Japanese who were killed working for the railroad. And because practically all of them were illegal aliens brought here in behalf of the Great Northern, it would be to the railroad's best interest not to discuss or even acknowledge any catastrophe such as this. It is also worth remembering that it was the GN's policy to keep the Japanese laborers way from others and house them in box cars.

The reporter's second dispatch to the Times the same day stated that "thirty-five bodies have been recovered…The rest, being buried under hundreds and thousands of tons of snow must remain in their icy graves till summer." His next paragraph continued the mystery of the 'foreign laborers.'

"The list of dead and missing, given out by the railroad now number 88. Thirty laborers, unlisted, were also killed. Besides these, there are the laborers employed on the rotary snow plow that went down…their names are not known, but there is no question that 20 or 30 of these men are among the victims of the horror."(72)

Photo courtesy of University of Washington Special Collections Division

Photo by A. Curtis

Remains of Solomon Cohn, age 50, of Everett, Washington. His was the first body to be recovered after the avalanche had destroyed the trains.

Underwood had been at Wellington long enough now to include his own personal observations and the descriptions given to him by the survivors he had talked with.

Wellington – Thurs. March 3rd – 118 persons perished when the tremendous avalanche, more than a mile long, thundered down the mountainside Tuesday AM and carried 2 trains, 3 steam locomotives and 3 electric motors, besides buildings and snows sheds into the gulch below. 35 bodies have been recovered. A few more will be taken out...

A horror it is. The horror of it grows every minute. As if the apparent list of casualties is not enough, the last touch was added when a number of Italian workmen began robbing the bodies of the dead. This was Tues. AM, immediately after the catastrophe...a strict watch is kept and every precaution will be taken to prevent a recurrence of the outrage.

Those who are here among the survivors can find no words to tell of their awful experience. Even among those who emerged with little or no injuries there is the same feeling of utter lack of modes of expression or even of joy or relief that they escaped. On the minds of these has been indelibly marked a sense of absolute horror which seems to make them dumb and voiceless.

For a week, the 60 odd men, women and children, huddled in the sleeper and day coaches of the lost train, faced a horrible death such as came to the great majority of them. Since Tuesday of last week they had daily watched the awful snow slides strip great trees and great boulders from the mountainside and drive downward to the canyon with terrific speed. These slides occurred every few hours within plain sight of the marooned passengers. Daily the danger grew until the mental strain of the unfortunates became almost unbearable.

Hours passed and the slides came oftener and seemed even more terrible than before. Nights were spent in a ceaseless and wretched vigil, the passengers unable to rest and realizing more and more that they were caught in a trap.

After being there for several days, the emotional impact on Underwood began appearing in his reports. He was appalled by the behavior of some people who were stripping and stealing property from the dead. He emphasized this in his dispatches. GHOULS TO GET SHORT SHIFT AT SCENE OF SLIDE, was the headline for one of his stories. "Any man who attempt to loot the bodies of the dead at Wellington will be shot down like the dog he is and with as little ceremony. No orders have been given to our men covering this matter, but I know enough of the temper of our employees at the scene of the disaster to believe that ghouls will receive summary and effective justice.

So said William A. Ross, assistant general passenger agent of the Great Northern...plainly showing the effect of his mission of directing the recovery of the bodies of the dead and succoring the living."

Underwood's report of what Ross had to say went on, "Our men stopped three foreign-laborers and found that one had on three woolen undershirts he had stolen: another had a woman's jacket hidden under his coat, and the third had some silk which he had stolen from a trunk of one of the passengers," Ross said.

"The three were forced to disgorge and were driven from camp at the point of a gun. Of all miserable wretches in human form the ghoul that preys under such appalling conditions as now exists at Wellington is the most despicable."(72)

One of Underwood's final dispatches from Wellington read:

MELANCHOLY PROCESSION ARRIVES

Up until dusk yesterday a melancholy procession of people plodded up the steep and difficult path from Scenic. They came in search of their dead. Some broke down and wept bitterly at the sight of tiers of dead bodies, piled in an outhouse in back of the telegraph office. Others accepted their bereavement with resignation. (72)

By now, reporters from other newspapers were arriving also, but J. J. Underwood, the first one there, had seen and heard enough. But his reporting is, to this day, indispensable in helping to understand and determine what really happened at Wellington.

In fact, as mentioned earlier, the Great Northern recognized the Seattle Times for its accuracy of reporting. The March 4, 1910 edition of the newspaper featured the following article:

A Spokesman for the Great Northern today made the following statement to the Times for publication. "The Times is the only newspaper which has consistently published accurate, conservative accounts of the Wellington disaster and the events following it. Certain sensational statements in other papers should be promptly denied…Such stories are both willfully and unnecessarily false!" (72)

Leavenworth

Many towns and cities from Minnesota to Washington State owe their very existence to James J. Hill and the Great Northern Railway. In his driving ambition to forge through the Cascades, Hill kept his promise of better days ahead for those towns that were just starting or struggling to stay alive in the northern mountains of Washington.

Leavenworth is just such a town. It was built solely around the Great Northern's east entrance to the Cascades. The early station stop was platted in 1893, the year the railroad successfully crossed Stevens Pass, by a group of financiers headed by Charles F. Leavenworth. From the very beginning, the heart of the town's economy was provided by the Great Northern.

Leavenworth was built around the train's depot and roundhouse. As the railway grew, so did Leavenworth. From the very beginning, the town prospered from railroad money that arrived with the workers who came to construct the line through the mountains. With the employees, came their families; and those families required schools, churches, and numerous retailers. As more and bigger trains, with their heavier loads began crossing the Cascades, the railroad yard was enlarged for extra track sections to handle the additional rail cars and snow fighting equipment.

The timber industry was also an important source of growth for Leavenworth. The Great Northern was in continuous need for wood to construct more rails and bridges, in addition to the unquenchable need for timber back east. A large mill was built adjacent to the railroad yard for convenience in shipping. The location of the town's mill was also close to the Wenatchee River, where a dam was constructed to form a log pond, from where the logs were hoisted into the mill to be planed and made into lumber. When the mill was finally closed, the dam was also removed from the river, and what was once a sandbar, became known as "Blackbird Island." The little island is now part of a beautiful park at Leavenworth.

Leavenworth's setting in the Alpine-like region of the Cascades helped to keep the town from going bust when demand for timber started depleting. But its beautiful surroundings made it a natural stop for campers or travelers crossing the state. The town started growing again. Streets were built to handle increasing automobile traffic, a water system was installed, and then a sewer system. Streets and sidewalks were paved. Doctor and dentist offices opened as well as a small hospital. By the early 1920's, Leavenworth had become quite a town, with the addition of a bank, a few hardware stores, grocery and drugs stores, more schools, churches, cafes, and many taverns.

The fruit industry also expanded up the Wenatchee Valley from the lower areas near the Columbia River, and residents cleared more land for apple and pear orchards. Packing sheds were built along side the Great

Northern tracks in the little towns of Peshastin, Dryden, and Cashmere. All three consider by citizens of Leavenworth to be a part of their economic hinterland. The fruit industry provided more jobs in the orchards, in the packing mills, as well as in the storage and shipping facilities. The industry continues to be a major part of greater Leavenworth's economy.

For a number of years, championship ski-jumping competition was held at Bakke hill near Leavenworth. When the schedule for this type of competition was changed, the result pretty much eliminated Leavenworth as one of the country's fine jump sites. It also cost the town many jobs as well.

When the railroad finally closed the switch yard, and the lumber company shut down its saw mill, many more jobs were gone, and people who chose to stay had to find other ways of making a living. Some became loggers and truckers. Some people planted more fruit trees, but many residents could not find jobs and had to leave the small town located in one of the most beautiful natural settings in the country. Suddenly, almost overnight, many houses and businesses were up for sale. The economic situation was very bad in the late 1930's. It happened almost as fast as it prospered back at the turn of the century when the Great Northern 'created' it.

In the late 1950's, some of the local people realized they had to do something to bring more and better jobs to town. They were not about to leave such beautiful surroundings and let their beloved town go the way of so many others. They contacted the university of Washington in Seattle and received help in making a study of the area's assets and liabilities. Researchers from the University of Washington, after analyzing all the data, recommended to the people that Leavenworth was located in a good and unique area for their town to flourish in the tourist industry. The people from the university also advised them to pick a specific 'theme' for the town.

The Cascade Mountains, with all its beautiful, changing scenery during all four seasons, its steep, jetting peaks, lots of snow for winter sports, trails for hiking in the summer, and clear water streams for fishing, reminded the people of the European Alps. They decided on a Bavarian theme. In the 1960's, buildings in town started being remodeled and redecorated as a Bavarian village. New buildings have been constructed, as tourism has grown and become the number one source of revenue for Leavenworth.

Festivals and many other events are held throughout the year and attract growing numbers of tourists from around the country every year. This new industry, brought on by people who were not about to give up on their town, Leavenworth not only survived, but it now thrives as one of the Pacific Northwest's finest tourist spots. Jim Hill would be proud of the vision and fortitude the people of the town he helped to create have shown. Perhaps the ghost of Hill's determination has never left Leavenworth.

Wellington, The Rescue Continues

As if the avalanche and the tremendous destruction it caused was not enough for O'Neill, he was now having troubles with a number of the rescuers. The following is a telegram from H.H. Parkhouse in St. Paul, relaying to Louis Hill in California, the newest problem at Wellington.

St. Paul, Minn., March 3, 1910

Louis W, Hill
Casa Loma Hotel,
Redlands, California
O'Neill at Wellington last night. Badly delayed with rotary work account foreign extra gangs refusing to shovel snow. Has sixty white men. All injured in temporary hospital at Wellington attended by doctors and nurses. Estimated will take twenty to thirty days to open slopes. Still sliding and conditions very bad. Sultan and Skykomish Rivers raised one foot past twenty four hours. No danger from them yet.

H.H. PARKHOUSE

The searchers finally located O'Neill's private car on March 5th, along with a number of cabins that had been swept off their foundations. His car and the cabins were not as far down the gorge as had been previously thought. The next step for the rescuers was to find what they could of the No. 27 Fast Mail train. As it was placed on the outer track next to the cliff, it was surmised that the engine and its cars were hurled farther down the slope than anything else. When they were eventually discovered, the rescuers worst thoughts came true. The cars were all crushed under the debris of the passenger train coaches, a rotary, and the three electric helper engines.

By now, the injured victims who could be moved safely were put on sleds and carefully taken to Scenic. Bodies of the dead were also being hauled out of Wellington as there was no longer any room to house them. They were sent to Scenic in the same manner as the survivors, and then put on a special train to Everett. Still more and more bodies were being discovered and brought up the hill. To many, it seemed it would never end. There were extra workers down at the bottom of the gulch near the Tye river, digging, cutting, and sawing away the wreckage piled on top of what was left of the No. 27 Fast Mail.

Great Northern Engineer John P. Brady was personally involved in the transporting of the dead victims and gave this account some thirty-five years after the disaster.

"In the depot baggage room, which by a freak of nature was left standing, there were fifty-seven bodies which were being prepared for movement by sled down to Windy Point, three miles west. The track formed a horseshoe curve at that point; and as the track west of Wellington was still covered by the slide while the line was open from Scenic west, men had made a toboggan trail by sitting down in scoop shovels and sliding down through the deep snow. The remains of a number of persons had already been taken down that way. Wrapped in blankets and roped to improvised sleds for the descent to Windy Point, they were transported from there to the other side of the horseshoe at Scenic and then to Seattle by train."(10a)

It took two days of backbreaking work to finally reach the cars. One rescuer said, "We've finally found the last of the death chambers."(74) One at a time, the bodies of the train crew aboard the Fast Mail were taken out from the wreckage. Among the firemen, brakemen, and seven postal workers, the rescuers found the bodies of twelve more laborers.(69)

REMOVING BODIES DUG FROM WELLINGTON SNOW SLIDE, MARCH 1, 1910.

Photo courtesy of Museum of History & Industry, Seattle

Some of the first bodies to be recovered from the Wellington avalanche disaster.

If Superintendent O'Neill did not have enough on his mind, a dispute broke out between the undertakers who had arrived from both Everett and Seattle. Many of the trainmen who had been killed, lived in Everett in Snohomish County, the Great Northern's division headquarters. But the avalanche and Wellington were located in King County, from where the Seattle undertakers had come. In the midst of all the death and destruction surrounding them, the men from the different funeral homes could not come to an agreement where the bodies should be taken, Everett or Seattle.

Although the conflict almost resulted in physical violence between the undertakers from Jerread's Mortuary in Everett and those from Butterworth's in Seattle, the solution was made at the Great Northern offices in Everett. Quite simply, if the bodies of the dead had resided in Everett, Jerread's would take charge of them. Most all these victims were employees of the Great Northern anyway and had lived in Everett as mentioned. All others would be taken to Butterworth's Mortuary in Seattle. Most of these were passengers.

On March 6th, O'Neill found enough time to send the following telegram to the Great Northern home offices in St. Paul, to help the officials there understand what had happened at Wellington and why. In many ways, it repeats what he sent in his telegram of March 4th.

"Snow slide Wellington extended from west end of depot to snow shed 2.1 third shed west, portion shed two east end gone out, shed 2.1 moved some and timbers bulged – depot not damaged. (This slide 6,367 feet wide). Motor shed, all motors, water tank. All trolly supports and wires gone – slide seemed to part at coal chute but took everything each side. Impossible to have placed train No. 25 either in snow shed or tunnel, track so badly obstructed and bad storm snowed in train quickly – train was in tunnel one night but passengers complained about being in tunnel and train was moved out following morning. Train was moved to this site and placed just in the clear on No. 1 track, No. 27 on No. 2 track. When storm began 35 tons coal in chute. And 2 ½ [coal] cars on track – soon as we found supply was getting low we killed all the engines not needed consisting of five and took what coal they had for snow machines. Weather so severe it was impossible to accomplish anything – slide east of shed 3.3 came down three times, 1500 feet long, twenty to thirty feet deep [Windy] point caused about all our trouble as we cleared it three times and it is as bad as ever now. Have wired my office to give you names of all injured, those recovered and missing."

J.H. O'NEILL

It was also on March 6th that the less seriously injured decided they would wait no longer for a train to get to Wellington to take them away from this nightmarish place. Seven men left the hospital/bunkhouse to hike to Scenic. Most were Great Northern employees. It still was not clear to anyone at Wellington when the first rescue train would actually reach the scene of the disaster. Many who had survived with little or no injuries had decided to walk away from the white horror as early as March 4th. By then, it was obvious there was little else they could do. But when O'Neill got wind of this, he instructed his employees to begin helping take out the bodies on sleds, if they were indeed determined to hike out of there to Scenic. They could at least help in that way if they were determined to leave, O'Neill thought.

There were now trains at Scenic waiting to take the survivors and the dead back to Puget Sound. Clearing the tracks and getting the trains to Wellington was taking much longer than expected. It would still a lot more time and the first train to reach Wellington would not come from Scenic, but from the east.

The first rescue train to reach Wellington came through the Cascade Tunnel from the east on March 9th, lead by Rotary X-808. On board the train was E. L. Brown, and on board the rotary, J. M. Gruber. They found O'Neill, still in charge of the rescue operation, only by this time it was primarily that of hauling bodies out of Wellington as quickly as possible on the improvised Alaskan sleds described earlier by Engineer Brady. O'Neill was certainly glad to see them. The nightmare that began weeks earlier was having a definite effect on him, both physically and mentally. Gruber explained to him that they would have arrived sooner except for the extremely heavy and wet snow they encountered between Berne and Cascade Tunnel Station. The big delay, however, was the ice on the tracks. The rescue trains could make maybe ten feet if they were lucky, before they had to stop and let the men down onto the rails to pick off the ice. Rotary X-808 was off the track several times due to the ice. Gruber and Brown also told O'Neill that they had to use about six hundred kegs of blasting powder to clear the huge slide at Berne. They had another five hundred kegs with them to use at Wellington and westward, if they were needed. Having seen the conditions between Wellington and Scenic, O'Neill assured them they would definitely be needed. Gruber instructed a telegrapher to order as many kegs of black powder and boxes of dynamite be delivered to Wellington as quickly as possible.

The newly arrived Great Northern officials were staggered by the number of bodies they saw. O'Neill told them how many had already been removed from Wellington and that there had been talk among the undertakers of packing the remaining bodies in snow until a rescue train arrived. There were still nine survivors in the temporary hospital, and Gruber immediately ascertained from the doctors that all nine were well enough to be transported out of there to a real hospital for better treatment. Gruber ordered a special car to be attached to the locomotive that had brought him and Brown to Wellington, and to transport the victims back through the tunnel to Wenatchee.

Wenatchee

In part, the city of Wenatchee owes its existence to the difficulties settlers had in the late 1800's, with reaching the county seats of Kittitas and Chelan counties. In order to be the first people to stake claims on the fertile property near the Wenatchee River in North Central Washington State, the settlers had to travel to the county seats of either Kittitas or Okanogan counties. The traveling was difficult and time consuming. To make matters worse, many times the would-be landholder found out to their dismay that they had filed for their land in the wrong county. This inconvenience to the Wenatchee Valley people became so irksome, they demanded the creation of a new county for their own. In 1899, a bill was introduced in the state legislature that created the new county of Chelan, named after the Indian tribe in that area called the "Chelanics."

The city of Wenatchee was named by its founder, Don Carlos Corbet, after the Indian Chief, "Wenatchee." There is no specific English translation of the word. The closest translations are, "good place," or "boiling waters." Local Indian lore, however, claims that the name comes from a poetic description of the area, "Wa-Nat-Chee," meaning robe of the rainbow.

In 1891, the Wenatchee Development Company was organized to plot the town. In May of 1892, the Development Company ordered a change in town site, locating it approximately one mile north of the original location. Within five days of this order, more than $100,000 worth of property was sold in the new town site. To entice development and growth in the new town, the Wenatchee Development Company moved buildings from the old location to the new site, free of charge.

On May 1, 1892, the town of Wenatchee began its venture of becoming an important commercial center in Eastern Washington when the Columbia Valley bank opened for business. However, it was not long before the new settlement suffered its first setback. Only weeks after the bank began operations, on May 27th, the townsfolk witnessed the scene that almost destroyed their vision of Wenatchee becoming a major economic community. On that day, much of the new town was destroyed by fire. Tens of thousands of dollars in damage nearly devastated the town. The original cause of the fire has never been determined.

But Wenatchee survived with the arrival of the Great Northern Railway later that year, and the town incorporated on December 17, 1892. It was made a major division point for the railway, which constructed one of the largest train yards in Eastern Washington. Wenatchee also became a primary base for steamboat operations on the Columbia River, and its tributaries in the Okanogan country.

The backbone of the regions economy, before the arrival of the Great Northern, was primarily agriculture, with more than 70 per cent of the monetary value coming from the growth and harvesting of fruit; primarily apples. There were other crops, such as cherries, pears and peaches, and with the coming of the Great Northern, farmers prospered greatly. Jim Hill had kept his word of transporting their harvests via the Great Northern at the cheapest rates of any of the other railroads. Soon fruit processing and packaging plants were built and Wenatchee was on its way to becoming one of the dominant cities on the eastside of the Cascades. The Great Northern also contributed to the city's growth by investing large sums of money in the building of a number of irrigation projects to help promote the growth of farming in the valley.

By the Fall of 1894, Wenatchee boasted a new brick school house, two general merchandise stores, one grocery store, as well as three hotels, a restaurant, bakery, two butcher shops, livery stable, brickyard, a newspaper, a wholesale liquor store, and four saloons.

Wenatchee did have its run-ins with the Great Northern, however. When the harvesting became so abundant, especially apples, the railroad decided to greatly increase its freight rates to the farmers. Many of the farmers felt betrayed. In the late 1800's, the farmers and other citizens of Wenatchee fought hard to get the railroad to build through their town, and did everything they could to keep it there. But by the early 1900's, with the constant rate increases by the Great Northern, the people turned and fought against the railway's financial exploitation of their town. The people concluded that the best way to battle the Great Northern's freight increases, was to someway construct (with the help of other nearby communities) a highway of their own across Stevens Pass. This would provide them with an alternate means of transporting their goods via trucks. All of a sudden, officials of the Great Northern saw a new form of competition that would need to be addressed.

Stevens Pass highway was more important to the people of Eastern Washington than it was to the people of Western Washington. Even though only a third of the state's population lived and worked in Eastern Washington, four out of every five acres of farmland under cultivation were located in Eastern Washington. The Great Northern decided to slow down the rate hikes. Things got better quickly between Wenatchee and the Great Northern. They both realized that they needed each other.

On November 1, 1924, the first automobile to cross the newly completed Stevens Pass Road over the Cascades Mountains had arrived at its destination. The motor car, driven by C. C. Collins of Seattle, and Bailey Hilton of Everett, had left Everett at five o'clock on the morning of Friday, October 31st, and got to Wenatchee late Saturday evening, November 1st.

Driving through the mud and snow between six and eighteen inches deep, crossing railroad trestles, and driving through the Great Northern's old and abandoned Horseshoe tunnel, was the most thrilling adventure of their lives, the two men exclaimed upon their arrival. It marked the first successful automobile trip between Puget Sound and Wenatchee over the newly constructed Stevens Pass Highway.

Unlike many of the towns that grew up along the route of the Great Northern, many of which later went into decline, Wenatchee's strong and diverse economy was the key factor in maintaining it stable population.

The abundance of cheap hydro-electric power, due mostly to the completion of the Grand Coulee Dam, as well as Rock Island and Rocky Beach Dams, helped Wenatchee develop a new source for it's economy. During the 1940's aluminum became extremely important to the war effort, and companies such as ALCOA (Aluminum Company of America), Reynold's Aluminum, and Kaiser Aluminum, built operations in Wenatchee, as well as Spokane and Tacoma.[97]

Today, agriculture remains the foundation of Wenatchee's economic health. However, health care, retail trade, and especially tourism are also major sources of revenue in this city of 50,000 people. Wenatchee continues to be served by the Burlington Northern Santa Fe Railroad, as well as Amtrak's "Empire Builder" from Seattle to Chicago.

Chapter 6:

Wellington, The Avalanche Aftermath

E. L. Brown sent his first telegram since arriving on the scene at 4: 10 P.M. on March 9th to the home office in St. Paul. He explained to the officials back east that there remained one continuous snow slide from Wellington, westward for nearly one and a half miles. He also informed them that Mr. Gruber had ordered a sleeper car for the remaining survivors at Wellington, and that they would be on there way to Spokane the next morning.(62a)

Meanwhile, in Everett, the first Great Northern official to return from Wellington since the fatal avalanche was W. J. Manley. He arrived on March 5th. Manley had been acting as trainmaster under the supervision of James O'Neill. Mr. Manley's account is worth reading." He told the Everett Herald.

Trainmaster A. P. Blackburn's body was found in an attitude as if he had been sleeping peacefully [when the avalanche hit], his face was in his hands when the catastrophe occurred. His next statement is a bit gruesome, but was never denied by anyone at the scene. "During the first day of the tragedy," Manley told the reporters, "several temporarily crazed persons attempted suicide by cutting their throats with broken pains of glass, evidently fearing they would not be liberated from the death trap in they found themselves."(66) Most of the accounts and descriptions from many of the witnesses to the disaster were ghastly, grotesque, and grisly; but perhaps it was a mental relief for those who gave their personal testimonies, of their horribly horrendous situation stranded in the Cascades for over a week.

Manley also indicated how much trouble the workers were experiencing in clearing the tracks. The snow, in places, covered the tracks up to forty feet deep, he contended. And the rotaries were practically useless due to the depth of the snow, mingled with large rocks and broken tree trunks. However, the most significant problem, he pointed out, was the thick, hard ice on the rails. Manley continued to be a very reliable source of information to other newspapers as well. But finally, he had enough of the reliving of the horror and went to Peru, to become the Superintendent for the Cerra de Pasco Railway.

At Wellington, O'Neill was proposing an idea to his superiors, Brown and Gruber. Since so many bodies had been recovered, and still they had no way of knowing how many more were embedded in the 15 to 60 feet of snow, perhaps they could melt away the snow by using sprays of steam generated by locomotive boilers. This way, more bodies could be located faster than digging, and could then be turned over to the undertakers from Puget Sound that were still at Wellington. Brown and Gruber explained that it might possibly work if the area was not that vast. Right now, the depth of the snow, which was still a big problem, was not the biggest problem. It was the more than sixty acres that the slide covered, in which the wreckage was scattered and buried. In all practicality the idea would not work. Besides, they decided that O'Neill's original thought of waiting for the snow to melt in the Spring, was probably the most prudent course to take. In the meantime, and of utmost importance, the tracks had to be opened to Puget Sound. Every day the trains could not cross the Cascades in either direction, was costing the Great Northern a fortune.

It was March 9th and Gruber decided he had to contact Louis Hill to inform his boss when they expected to have the tracks cleared so the Great Northern's commerce could again commence. He sent a one sentence telegram to Hill in California cautiously predicting that he "expects to have line opened by Sunday [March 13] at latest."(61) Whether Gruber actually believed this is a matter of speculation. He had seen from himself how devastated the summit was by the avalanche, but perhaps it was important to keep Mr. Hill optimistic.

Later that day, O'Neill noticed the strain on the faces of the men still working to recover bodies. He had not noticed it a few days earlier. Their expressions were now stony and solemn, without expression. There was very little talk among any of them either, and when there was talk, it was in a short and quiet, monotone.

Later that same day, one of the rescuers came into the telegraph office where O'Neill, Gruber, and Brown were and described how incredibly powerful the avalanche must have been. He had just climbed back up the hill, where at the bottom, he told them, was one of their locomotives standing on its head in the deep snow, with the body of the giant iron engine twisted half way around. Everywhere there were strips of steel and iron, whipped around and embedded in large tree trunks. Between all this tremendous destruction, was scattered the many personal effects of the victims, from pieces of torn clothing to suitcases that had been torn apart.

The sight of all this devastation, with the scattered belongings of the dead, had caused the attitudes of all the search party members to become one of "deepest respect and utmost decorum" in respect for the victims of this horrible holocaust.

The rescue work continued as late into the night as possible, but there was much more that could be done until the late Spring or Summer. By then the snow should be gone and expose what the great avalanche had left. O'Neill, Gruber, and Brown decided they would start lending their assistance to the work of recovering whatever they could, in the morning.

Thursday, March 10, 1910, J. M. Gruber awakened early and headed east to Cascade Tunnel Station. Whether he rode on a rescue train or walked the length of the tunnel is not know. He wanted to see for himself if there had been any more slides east of Cascade Tunnel, and if so, how large and how far east were they. There were still no communication wires between the two towns on each side of the tunnel, so the trip was necessary. There he sent a telegram to officials of the Great Northern in St. Paul

Cascade Tunnel march 10-10

Got out nine bodies yesterday making sixty eight all told. Still missing a Mr. Thompson of Bellingham [Washington], Davis, a Real estateman of Seattle, a man named Topping of Seattle, Three brakeman and one engineer. Think there are some more Italians, Mr. O'Neill thinks about a dozen including these mentioned above not yet out. Have had 55 to 60 men working at the wreckage recovering bodies. Will increase it to 70 or 75 today until our outfit cars arrive... there are not sufficient accommodations at hotel and other places to care for more men. Found considerable obstructions to rotary. Think that bothers about us as anything is ice over the rail which gets rotary off track occasionally and requires picking out. Also ran into Considerable number of trees and several telegraph poles parts of the motor shed timbers and tools, Will walk down to the front again this morning where Mr. Brown is and will make further reports during the day. J M Gruber

----

These early telegrams, as well as newspaper reports and other personal accounts, were inaccurate and confusing. But this was a different era in travel in America. Passenger manifests were either not complete or not kept at all. This is no ones fault, it simply was the way the trains operated in this country in the early 20th century. But it does help explain that the number of people who survived, or were killed; missing and injured, can never be accurately determined. For example, Mr. Thompson of Bellingham, was the Reverend J. M. Thompson, 57, of Bellingham. Davis, the "Real estateman" of Seattle, must have been George F. Davis, 35, of Seattle, but was a motorman employed by the, Seattle, Renton, and Southern Railroad. And finally, the man named Topping, was Edward W. Topping, 29, a salesman for the Safety Door Hanger Company from Ashland, Ohio. On two of the railroad's official list of dead, Mr. Topping is referred to as E.H. Topping and E.U. Topping.

Gruber's second telegram sent to St. Paul that day was sent the following day from Wellington.

Wellington mch 11-10

Rotary from west reached Point 350 feet east Shed one last night, there they struck badly bent rail which they are replacing this morning. Rotary on east end reached Tank where they are clearing away debris and should be by it at nine A.M. this and a box car across main line buried under snow caused much delay. The box is one of the cars slide took off of coal chute incline. All told 1500 fifteen hundred full of large trees and stumps. Have several powder crews blasting, have plenty of powder on hand. Still think we will open main line some time saturday, be quite a job to get passing tracks and other tracks clear but in mean time will run trains light enough so they can run Wellington eastbound for coal and water, Gang of carpenters clearing away for tank which will be erected soon as material reaches here. In meantime arrangements being made to take water through in shed to Where there is good flow of water. Four bodies recovered yesterday: J.E. Wells, Rev. Thompson, Mail clerk Towsley and fireman Ross...seventy one to date by coroners figures, my previous wire saying 68 incorrect.

J M Gruber

J.E. Wells was Julian E. Wells, a 19 year old brakeman from Seattle. Mail clerk Towsely was Hiram Towslee, a 36 year old mail clerk on the

No. 25 train, from Fort Steilacoom, Washington, and fireman Ross (first name began with letter 'L') was a 25 year old Great Northern fireman from Paintsville, Kentucky.

The lists of victims among the railroad, newspapers, and mortuaries all differ. People at Butterworth's Mortuary in Seattle tried to explain the confusion. In addition to mentioning how the Great Northern had compiled their official list from "the registers at the eateries" at Wellington, Butterworth's also claimed the confusion came about in part because many of the "railroad employees used more than one name. Bovee, for instance, being reported under his own name and also that of Kelly."(10)

"Mistakes were made in several of the earlier identifications [also]. The body of a fireman identified 10 days ago as Johnson, is believe now to be that of Sidney Jones. All the railroad workers recognized the body as that of the fireman and someone gave the name of Johnson, but no such name is on the official list. Fireman Sidney Jones is missing."(10) This was the statement issued by Butterworth's and Sons in Seattle in the middle of March 1910.

The body of fireman Sidney S. Jones, 25, from Everett, was eventually identified. And Butterworth's records remain correct regarding no one named Johnson appeared on the Great Northern's official list. However the mortuary's records listed six bodies never claimed or identified.

The use of black powder and dynamite started almost immediately after Gruber and Brown got to Wellington, as Gruber mentioned in his telegram of March 11th. Many of the sheds west of Wellington had been badly damaged, some completely destroyed by boulders and broken evergreens. So it was not just a matter of clearing the snow from the tracks, but blasting the destroyed snow sheds and their debris out of the way. Gruber knew in the back of his mind that Louis Hill and his father James Hill would want the tracks open as quickly as possible.

That same day, March 11th, rescuers discovered nine more bodies in the valley two hundred feet below Wellington. There were now only about sixty men searching the wreckage site, all others had been transferred to locations west of Wellington to clear the rails and get the trains moving across the mountains.

The previous day, bought another incident at Wellington regarding the presence and the large force of Japanese laborers who were there to clear the mainline. It began when one of the American foreman got into a dispute with a Japanese 'bookman,' was serving as an interpreter.

The foreman had wanted all the Japanese crew, who had just arrived aboard a Leavenworth work train, to continue working straight through the night without any rest. This did not go over well with the Japanese 'bookman,' Jim Wanato. Wanato told the American that his men needed rest and instructed his people to stay aboard the boxcar they were living in. Of course the foreman's will prevailed in the dispute and the Japanese ordered out of the car and began the back breaking work of shoveling snow off the tracks throughout the night.

The next morning, Wanato grew insulting in talking with the foreman, which caused the unnamed American boss to lose his patience with his 'bookman' and he started towards Wanato intending to settle the matter physically. But the Japanese quickly pulled a revolver and opened fire on the foreman. Fortunately for the Great Northern official, Wanato's aim was bad, and he missed his target by about a foot, witnesses claimed. (72)

According to accounts given to other newspapers, "White men rushed in and put an end to the affair and for a moment it looked as if a race riot would be started." Ironically, J. M. Gruber was at the scene and got directly involved in the altercation. It fact, it was said he held the situation in control until Sheriff Ferguson arrived. Ferguson, after hearing from a number of witnesses took Wanato into custody and sent him back to Leavenworth to be held for "shooting with intent to kill." Order was restored, the Japanese laborers returned to shoveling snow, but charges were never filed against 'bookman Jim Wanato.

Progress was finally being made clearing the tracks westward from the summit. Superintendent Gruber now focused his efforts on clearing out the Wellington yard and repairing the tracks so trains would be able to get into what was left of the town and proceed east and west through the tunnel.

On March 12th, Gruber sent the two following telegrams to Louis Hill who was now back in St. Paul.

Wellington match 12-10

L.W. Hill, stpaul

Rotaries met at seven this morning. No 1 and four will come via our line today, three bodies recovered yesterday, Bkman W E Cracraft, A Bowles, A Passenger and one unidentified, will have to begin at once clearing side tracks at Wellington in order to get tracks for trains to meet at cascade tunnel yard of course is pretty well filled up with outfits. Have two more tracks to open up over there. That work going extremely slow acct several inches ice over track and having to pick every bit of it out ahead of rotary.

J M Gruber…..1045am

Wellington march 12-10

L.W. Hill, St. Paul-

We used one thousand keg black-powder and about 50 boxes of dynamite yesterday and have to do a lot more shooting on the side tracks Wellington as we will find a lot of logs as on main line. There are some rails down the bank taken by the snow slide probably off from No. 2 track.

J.M. Gruber….10:49am

It looked as though Gruber's prediction of having the main line cleared to Wellington from the west by March 13th would be accomplished. But, as usual, another slide took place near Alvin, knocking the rotary there, off the tracks, and killing one worker. The Oriental Limited, on its way east, was halted at Alvin, and the passengers, like so many in the past, had to get off the train and hike into Wellington. It took only two days to clear the way from Alvin to Wellington.

One of Gruber's last telegrams to Louis Hill from the Cascade Mountains was sent from Scenic on March 14, 1910.

Scenic. Mch 14 10   **L.W. Hill,**

                                                       StPaul

If rotary which is off track in cut at west end of Tunnel just east of Bridge 398 is re-railed so it can begin work say about Ten O'clock I think we will have line open by Two or Three O'clock this P.M. Have had a hard time with rotary which as wired you was partly covered over with the slide after it was off the track with ice, Mr. Emerson

and Kelly have gone up the hill this morning to assist in getting it on, Halford quarry crew that went to their camp last night not here yet this morning at Eight O'clock having been caught behind a rock slide east of here but Dalquist's crew arrived this morning and are doing the shooting, the Northern Pac rotary which we have on the west end is almost useless.

J M Gruber.

So on March 15, 1910, the way was finally cleared to Wellington from both directions. The Great Northern went to work immediately restoring the town and cleaning up the mess that remained. Officials noted that the passenger trains were carrying an extraordinary number of people. They could only conclude that many of them were sightseers wanting to view the devastation first hand.

One of the first through trains brought the rest of the recovered bodies at Wellington, back to Puget Sound, along with many personal effects and sacks of registered mail along with bags of letters sent via regular mail. Most of the mail had been lost, however.

Only a few days earlier, Lucius Anderson, the porter on the Pullman car, "Winnipeg," which was destroyed in the avalanche, positively identified the bodies of Bert Mathews of Cincinnati, Ohio, and Edward W. Topping, of Ashland, Ohio. Topping's father, William, and his brother Roger, had made the trip west to claim Edward's (Ned's) body. The terribly mutilated forms of both Topping and Mathews were not recognizable by either Topping's father or brother. The two dead men were approximately 5 feet 8 inches tall and weighed 170 pounds. The two surviving Toppings could only rely on porter Anderson's way of telling the two apart. He had retrieved Topping's wallet from his trousers and gave it to his father.

Edward (Ned) Topping's story does not end with the recovering and identification of his body. Attorneys on behalf of Topping's two year old son in Ashland, Ohio, would bring legal action against the Great Northern within a few years. They would charge the railroad with general negligence. First, however, there would be the coroner's jury investigation.

The Coroner's Inquest

In the early 1900's there were no such professions as medical examiners and forensic scientists. When a death occurred that called for some investigation, the city or county coroner would appoint a "coroner's jury" to investigate the death or deaths, and report on their findings.

The coroner's jury to investigate the Wellington avalanche disaster consisted of five jurors and foreman, C. S. Wilson. They began their work on March 18th and reached their findings on March 23, 1910. For their efforts, they were each paid $11.00.

But despite their small pay, they were all dedicated individuals who earnestly sought the truth as to what happened on Stevens Pass. The estimated number of witnesses called by the coroner's jury to "fix the responsibility for the death of John Brockman and 87 or more others," ran between 28 to 40 people. Record keeping in those days was poor, and it is not sure just how many witnesses ever testified.

As it turned out, John Brockman, who was killed in the avalanche, was a very wealthy rancher from Wenatchee, Washington. He left quite a large estate, and quite a number of people showed up at Butterworth & Sons Mortuary in Seattle to claim his body, and also the inheritance. Obviously, they could not all be relatives, as many of them could not even identify the right body. City and county authorities were concerned that this might become a common practice regarding other victims also. There were still a number of bodies of unclaimed or unidentified dead at the mortuary, with probably more to come. Therefore, in an attempt to prevent this callous conduct to continue, the coroner's office assigned a jury to look into the matter of all the Wellington victim's deaths, and render an official conclusion as to liability.

The Seattle Post Intelligencer reported that witnesses would be called, including all survivors of the disaster, officials of the Great Northern Railroad, rescue workers, and "right-of-way" men. Coroner James C. Snyder, of King County, asked Deputy Sheriff Joe Hill to send out subpoenas to 40 individuals instructing them to show up at Forester's Hall, 1923½ 1st Avenue, in Seattle at 11 o'clock on the morning of March 18, 1910. Members of the Washington State Railway Commission were also in attendance, H. A. Fairchild and J. C. Lawrence. The law required members of this commission to investigate all fatalities on railroads in the state. Deputy Prosecuting Attorney Alfred Lundin was also there along with Superintendent J. H. O'Neill. Lundin would be the person to question O'Neill about his recollections and involvement in the disaster.

"Every phase of the accident at Wellington and its causes will be gone into thoroughly," Coroner Snyder assured the public. "Guests at the Scenic Hot Springs Hotel will be asked in regard to the statement that the Great Northern permitted forest fires to rage on the mountainsides last summer without making an effort to extinguish them."(69) It has been claimed that these fires destroyed trees and shrubbery which in the past years has prevented just such an accident as that in which 87 lives were lost," Snyder continued.

There was one other reason for Coroner Snyder to call this inquest as quickly as possible, and that was to help the general population come to grips with the horrendous happenings less than one hundred miles away. By now, the first photographs were being printed in the newspapers all over Puget Sound and the people were outraged and sickened by the sight. They too wanted to know how this destruction in lives and property could have happened.

Another Post Intelligencer story reported "the coroner stated that he would inquire into the statement that on Monday night, Feb. 28th, a meeting of the passengers was held with representatives of the Great Northern and were asked by the passengers to be given guides to lead them out of Wellington and over the tracks to Scenic Hot Springs Hotel.

"Only one of the passengers who attended the meeting is alive to tell of it. He is Henry H. White, a traveling salesman employed by the American Paper Company. Trainmaster, A.H. Blackburn of the Great Northern, who is said to have refused the request, met his death with the passengers."(69)

For the next several days, the jury listened to the testimony of all those who bothered to show up and give their account of the tragedy. Lundin asked O'Neill to talk about the coal situation at Wellington. Why wasn't there enough to keep the rotaries going and the trains heated? O'Neill's reply was reported in the Seattle Times.

"O'Neill, while admitting that the fuel supply for the plows became exhausted, insisted that he had made the best fight possible,

going over the ground several times in order to keep the track clear from February 23 until February 26, when the coal ran out.

"O'Neill also testified that, 'I gave orders for the removal of the trains from the tunnel and never discussed the matter afterwards with Conductor Pettit [who began his hike to Scenic with others on the 28th of February, but went back to Wellington where he was killed in the avalanche], of the passenger train, or with [Conductor Walter] Vogel, of the mail train. They did not argue the matter with me and I do not know whether or not the passengers discussed the change and asked Pettit to take them back into the tunnel. Pettit was carrying out orders that I gave, thinking I was doing the best thing possible under the conditions. The passengers did not discuss the order with me. I alone an responsible for the removal of the trains as indicated."(72)

After hearing all the witnesses' the jury then boarded a train to have a first hand view of what was left at Wellington. Upon their return to Seattle, the jury wrote its decision. The verdict rendered can still be read in the archives of the King County Medical Examiner's Offices in Seattle. The jury's conclusion is printed in its entirety below.

CORONER' JURY INVESTIGATION
DATE OF INVESTIGATION: MARCH 18 THRU 23, 1910

"John Brockman and 87 or more others came to their death on the 1st day of March, 1910, by reason of a snowslide at Wellington, King County, Washington. The cause of which was beyond human control; that the said John Brockman and the 87 or more others were upon two trains of the Great Northern Railway Company, which trains, being snowbound, stood upon the siding to the west of Wellington depot. The railway officials, in placing the trains where they did, believed from past experience that the location of said trains were in a safe place. We find that the trains were not placed in the safest place to avert a possible accident, as the trains should have been, as the company had other sidings east of said depot on which the trains should have been placed that are safe from snowslides.

The evidence shows that the Great Northern Railway Company did not have sufficient coal at Wellington to cope with all possible emergencies. The evidence also shows that by reason of the small wages of only fifteen cents an hour for shoveling snow, out of which the laborers had to pay four dollars and fifty cents per week for board,

about 35 laborers left Wellington who should have been retained regardless of wages for the purpose of providing for the safety and welfare of the passengers."
VERDICT OF JURY A INQUEST
FOREMAN: C.S. Wilson
JURORS: James Hopkirk, Dan Harris, Ino E. Davis, Grant Sweet, J.A. Caldwell (47)

The Great Northern continued its policy of very little pay for backbreaking work, even after the avalanche. According to the Leavenworth Echo of Friday, March 18, 1910, the laborers from that town, were induced by the railroad to go to Wellington on the false promise of earning between $3.50 to $5.00 per day in helping with the rescue efforts. When they arrived at the disaster site, they found out the truth; that they would be paid only 15 cents an hour (just as the Coroner's Jury reported), with time checks taken regularly. Consequently, these volunteers from Leavenworth, almost to the man, refused to stay there. In fact, they were forced to walk out as the railroad refused them return transportation on the same train that brought them there.

On March 15th, just three days before the Coroner's Jury Inquest convened, the Great Northern Railroad and Butterworth's Mortuary in Seattle, announced that all the unclaimed and unidentified bodies from the Wellington avalanche would be buried in a "common plot" dedicated to that purpose, at Mount Pleasant Cemetery located on top of Seattle's Queen Anne Hill. The railroad said it would pay all the expenses.

The Seattle Times reported on page one of its Tuesday, March 15th edition:

ELEVEN BODIES WILL REST IN COMMON PLOT

Unclaimed and Unidentified Dead of Wellington Avalanche to be Buried at Expense of Great Northern
The present accounting indicates that not less than eleven bodies will share the common plot, but the number may be increased. The Great Northern, through Claim Agent Flynn made tentative arrangements with the morgue management today for public burial, the Great Northern purchasing the burial plot and assuming all the expenses of the interment.

There was confusion then, and there remains confusion to this day as to just how many bodies were buried at Mount Pleasant Cemetery. As plans for the mass burial were being put together, both G. M. Butterworth of the mortuary, and Claim Agent Flynn for the Great Northern established the fact that eleven unclaimed and unidentified bodies were currently at the morgue. But Flynn also had a list of nine more missing persons. Butterworth thought that some, if not all the people on the Great Northern's missing list, could be the unidentified at his mortuary.

However, according to whatever records are examined (whether the railroad's, the mortuary's, or the cemetery's), the number of bodies simply does not agree. Butterworth's records showed a total of eleven at their morgue; seven identified but unclaimed bodies, and four unidentified and unclaimed victims. Flynn of the Great Northern carried a list of the names of nine persons. He had their names, but only four of them could possibly be among the unidentified at Butterworth's, as the other seven had been identified. The chances were also probable, due to faulty record keeping by the Great Northern, that none of the names of the missing were among those at Butterworth's.

So how many victims of the Wellington avalanche are actually buried in the 'common plot' dedicated for that purpose? Again, it is impossible to say, for two reasons. Some of the records of Mount Pleasant cemetery were destroyed in a fire in the 1940's. Secondly, what records they do have are quite surprising. According to Mr. William N. Edwards, the President of Mount Pleasant Cemetery Company, regarding the Wellington common plot, "The Great Northern Railroad arranged for a section of land which accommodated 16 adult graves. The permanent care of these graves at $75.00 has never been paid. This totals $1,200.00." His letter to the author, dated October 24, 1988, goes on to state, "A small monument measuring 2'6" x 18" was placed in the center of the plot and there are five other permanent markers in the plot as well...the Great Northern Railroad was responsible for the care of the plot."(16)

Notably among the Butterworth records, there is listed a John Earl Wells, age 19. What catches the eye on Mr. Wells' death record is that his body was claimed by his brother, Fred, and he requested on behalf of the Wells family, that his brother be buried at Lake View Cemetery on Seattle's Capitol Hill. Since his burial was separate from the rest of the Wellington victims, the cost of burial was higher, $268.00 to be exact. Handwritten at the bottom of the death record are the words, "the Great Northern will only pay $150.00." Young Mr. Wells' brother, Fred, was billed the balance of $118.00. This disturbing notation showed the lack of compassion by the railroad for all of the victims of the avalanche. But this cold, unemotional attitude in handling its responsibilities, is even more abhorrent in this case due to the fact that John Earl Wells was actually the 19 year old Julian Earl Wells, the brakeman for the Great Northern Railway killed doing his job while stranded at Wellington.

Anyone interested in visiting the Wellington burial site at Mount Pleasant Cemetery will have to look long and hard to find it. The Great Northern did not place a marker or monument on the site, as this was against the policy of the railroad at that time.(8) The Great Northern did not supply and ground markers for any of the buried either, whether they were passengers or employees. This too was not the railroad's policy. There is one ground marker on the site for Luigi Giammarusti, who was a 45 year-old laborer employed by the Great Northern. The cement stone was purchased and placed their by his family living in Spokane, Washington. As there are no other markers anywhere in the Wellington common plot, it will have to remain an unsolved mystery as to just how many victims are buried there. The records of Mount Pleasant, Butterworth, and the Great Northern cannot be reconciled.

What does stand out, however, to anyone visiting the site, is the headstone, measuring 2 ½ feet high and 18 inches wide, that is placed in the middle of the plot. The front of the granite stone, facing the street, written in four Japanese characters is translated, "All gather/meet in a single place."(49) On the back of the stone are listed the names of 23 Japanese. Twenty-three Japanese buried together in one single grave, with no date given or any explanation for the grave. There are records that indicate the stone was placed there in 1938 by the North American Japanese Chamber of Commerce. The story is that these 23 laborers worked for the Great Northern Railway, and were all killed while riding on a locomotive that derailed somewhere near New Westminster, British Columbia in Canada. Supposedly, the accident happened on January 28, 1909, one year before the Wellington disaster. There is no official written record that can be found regarding this accident. However, the Japanese in Seattle kept an 'oral history' of many happenings in connection with the Northern Pacific and Great Northern. The stories were passed from one generation to the next.

The rest of the story of the 23 dead, contends that in addition to the 23 killed, 15 survived. They were all working on the new extension line of the Great Northern from the Fraser River to New Westminster when the accident occurred. "Therefore, it may have been "Tobo," [the named used by the Japanese of that era that pertained to all the labor contractors in the Northwest. It was not flattering], that sent those twenty-three to New Westminster.(44) According to Kazuo Ito, who did remarkable research on this story, "It is also recorded that Tetsuo Takahashi, President of Tobo, went to Vancouver in regard to the accident. After all, the Great Northern Railroad in the end agreed to pay $1500 in damages to each of the families of the victims. The accident must have shaken up the Japanese community in Seattle at the time."(44) However searches through the Great Northern Corporate papers, and the help of the Japanese Methodist Church, the Seattle Betsuin Buddhist Temple, the Wing Luke Asian Museum, and the Japanese Community Service of Seattle, nowhere indicates that the railroad ever paid the damages they promised.

Chapter 7:

Topping v. Great Northern

Immediately after the avalanche, the Great Northern began to rebuild Wellington to its former self. To help erase the blight the disaster had placed on the railroad, the town's name was quickly changed to Tye, after the river the site was built above. Any signs, maps, railroad schedules, brochures, and all other Great Northern publications that still contained the name Wellington were confiscated and destroyed. Employees were instructed to never use the name Wellington again.

The railroad had to regain its image and reliability as one of the safest railroads in the country, both to the public and to the businesses along it thousands of miles of track. But to the survivors, and relatives of the dead, just simply changing the name of where the most terrible avalanche in the country had taken place, was simply not enough. People from around the nation who had been affected by this disaster believed the Great Northern was responsible, at least to some extent, for the deaths and injuries to all those who suffered through the Wellington horror.

It is fair to say, that the avalanche itself was an act of nature, and an act of God, a magnitude of incomprehensible devastation. But, anyone who has ever visited the former Wellington site, can easily see for them self how the coroner's jury concluded that the trains should have been placed in a safer location. Unquestionably there were other less precarious locations at Wellington where the trains could have been moved. Certainly, not left at the base of Windy Mountain. In fact, the Great Northern, without officially conceding the fact, admitted the trains were in the wrong place, by later constructing the enormous, double-tracked concrete snow shed at the very place were the doomed trains had stood. This imposing sight can still be seen today, just on the west side of the summit from U.S. Highway 2, the Stevens Pass Highway.

Other factors need to be considered also. There should have been more coal at Wellington, as the coroner's jury pointed out. The hundreds of men originally employed to shovel snow, should have been paid higher wages in order to keep them on the job, rather than let them walk out, leaving the trains and the town completely stranded.

The Great Northern announced that it would financially settle, in a fair and equitable way, all personal injury and death claims resulting from the Wellington disaster. But how serious the railroad was came into doubt when the Great Northern had to be taken to court before it would pay out, on its own accord, any compensation to the victims and their families. It should also be kept in mind, the records at Butterworth's, where on the death reports, the Great Northern would not pay for all the funeral expenses of one of its own employees, and never paid for the upkeep of the Wellington plot at Mount Pleasant.

What was considered the test case for litigation necessary to determine the true financial responsibility of the Great Northern began in February of 1913. Lawyers, on behalf of William Topping, who being born on April 22, 1908, was only three weeks shy of his second birthday when his father, Edward (Ned) Topping was killed in the disaster, filed a wrongful death and negligence lawsuit against the Great Northern.

The trial that was finally held in King County Superior Court in Seattle actually began on February 19, 1913 in the Ashland County Court in the State of Ohio. It was a petition for the appointment of a legal guardian for Ned Topping's son, William. The petition was granted and W. V. B. Topping, the deceased's father and grandfather of William Topping became the boy's legal guardian. The lawyers representing William Topping's grandfather, W. V. B. Topping, on behalf of his grandson, were Fred Williams and L. F. Chester. The Great Northern's defense team consisted of F. V. Brown and Frederic G. Dorety Esq.

The first legal actions against the Great Northern were filed "In the Superior Court of the State of Washington, in and for the County of Spokane." The first petition claimed that Ned Topping was killed "through the negligence of the defendant's agents and servants, for whom defendant is responsible."(48) The Great Northern attorneys countered with what only can be called a legalistic delay tactic. The original charges against the railroad mentioned that the Wellington disaster happened in Snohomish County, Washington. This was an easy mistake for the attorneys from Ohio. After all, the home offices for the Great Northern were located in Everett, in Snohomish County, and the path of the railroad across the western slope of the Cascade Mountains was primarily through Snohomish County. Wellington, however, was located in King County, just a few miles outside of Snohomish County. It was an honest oversight and insignificant mistake, but enough for the railroad's attorneys to cause all kinds of legal maneuverings.

F. G. Dorety, representing the Great Northern, filed an affidavit in support for 'bill of particulars' with the Washington State Superior Court in Spokane County. In it he claimed, "That he is one of the attorneys for the defendant in the above entitled action; that he knows of no wreck or derailment occurring on the line of the Great Northern Railway Company in Snohomish County, on or about March 1st, 1910, and that he has been unable to learn of any such wreck or derailment from the operating officials of said road; that, in order to prepare for an adequate defense of said action, it is necessary that said defendant's attorneys be advised as to which train of the defendant is alleged to have been wrecked in said county on said date, and as to the alleged circumstances of said wreck."(48) This tactic was not the Great Northern's finest hour and did not go over well with the public or members of the bar. But the matter was straightened out very quickly and the trial would begin in Seattle very soon.

Topping's lawyers went right to work calling witnesses to explain how awesome the storm was that raged at Wellington, all during the week that the trains were stranded there. Witnesses also testified how the blizzard remained relentless and became so severe that practically everyone in town was fearful for what might (and ultimately) did happened.

They filed a motion for an order to the Great Northern to produce "papers and documents for inspection." They wanted all profiles, plats, documents and writings showing the topography of the country between Leavenworth and Skykomish. The railroad was also instructed to turn over all information on the location and extent of snow sheds on March 1, 1910, and all maps and profiles showing the topography of the "contiguous mountains where slides have occurred during the last ten years, so as to interrupt and impede traffic." All telegrams, telegraphic dispatches, letters, memoranda, and all written communications between officers, agents, and employees of "said railroad company during the last ten days of February, 1910, relating to the operation of trains between Leavenworth, Washington, and Everett, Washington."

They also demanded the telegrams of Basil Sherlock. The lawyers were particularly interested in his telegram sent to Everett on the night of February 27th, in which Sherlock said, "That train is down there in a dangerous place, and if it goes down the bank, it will cost the company millions of dollars." They requested that Sherlock's telegram sent the same night referring to the fact that the passenger train could be put in the snow shed, on the mainline, or in the tunnel. They also wanted all of the other written reports and statements of and concerning the avalanche that were signed by B.J. Sherlock.

In addition, the Great Northern attorneys were inundated with demands to produce all other books, records, and files in connection with the disaster. The demand were included in fifteen additional paragraphs that took up 4 pages of the 6-page motion to produce papers and documents.

The attorneys explained to the jury how the trains were placed at the very base of an incredibly steep mountain just to the west of the town of Wellington. Windy Mountain was indeed precipitous and dangerous in these weather conditions. The timber that once densely covered the mountain had been burnt away a few years earlier prior to the disaster, therefore enhancing the chances of a major avalanche. It was the large, dense forest of huge evergreens that was needed to help hold the fallen snow in place. Topping's lawyers also explained that the Great Northern had knowledge of the danger at the point where the trains were placed at Wellington, even before they were sent through the Cascade Tunnel from the east portal.

Upon immediate examination of the weather situation and the condition of the rail tracks, Williams and Chester contended that the Great Northern officials did not use their best judgment and should have sent the trains back to Leavenworth immediately, instead of through the tunnel to Wellington. They also accused the defendant railway of being negligent by not building enough snow sheds along the base of Windy Mountain, and not placing the trains within one of the snow sheds that did exist at the time.

The lawyers produced telegrams and dispatches that showed even many Great Northern officials were worried as to the placement of the trains. Other telegrams that reflected concern as to how long the mainline to Puget Sound would be tied up were also offered as evidence. It also came out at the trial how Trainmaster Blackburn, was given a written petition by the passengers aboard the No. 25 Spokane Local, requesting him to move the train to a place of safety.

More witnesses painted a picture for the jury of disagreement and confusion on the part of many of the railroad's officials regarding just what to do with the stalled trains and their passengers. After several days at Wellington, when it became apparent that the railway people had no idea how long it would take to clear the tracks and get the trains to Puget Sound, they agreed among themselves that the trains should have been held at Leavenworth. There should never been an attempt made to send them across the Cascade Mountains during the worst blizzard in decades. But since they were now at the summit, the Great Northern staff had no idea what to do except wait out the storm.

It also came out at the trial that the Great Northern officials in Spokane and Leavenworth knew that a number of rotary snowplows were either stuck in slides and could not be extracted from the deep snow, or off the tracks completely, and yet they went ahead with sending the trains into the mountains. The lawyers contended that with the tracks being impossible to keep cleared, the trains should never have sent to Cascade Tunnel Station or to Wellington, since no supplies of food or coal would be delivered to the isolated towns. By the time of the disaster, there was hardly any coal left in the coal chutes or bunkers at Wellington. Food was also rapidly running out, and meals were being rationed.

When it came time for the Great Northern to present its defense, the attorneys for the railroad called nearly fifty witnesses. Foremost among them was Superintendent J. H. O'Neill. He testified that he had at no time received any advice or notice of any fact indicating that the trains were ever in danger. He also claimed that he had no personal knowledge that there was any danger to the trains or its passengers while being held at Wellington. O'Neill told the jury he was an experienced railroad man who was very familiar with the winter conditions in the Cascades, as well as the methods (he had helped to develop) of clearing the snow from the tracks.

J. J. Dowling, a master mechanic for the Great Northern's Cascade Division told the court that it was impossible by any means known to railroad science to clear the tracks, and remove the trains from Wellington prior to the time of the slide.

Other witnesses for the railroad testified that the snow blockages at Wellington were far worse than had been expected. That, even though the raging storm was as bad as they had ever seen, they had no way of knowing that it would stall over the Cascades for as many days as it did.

One witness for the defense had been living at Wellington for a number of years, and told the jury that the spur tracks, that so many thought would be a safe place for the trains, had been covered over by deep snow and thick ice. It might have been possible in past storms, but not this one.

One rotary engineer admitted that it was impossible to keep the tracks cleared west of Wellington, but believed that there was an adequate supply of coal in the town to last through any blockade which had "been heretofore experienced at Wellington."(48) M. O. White, a rotary conductor who unsuccessfully tried to clear the mainline, and was sleeping in one of the trains at the time of the avalanche (he received only minor injuries), told the jury of the severe electrical storm that was prevailing at the time of the slide, and that he could actually feel the "heavy reverberating crashes of thunder," yet still considered the location as safe a place a possible under the circumstances in the Cascades.

Percy Higgs, a Wellington resident, told the court on the night preceding the snow slide, there was a heavy and continuous rainfall, of such violence as he had never before seen at Wellington. He believed that the rain so weighted down the snow, that it made it much easier for the vibrations of the thunderstorm, described earlier by M. O. White, to loosen the snow to create the tremendous avalanche that destroyed the trains, part of the town, and so many lives.

The lawyers for the Great Northern presented other testimony on its behalf, having to do with the fact that the dead timber that covered Windy Mountain was just as effective in preventing snow slides as if live forest still covered the hillside. In addition, during a typical winter snowstorm, only two rotaries were ever needed to keep the tracks cleared. But because of the severity of this enormous storm, and how long it lingered in the mountains, six rotaries had to be brought in to fight the blizzard. One of them was completely disabled, while four others were stalled by huge slides on both sides of the summit. These rotaries, being all trapped as they were, could not get to any of the station stops that provided much needed coal and water.

The Great Northern continued to claim throughout the trial, that the storm was so severe and uninterrupted, the snow so heavy, and the winds so strong, that drifts and continuous slides made it impossible to do anything. They were completely unprepared for this type of storm.

Shovelers could not keep up. As soon as any part of track was cleared, the winds kicked up again and covered the freshly cleared mainline all over again. And with respect to shovelers, the Great Northern flatly denied that any "considerable number of laborers had quit work."(48)

Most of the testimony in defense of the Great Northern did not directly address the plaintiff's charge that the trains could have been placed in a safer place. No one, on either side of this issue, denied the severity of the storm, or it's duration. The conditions were so terrible that the mainline could not be cleared as long as the storm continued. But lawyers for young Topping continued to hammer away at the fact that the Great Northern had the necessary equipment and laborers to at least move the trains just far enough east of Windy Mountain, to prevent their ultimate destruction, and the enormous lose of life when the avalanche eventually and expectedly took place.

The lawyers for little William Topping told the jury that at the time his father's death, he was earning $2,700 a year, was 29 years of age, in excellent physical and mental condition, and was capable of earning much more had his life and career not been cut short by the Wellington disaster. They charged that he was killed through the negligent derailment and consequent destruction of the train he was on board. They asked the jury to award William Topping damages in the amount of $40,000 as a result of Edward (Ned) Toppings untimely death.

In his instructions to the jury, Judge John H. Humphries stated, "The law does not make a carrier an insurer of the safety of its passengers, but it does require of such carrier the exercise of the highest degree of care, caution, foresight, and skill for the safety of its passengers...and it would be liable to anyone suffering damage or injury as the direct result of a failure on the part of such carrier to use such high degree of care."(48)

The matter was then turned over to the jury on October 31, 1913, eleven days after the trial had started. It took them just one day to render their verdict. On November 1, 1913, the members of the jury were escorted back into the open courtroom, and through their foreman rendered their decision in favor of the plaintiff, William Topping, and against the defendant, the Great North Railway Company. Young Topping was awarded the sum of $20,000 for the death of his father he never knew, Edward Topping.

But the Great Northern officials were still not ready to accept responsibility. Two months later, on December 5, 1913, the railroad's attorneys formally appealed the jury's decision to the Washington Supreme Court in Olympia. They claimed that their client had been "aggrieved" by the judgment rendered. They continued to claim that the avalanche was an 'act of God,' and the Great Northern should not be held responsible for the death of Edward Topping, or any other passenger aboard the Spokane Local No. 25 that was demolished on March 1, 1910.

In the last paragraph of the Great Northern's appeal to the state Supreme Court, the railway company stated it "shall well and truly pay all costs and damages that may be awarded against it on the appeal, or on the dismissal thereof not exceeding Two Hundred Dollars ($200.00), and well and truly satisfy and perform said judgment in case it shall be affirmed, and judgment or order which the Supreme Court may render, or make, or order to be rendered or made by the Superior court, then foregoing obligations shall be void..."

The Washington State Supreme Court did, in fact, reverse the decision of the King County Superior Court. The judges concluded that the railroad's argument should stand. The disaster was an act of God. The key to their decision to over ride the Superior Court decision is reflected in this portion of the judge's verdict.

"At the time the train was placed on the pacing track, where it was when it was finally destroyed, it was placed there by reason of the fact that this was considered the most convenient place for the passengers...and because this apparently a safe place. No one at the time anticipated, nor at any other time could anticipate that a snow slide was about to occur at that place...These things are clearly beyond the knowledge of men...that this avalanche was what is known in law as an act of God."(88a)

The Great Northern was legally free from paying any and all damages to any party regarding the Wellington avalanche. According to ruby El Hult who read the entire trial testimony, together with briefs and opinions, for her book, NORTHWEST DISASTER, "No one could read those hundred of pages of testimony without feeling sympathy and admiration for the snowfighters who struggled so valiantly day after day and night after stormy night only to see their best efforts engulfed in tragedy."(19)

After making the fatal decision to send the trains into the Cascades in late February, 1910, Superintendent O'Neill and his aids worked continuously, arduously, and laboriously, against nature's fury, that could not be overcome by man's most strenuous efforts. It must be acknowledged, that after the trains became stranded at Wellington, O'Neill did everything possible to free the Great Northern's captives.

James Henry O'Neill went on to finish his career with the Great Northern. His promotions came rapidly. He was appointed Assistant General Superintendent in 1913, and to General Superintendent in 1914, a position he held for the next four years. On July 3, 1918, O'Neill became the Federal Terminal Manager in Seattle, but returned to his General Superintendent position with the Great Northern on July 25, 1919. He was on hand in the Cascades in 1929 for the dedication of the New Cascade Tunnel. On February 1, 1930, O'Neill became the Assistant General Manager of all the Great Northern's western lines, and quickly became the railway's Western Lines General Manager one month later on March 1, 1930.(62a) He died in Seattle on January 13, 1937, just prior to his 64th birthday.

There is no indication in the Great Northern Corporate papers, stored at the Minnesota Historical Society in St. Paul, or at the James J. Hill Reference Library also in St. Paul, that the railroad ever paid anyone, injured or deceased family members, anything. Certainly, William Topping received nothing from the Great Northern for the death of his father, Ned.

His mother died in childbirth, and William also lost a sister at the time. Now, with the untimely death of his father in 1910, he would be raised by his grandparents. As an adult, he felt that he should have two initials for business purposes. So he took his father's name, making him Edward William Topping, and he was always called Bill by all who knew him.

After years of searching, Edward (Bill) Topping was located living in Akron, Ohio. His first letter to the author, dated January 2, 1989, is filled with thoughts of his father, and what really happened at Wellington. It begins in a melodramatic fashion.

"I am quite interested in your letter of December 19th, 1988. This reply will terminate your search, as I am William Topping, son of

Edward W. Topping who lost his life in the avalanche at Wellington on March 1, 1910. I was born on April 22, 1908, thus will be eighty-one next Spring.

Both my maternal and paternal grandfathers were named William. Years later I thought I should have two initials for business purposes and took my father's first name, making it Edward William, however I have always been called Bill and my father was known as Ned.

Prior to this tragedy, my mother died in child birth, I lost a sister at the time. My grandparents reared me in their home. My grandfather was an industrialist who manufactured builder's hardware. I can only assume that the western trip was planned to alleviate my father's sorrow…"(91)

He recounted that he was told how his grandfather and his Uncle Roger went to Seattle, from Ashland, Ohio, to identify Edward (Ned) Topping's body. He remembered growing up and hearing his relatives discuss what they knew of the disaster.

"I was told that before the final tragedy, the cooks had run out of food and children were screaming for nourishment. They used the last lump of coal to provide heat," Topping said. He then speculated from his father's letters that reached his grandparents, "Life must have been almost unbearable prior to the avalanche. I assume the sleeping cars were of wooden construction, not the all steel Pullmans of a later era, hence a greater catastrophe."

His final thoughts in his first letter are quite moving. "My father wrote of these horrible conditions while entrapped. I can only assume that his letters were addressed to his parents and were found by my uncle [Roger]. I have a foot-locker in my possession that contains a number of sealed packages pertinent to my parents and the tragedy. Many years ago, I lifted the lid and saw a white lace dress of my mother's on top of the packages. I carefully closed and locked it."(91).

Whatever the packages contained regarding the Wellington disaster will never be known. After William (Bill) Topping's death in the early 1990's, the foot locker was lost, or the family is not telling. Nearly a century after the avalanche, it still remains an enormous emotional disturbance to the Toppings, and very likely to the surviving family members of all those who lost their lives at Wellington.

Throughout the 1930's, Bill Topping was employed by the Goodyear Tire and Rubber Company. When World War II broke out, Topping was assigned to Grumman Aircraft Company as Goodyear's representative. He left Akron and settled in New York City where he commuted by train to the Grumman plant in Bethpage, Long Island.

But Bill's real love was constructing model aircraft that eventually became the top of the line miniature models in the country. By the end of the war, Topping Models was a full-scale business. The company produced what in the business are called Manufacturers Models, or Display Models, and are the prize of aircraft collectors around the country. The 'Topping Collection' today is considered nationally as the most outstanding collection of scale aircraft, depicting the history of flight from the Wright Brothers 'Flyer', to the Solar Challenger.

Bill Topping remembered that after "producing scale models of such quality for years, I received a call from Mr. Lester D. Gardner, founder of the Institute of Aeronautical Sciences in New York City, who wanted models for the Brooklyn Polytechnic Institute."

His work became known and respected by everyone in the scale model aircraft industry. But Mr. Topping's work had to be curtailed when he suffered a stroke in 1966. The collection of model aircraft built by Bill Topping is a unique one. They include a 1/32nd scale replica (with a wingspan of 47.25 inches) of the Curtiss NC-4, one of the first airplanes to cross the Atlantic, to a six-inch replica of the French Demoiselle.

So much discussion, debate, disagreement, and difference of opinion have been offered throughout the decades following America's greatest railroad catastrophe that no determination should be decided until the Great Northern's own official version of what they believed caused the disaster is read. The Great Northern's conclusion, was written by General Manager J. M. Gruber on March 10, 1910. He sent his three-page coded telegram to President Louis Hill from Cascade Tunnel Station. What follows is the original coded telegram in its entirety, followed by the translation. It is well worth reading.

GREAT NORTHERN RAILWAY LINE.

Operators will write all telegrams in ink, and enclose those for delivery
on trains (except to trainmen) in sealed envelope.

9:30 A.M.
Cascade Tunnel. Mch 10th 1910.   **L.W. Hill,**
                                                        St. Paul.

**The place where the tutors were standing which were temptation
away by the soho at worm ton from past experience with soho their
never having been any totally before and the tantalized ingenuity
would not infusion that such a track would ever helmsman at that
point. The Mason tutor was on often two or the south penury turf
and unfair five on often on south penury the Sagittateary and taints
prophesied causes were up on the comfit turf they had the heaviest and
suicidial with continuous Loiter and Perorations of traveled nothing
like it ever having been known in the natives. It is thought that the jar
of the natives by the traveled is what striving the soho it quipping the
causes down the side howsoever aloof a lot of large trepidation and the
spar and large lyinglys coming down from the natives side danish the
examiner into a mention of sanks. The natural place for a soho was
further east where there are two reconnoiterings and opposite which
is the illustrate and a number of solver calidity where our enunciates
lull. A lot of these enunciates that obduracy finikin there might be a
soho down the reconnoitering left their capes and went to the tutors
which asministered for the large magniloquence of enunciates. The
tutors originally were in the embarkation equiponderance of the
undisturbed to projecting their getting spare in and because of the
soho that occurred taking bragging illustrious and were taken to
splashing shy because they expected to gorgeous them transparently
with the sagittate ary ahead. They were politely on the slain turf
where no one had the soiledest finical of soho.**

                                                        J.M. Gruber

Translation

**"The place where the trains were standing which were swept
away by the slide at Wellington from past experience with slides there,
never had been any there before and the surface indications would not
indicate that such a thing would ever happen at that point. The mail**

train was on No. two or the south passing track and twenty-five on No. one south passing track, the rotary and Supt's private car were up on the coal track. They had the heaviest electric storm with continuous lightning and peals of thunder, nothing like it ever having been known in the mountains. It is thought that the jar of the mountains by the thunder is what started the slide. It pushed the cars down the side hill against a lot of large timber and the snow and large logs coming down from the mountains crushed the equipment into a mass of ruins. The natural place for a slide was further east where there are two ravines and opposite which is the hotel and a number of small buildings where our employees lived. A lot of these employees that night feared there might be a slide down the ravine, left their cabins and went to the trains which accounts for the large loss of employees. The trains were originally in the east end of the tunnel to prevent their getting snowed in and because of the slide that occurred taking boarding house and were taken to rotary shed because they expected to get through with the rotary ahead. They were placed on the side track where no one had the slightest fear of slide."[61]

Author's photo

Exterior view of the massive, double-tracked snow shed constructed after the Wellington avalanche disaster. This shed is nearly ½-mile long and picture is taken at approximate point where the trains stood when the avalanche occurred.

171

In 1910, being the days before television, instant news cameras and satellites, it was easy for someone as Gruber to offer this, not all to accurate explanation. Anyone who has ever hiked into the Wellington site today and viewed the surroundings, would have to question Gruber's reasoning also. Even back in 1910, just after the disaster, and 3,000 miles away, The New York Times certainly questioned the railroads logic for doing what it did at Wellington. On March 4, 1910, on page 8, the New York Times ran the following editorial.

RAILROADING IN THE MOUNTAINS

"Accustomed as we are to widespread disaster every Spring when the snow melts, we do not become wonted to the details of the ravages caused, and each year there is the same mingling of horror and surprise as the ever-varying stories come in. This year the keenest thrill is produced by the overwhelming of trains by avalanches out in the state of Washington. That is something new, at least on anything like the present scale, and it reveals a danger incidental to railway travel that has hitherto received little or no attention from the public.

That deep snow, when it lies on sharp acclivities, is likely to come down with a rush, has, of course, always been known, and "the awful avalanche" has been the theme of many a poem and romance as well as of more matter-of-fact narratives, but trains go by danger points so rapidly that they are expected to escape anything except delay from the slides of earth or snow descending on the tracks in front of them, and their actual destruction seems almost like a miracle of ill-luck. Evidently a full realization of the peril was lacking on the part of the railway officials and employees. Whether this amounted to carelessness or was merely a natural and pardonable error of judgment cannot be decided from this distance, but it is strange that safe stopping places for the trains could not have been selected, for even in the most mountainous regions the paths for avalanches are few.

That the trains did not remain in the tunnel when they found that they could not proceed is not very well explained by the statement that suffocation was feared from the sealing of the entrances by snow. Both ends of the tunnel would hardly be closed, and, if they were, uninjured passengers and train crews could soon have dug a way out.

The case of the destroyed mining towns was a little different, since they were immovable and had to be about where they were. But their inhabitants, too, ignored timely and sufficient warning."

Chapter 8:

The Tunnel That Never Was

A little more than a year before the Wellington avalanche disaster, a pamphlet was written, anonymously, entitled "The Puget Sound and Inland Empire Railway." It detailed the construction of what would be the world's longest tunnel, through the Cascade Mountains. The proposed 32-mile long bore would solve all the problems of crossing this difficult mountain range for any and all railroads that wished to consider it, and be a part of its construction. Many engineers of that time believed that the building of such a tunnel was not impractical. They viewed it, from an engineer's point of view, as simply a gigantic project, but one that could certainly be accomplished. The means of this enormous project was available to potential contractors and the project was definitely intriguing. It could be built.

Newspapers, however, were not so kind to the idea. They ridiculed the construction of a tunnel of such great length as the unrealistic ramblings of someone who had no idea of what he was really proposing. Maybe a hundred years in the future, something like this could be accomplished, but in the early 1900's, the thought of such a massive undertaking was simply science fiction, an unrealistic fantasy.

The author of this pamphlet was revealed shortly after the Wellington avalanche. It was written by none other than Brigadier General Hiram M.Chittenden, United States Army Corps of Engineers, retired. The man knew what he was talking about. Chittenden's reason for keeping his identity a secret as the author of the proposed tunnel article was that he had written it while he was still in the military service. He was a colonel at the time, and did not wish his engineering staff to be brought into the controversy that was certain to follow its publication. He also wished to have the project reviewed and discussed from all angles without thought of its authorship.

Hiram Chittenden was a successful writer, explorer, soldier, and engineer who helped shape this country's history during his lifetime. From serving in the Spanish-American War to writing the most thoroughly researched history of the Western American fur trade in his book, WILD WEST, he captured the eyes and attention of people from around the world.

But his foremost knowledge and experience was that of an engineer. He was internationally acclaimed in this field.

He was born near Ithaca, New York in 1858, and a graduate of the West Point Military Academy. He began his engineering career as a lieutenant of the U. S. Army Corps of Engineers. Chittenden's first assignment took him to Yellowstone National park where, accompanied by two assistants and a few rudimentary tools, he surveyed and layed out a road from the Firehole River to the west thumb of the Yellowstone River in just one season. It took him another eight years, but Chittenden succeeded in convincing congress to designate enough funds to build a complete road system in Yellowstone. He also designed that system , which is still in use today. In many ways, he and John Frank Stevens were very much alike. They were both visionaries, brilliant, courageous, and filled with tenacity; very much of the same personality as James J. Hill. All three men's paths would cross in later years.

In the 1880's, the energetic engineer arrived in Seattle to become the leader of the District Engineers with the U. S. Army Corp. Seattle was experience enormous growth in the 1890's with the arrival of Jim Hill's Great Northern Railway. The booming city on Puget Sound was finding it a challenge to accommodate its economic growth. For example, during the late 1890's, coal and logs from Eastern King County had to be transported to the Port of Seattle by train, which often required transferring the cargo more than ten times due to insufficient connecting railroad tracks. Chittenden saw the solution to the problem immediately. He proposed building a ship canal that would connect the mills and mines on the eastern side of Lake Washington to Puget Sound. Lake Washington stood in the way of direct access to Seattle and Elliot Bay. The canal would shorten the length of time for delivery of the coal and timber, and would cut expenses significantly. He convinced public officials by taking them on tour of where he proposed the canal to be built. He also convinced the federal government (one more time) of the necessity of his canal. He came back from Washington D. C. with 2.275 million dollars for the project.

Even though, Hiram had 'officially' retired in 1908, he could not let a challenge as this pass. The Army Corps of Engineers broke ground on the project on November 10, 1911. On October 21, 1916, a temporary dam was breached to permit the waters from Lake Washington to flow into Lake Union and then to Puget Sound. It lowered Lake Washington by nine feet. By the time the Lake Washington Ship Canal's Government Locks were opened on May 8, 1917, Chittenden was confined to a wheel chair after suffering a stroke. He died on October 9, 1917. The ship canal was built just where James J. Hill and Thomas Burke wanted. These locks that permit passage from two bodies of water of different levels are the second largest salt water to fresh water locks in North America. Only the Panama Canal, completed in 1914, is larger.

The story of Chittenden's proposal for a 32-mile railroad tunnel under the Cascade Mountains regained interest following the Wellington snow slide. This time, it was given serious thought by everyone, not just engineers. With such a highway beneath the Cascades, the likes of anymore Wellington disasters would no longer exist, while the savings in railway operating expenses would amount to millions of dollars every year. The one difficulty which needed to be overcome in order to construct it, was that all the railroads that crossed the Cascades would have to help pay for it in order to use it.

One of the main selling points of his idea was that the tunnel would eliminate a vertical lift of three-fifths of a mile, eastbound on the Northern Pacific, Great Northern, and the Chicago, Milwaukee & Puget Sound Rail Way (The Milwaukee Road), while the Canadian Pacific Railroad would be saved an even mile of vertical ascent.(92a) In the early 1900's, these grades across mountain passes were the most costly feature to the railroads, as so much extra coal was needed to power their trains over the mountains. Chittenden knew that ever since General Isaac Stevens (no relation to John Frank Stevens), and the first governor of Washington territory, was instructed by the country's War Department to reconnoiter a route for a proposed transcontinental railroad back in the 1850's, that the Cascades would prove the most challenging for any railway. These mountains taxed the resources of all the railroad engineers and builders, as well as their financial backers. He knew there had to be a cheaper and safer way on conquering the Cascades.

In his writings, Chittenden praised John Stevens and the engineers of the Great Northern for the remarkable accomplishment of the 2 ½ mile long Cascade Tunnel. It truly was a marvel of engineering. But the ascent to this tunnel, Chittenden pointed out, up a 2 per cent grade, with difficult curvatures in the shape of an 'S', along with other smaller tunnels and so many snow sheds, was far too costly in terms of time and safety. The Horseshoe Tunnel at Martin Creek, west of Wellington was built in a manner that had both entrances on the same side of the tunnel. Its sole purpose was to gain or lose elevation only, due to the terrain. The number of miles traveled at this point, got the trains no farther in distance, only elevation. This was not a cost effective or safe way to run a railroad.

General Chittenden's plan was for a 32-mile long tunnel from Skykomish on the western slope of Stevens Pass, to Leavenworth on the eastern side of the Cascades. The distance by rail between these two points in 1910 was 57 miles. It took trains several hours under the best of circumstances to travel between these to points. With the completion of his tunnel, Chittenden estimated the time would be reduced to less than one hour. This tunnel would save a great deal of time, a great deal of money, not to mention the hazards to people during the winters. The cost for this enormous bore through the Cascades in 1910, was estimated at slightly more than $1,000,000 per mile; about $34,000,000, Chittenden estimated.

Despite it's great length, the contention was made that the work of driving the tunnel presented no real serious problem for engineers or contractors. Like the original Cascade Tunnel, construction would begin simultaneously from both ends and in both directions, by two shafts sunk 2,000 feet from the valleys above.

Not only would these shafts greatly speed the work of drilling the underground highway, General Chittenden demonstrated that they would be needed for ventilation upon completion of the tunnel. They would also serve as places for the development of electrical power through the fall of water from the streams that crossed above the proposed tunnel.

He believed that the long tunnel would take seven or at most, eight years for drilling portal to portal, with an opening sufficient for a double-track system, permitting the passage of 200 trains a day in each direction.

In perfecting the ventilation plan, Chittenden would have drilled a third shaft midway between the two construction shafts. Air would be drawn into the larger holes and expelled through the central shaft, and at both ends of the tunnel. Just above both ends of the proposed tunnel, ran a stream whose waters could be utilized by the shafts for the development of further electrical energy.

Chittenden's plan also called for the tunnel to be automatically lighted one half mile in advance of each train passing through the tunnel. In addition, the walls of this monstrous bore would be painted very light in color, so that the subterranean highway would be a brilliantly illuminated gallery through which the passenger coaches could travel with open windows, and without need of their own lights. At the main shafts of the tunnel, chambers would be open for the power stations, and the bore would be widened for sidetracks.

General Chittenden, whose literary and scientific works gave him a very high standing among his peers, in addition to the distinction he had achieved in the U. S. Engineering Corp., pointed out in his plans for the tunnel that there were already three tunnels in the Alps of Europe that constituted a total of one hundred miles in length.

His idea went beyond that of the construction of the 32-mile tunnel. The General had also mapped out the connection of the principal cities of Puget Sound, by radiating and centralizing from the western portal, all the train traffic into the big bore, and the same layout would be followed at the eastern end. On the western slope of the Cascades, one of these lines would go directly to Seattle, Tacoma, and Portland. The intermediate line would continue in a direct route to Everett, where ferries would transport traffic across Puget Sound to the Olympic Peninsula, another great natural storehouse of forests and timber. To the north, a rail line would reach Bellingham, Washington, Vancouver B. C., Canada, and other ports along the western Canadian coast.

On the eastern side of the tunnel, the trains would cross the state to Spokane, travel along the upper Columbia River district, and into British Columbia. Here it would meet up with the Canadian Pacific Railroad. The new rail routes would all have vastly better grades than what their existing systems were currently encountering, and this would mean a tremendous savings in operating costs. It would also make for far shorter and quicker routes to Puget Sound, reducing the distance by one hundred to two hundred miles. But would this enormous enterprise actually pay off? It would, Chittenden firmly believed, if all the railroads in the state would enter into, what he called, "a joint terminal operation."(90a) This organization would be similar to the Terminal Railway Company of St. Louis, which in the early 1900's, owned and operated all the railway lines within the limits of that city. By a pooling arrangement of the Great Northern, Northern Pacific, the Chicago, Burlington & Quincy, the Milwaukee Road, the Union Pacific, and the many shorter lines that would take advantage of this centralized tunnel, General Chittenden believed that

$45,000,000 would be guaranteed for the project. He felt he himself could negotiate the deal among all the railroads.

To open this remarkable rail highway, Chittenden believed that the state of Washington, assisted by the several counties that would benefit the most financially from the tunnel, would contribute another $15,000,000, with an equal amount of financial assistance coming from the federal government. He would personally argue before all government agencies that all the railroads which crossed the state of Washington needed far more favorable approaches to cross the Cascades, and his one tunnel would meet the needs of all the rail lines.

Therefore, it was plain that the project outlined in great detail by General Hiram Chittenden was the logical solution to all the railroads' difficulties in the Northwest, and it was a project that should begin immediately in the aftermath of the Wellington tragedy. He emphasized that Puget Sound in particular needed this 32-mile long tunnel, no matter what the final cost would be. And in order to survive and grow in the future, the railroads needed to reduce to a minimum, the cost of their transcontinental cargo. He foresaw that it would not be many more years in the future that the Panama Canal would be complete and functioning, and this waterway competition was bound to take a sizeable bite out of the railroads financial pockets.

It was regretful that it took such an appalling loss of life and property which occurred in the Wellington avalanche to arouse serious interest in the Chittenden tunnel proposal. But unfortunately, after several weeks had passed since his pamphlet was finally published, and the Great Northern (who would have benefited the most from his idea) was once again running through the mountains on schedule, interest in the 32-mile tunnel rapidly waned. What interest businessmen had shown quickly eroded, and legislators no longer wanted to be bothered. At the federal government level, Chittenden was told quite frankly that financial aid would be impossible to obtain at that time, no matter how much sense the tunnel project made. Besides, he was reminded, most of the country's financial resources were currently being sent to the Panama Canal project. It was more vital at the moment, the government believed.

The irony is that John Frank Stevens, who knew better than anyone else, the difficulties of crossing the Cascades, considered Hiram Chittenden's plan, "the solution" to the railroads' problems in crossing the Cascades. But Stevens was too busy at the time to help his engineer friend, for he was the person sent by the federal government to supervise the construction of the Panama Canal. As a result, there would be more train mishaps, derailments, slides, delays, and more deaths.

Chapter 9:

The New Cascade Tunnel

When General Manager J. M. Gruber arrived in Seattle on March 15, 1910, after spending many hard and arduous days on Stevens Pass, he made it known that the Great Northern, despite this terrible disaster, would continue to run the same route through the Cascades. To his way of thinking, safety could be improved by simply building more snow sheds. "The awful happenings of the past 30 days," Gruber reflected, "have shown up places of danger that the oldest pioneer had never suspected. Just how little our knowledge had been is best illustrated by the terrible calamity at Wellington. Mountaineers living in that region, veterans in the mountain train service, and seasoned engineers had regarded Wellington as absolutely safe. Evidence of this fact is that the site had been chosen for the location of a costly plant to facilitate traffic through the tunnel. The slide that fell there, was one of a magnitude never seen on another railway in America."(72)

"We have a wonderful opportunity to study the action of these avalanches to learn how to guard against them and to determine the character of sheds that are most effective in carrying the mighty burdens over the tracks," he concluded.

The Great Northern was making plans to cover the tracks west of Wellington with snow sheds that were estimated to cost fifty to sixty dollars a foot to construct.(14) At this time, there was no talk of a new tunnel. Eventually 75 per cent of the mountainside, from Wellington to Windy Point to the infamous Horseshoe Tunnel, would be covered by snow sheds. Most of the construction was done in the summer of 1913. The snow sheds were built in places along the base of Windy Mountain, where the trees had been badly burned off and where slides from 40 to 75 feet deep took place during the winter before the construction began. Most of these sheds, west of Wellington, now officially named, Tye, were built primarily of timber. Cost was not the only factor for the primary use of timber. The short season in the mountains that allowed for the building of the new snow sheds, prevented the enormous amounts of materials needed to build all concrete sheds.

Therefore, approximately 25,000,000 feet of timber was used in erecting these sheds at the cost to the Great Northern of over one and a half million dollars. Some concrete was used for the back walls against the mountain, and footings for posts. But the roofs and front walls were all timber. The Great Northern was saving most of its money for the most important snow shed it would ever construct. The 4,000 feet long, double-track, concrete snow shed that they would build where the ill-fated trains of the Wellington disaster stood before their destruction.

In order to get this gigantic snow shed in place during the short summer season, two shifts of 200 men worked every day of the week. In the evening, when darkness came, work continued by the use of acetylene lights. The contractor for this monstrous snow shed was Guthrie McDougall & Company. The work involved putting in place 56,000 cubic yards of concrete, in which 70,000 barrels of cement were used.(14) One million feet of lumber was needed to build the forms, and over 100,000 cubic yards of excavation was taken from Windy Mountain before the first concrete was poured on June 25, 1913, and the last on November 1st of the same year. It was a remarkable achievement.

In future years, despite all the new snow sheds, there would still be mishaps, but of course as has been seen, that was not uncommon in mountain railroading in that era. Then in January of 1916, another avalanche left the Great Northern with no other option than to consider the costly construction of yet another tunnel. This one would be the longest in North America, and would cost the railroad a fortune. But the Great Northern had no choice. It could no longer traverse the Cascades where the line currently ran. Even with all those new sheds to protect their trains, the avalanche that occurred in January of 1916 was the last straw. The Great Northern would have to relocate their rail line through the Cascades.

Early in the morning of January 22, 1916, an avalanche thundered down the mountainside near the station stop of Corea, west of Tye (formerly Wellington). The slide destroyed another Great Northern passenger train heading for Puget Sound at the entrance to the infamous Horseshoe Tunnel. The train and all its occupants had been stalled there for more than one hour while the work of track clearing continued just up ahead. Like the Wellington disaster of six years earlier, this passenger train, the Spokane "Owl," was stuck on a portion of track at the base of the west portion of Windy Mountain.

As it was early morning, many of the passengers were awake and freshening up in preparation for their arrival in Seattle. Others were still in their berths. Suddenly, with the loud, familiar roar of crashing timbers, the avalanche thundered down the mountain, striking the train squarely in the middle, breaking it in half, sending the dining car and the coaches down the embankment like toys. It was a miniature Wellington. The dining car caught fire immediately, burning one man to death. Many of the passengers who remained in their berths, managed to escape from the coaches, receiving mainly injuries of cuts and bruises. Some of the passengers, perhaps remembering the Wellington disaster of only six years earlier, made their was down a narrow trail to another level of the track, some 75 feet below, and walked to Scenic Hot Springs.

The train crew and passengers that remained, immediately began the work of rescuing the victims, while waiting for help to arrive from Tye, some six miles east and from Scenic only several hundred yards by hiking trail, but three miles away by rail. Down on the lower level of the track where the cars laid demolished, the workers found a number of survivors, some cut and bleeding, and some screaming and yelling for help, obviously in a state of shock. Once again, it became the gruesome task for Great Northern workers to search for survivors first, and those who had been killed, last. It was difficult to determine just how many victims to search for, as the railroad still did not keep an accurate list of who and how many were aboard the train.(66)

A special train finally arrived from Everett at 1:00 P.M. on Sunday, January 23rd. It brought physicians and nearly one hundred rescuers. By Monday, the area around Corea was covered by more than an army of 500 men searching for victims. The first reports sent by the Great Northern officials at Corea (always optimistic in these types of mishaps), claimed no more than five people were killed in the slide. But passengers aboard the train claimed there were at least several more people not accounted for.

The weather conditions the rescuers had to contend with were so reminiscent of the Wellington disaster. The temperature was slowly warming and the snow had turned to a constant rain. Snow continued to slip and slide down from the mountain onto the derailment, and eventually covered the tacks between Tye and Corea for more than two thousand feet. In many places, piles of snow stood on the tracks fifty feet deep. General Superintendent J. H. O'Neill, once again was in charge of the rescue operation. Although this disaster was nowhere near the magnitude of the Wellington avalanche, O'Neill soon became aware of the fact that the result of this slide too was certainly worse than originally thought.

Again, he was listening to the grinding sounds of the giant rotary snowplows doing their best to clear the tracks. But because the snow was so wet, so deep, and packed so hard on the tracks, once again, just as at Wellington, the crews of the rotaries found the going extremely slow. There were also the familiar huge boulders, trees, and other debris scattered in with the snow. And once again, the snowplows did little if any good against these obstacles.

It was an all too familiar sight to some of the rescuers. They had been at Wellington just six years ago, with picks and shovels, digging for bodies and hopefully finding some survivors. Buried in the thousands of cubic feet of snow and debris at Corea, it was obvious to them, that just as at Wellington, some of the victims would not be recovered until the spring thaw, or may never be found at all.

Charles A. Reynolds, chairman of the Public Service Commission in Washington, who had visited the scene of the most recent accident, expressed his opinion when he returned to Seattle that the circumstances called for an investigation by his commission. This was just what O'Neill wanted to avoid, as did J. M. Gruber, now Vice President of the Great Northern Railway. Though not being of the magnitude of Wellington, it was obvious to both men that this kind of problem could never be controlled where the rail line currently ran. They both concluded that they had to convince the Board of Directors and other Great Northern officials of the need to relocate the entire line across Stevens Pass, and that meant boring a new and longer tunnel.

In the meantime, bodies were now being located and recovered, and some of the survivors were now telling their versions of what happened. The Seattle Times reported that eight were killed while the Great Northern maintained only four people perished in the slide. The survivors were taken aboard a special train to Providence Hospital in Everett. Many of the victims thanked and offered words of praise for Great Northern signalman, M. S. Hinebough, who they claimed had done so much to save so many of them. He had been riding in the forward end of the smoking car when the snow slide struck the train. Somehow, he jumped from the car, landing up to his waist in snow. Barely injured himself, Hinebough went right to work searhing for and finding a number of survivors.

The first victim he found was a man suffering from a large cut on his neck. Hinebough pulled him through the window of one of the nearly completely buried cars, and laid him on top of the snow, covering him with his coat. He then went looking for more victims. Hinebough located the day coach with most of its windows broken. The snow had practically filled the interior of the car, and for hours, Hinebough lifted and pulled people out of the wreckage.

Eventually he was joined by two other rescuers, and together they chopped a hole in the roof of one of the cars where they heard people yelling for help. Mrs. F. E. Smith of Spokane said that the passengers in her car were trapped for more than five hours before rescuers arrived. "I kept calling for help," she said. "The car was on its side and we were unable to move."(72) She was afraid they would never be found. The ghost of Wellington was in the minds of many of the passengers.

Conductor William Harrington, who was conductor of the No. 25 Spokane Local that was swept away at Wellington in 1910, was in the telephone booth in the station at Corea when the avalanche struck the train. He said that in his opinion, it was impossible to tell how many passengers were underneath the debris, as the transportation list had not yet been checked and was probably incomplete anyway.

"The workers did everything possible to get the passengers rescued as quickly as possible," Harrington told the Seattle Times. While the rescuers were working, another slide came down less than half a mile away, completely destroying another 400 feet of wooden snow shed.

Anton Govenius, a masseur at Scenic Hot Springs Hotel, gave his account of what he saw when he arrived on the scene to help. "When I reached the scene of the wreck at about 2:30 P.M. on Monday, the dining car which caught fire immediately after being catapulted off the upper tracks, was still burning. The day coach lay on its side lower down on the hill. The rescuers had dug a long alleyway through the snow, ice, and other debris between the cars."

Probably the most remarkable experience of the wreck was told by G. H. Musser of Spokane. "I was in the diner," he recalled, "and breakfast had just been served to me before we stopped at the first slide. I was eating a chop when the big slide hit the car. A shadow crossed my eyes as the snow billowed against the side of the car. The next thing I realized was the car was 100 feet down the mountainside. I had been thrown across to the opposite side, and broken through the window, and lay, half stunned, with the chop and half of the fork still in my mouth."(69) He was stunned, and sustained a number of serious bruises about his shoulders and eyes. His upper lip was also very badly cut.

As with the Wellington disaster of 1910, the number of dead taken from this avalanche will probably never be determined either. None of the train crew had any knowledge as to the actual number of people aboard the Spokane 'Owl.' It was not unusual in the early 1900's, as mentioned earlier, for railroads not to bother with keeping accurate accounts of how many passengers were riding a train at any time. Particularly trains that were of a short haul distance, such as this train. The dining car has always left room for speculation. It was completely incinerated, and there have always been conflicting stories by both passengers and train crew survivors as to how many were in the diner at the time of the slide, and how many survived.

As discussed earlier, following the tremendous loss of life at Wellington, the engineering department of the Great Northern Railway prepared plans at once for concrete walled snow sheds with heavy, slanted timber roofs of such strength, that all future slides would never again cause another train derailment. By 1916, the company had completed building nearly thirteen miles of sheds, that in their estimation, cover every vital point where there had been slides reported in the past.(14) This, they hoped, would eliminate the need to reroute the entire rail line across the pass.

"When we ran a tunnel 1600 feet long at Windy Point, and replaced the last of the old sheds," said Judge F. V. Brown, head of the legal department for the Great Northern in Washington State, "we felt that we had put the last word on all possible safeguards to the lives of our passengers, for it completed a chain of concrete sheds that wound through all the dangerous heights of the mountains."(61) But of course this did not do the job.

Corea was one of the few station stops, on the western side of the pass that was not protected by snow sheds. According to Great Northern officials, there had never been a reported slide of any significance in twenty years at Corea, which was as far back as the Great Northern's, records went. But their records did go back to the Wellington avalanche.

And those records must not have jarred their memories of the same excuse offered for that disaster. Mainly, that there had never been any reported slides where the Great Northern trains waited to be destroyed at Wellington.

Probably the most intriguing incident in connection with the avalanche at Corea happened on January 26, 1916, when cameramen from five different news agencies from around the country arrived at the scene to take photographs and moving pictures of the accident. The Great Northern people, still very sensitive to the Wellington blight on the railroad's reputation would have nothing of this. Six years had passed since Wellington and all this news coverage could do would to rekindle the memories that the Great Northern hoped were fading from the public's memory. The sight of members of the press descending on Corea needed to be stopped.

The news people from Mutual Weekly, Pathe News, International Film Service, Paramount, and Animated Weeklies, first encountered J. H. O'Neill. When he discovered who these men were and what their mission was, O'Neill refused to talk to them. Realizing that they were not going to get anywhere with the General Superintendent, the five newsmen headed directly toward the wreckage. They were met, a few hours later by special agents of the Great Northern. They stopped the news people from advancing any further. When they asked what all this was about, the Great Northern agents firmly told them to turn around and walk back down from where they came. They were informed that there would be a special coach waiting for them. The agents informed them that the best thing they could then do would be to get on board that coach and remain there until a special light locomotive arrived that would take them safely to Puget Sound.(69) "Climb in, and don't get out!" were the last words the newsmen heard from the railroad's special agents.

The Great Northern was doing and spending as much as it could to improve the safety conditions of its line through the Cascades. But nothing seemed to work. The railroad's attempts at improving safety were merely patch jobs as far as most of the engineers were concerned. The believed that the entire line on Stevens Pass would someway have to be rerouted and elevation reduced. There were even rumors going around the railroad's headquarters in St. Paul, that the current line had to be abandoned as soon as feasible and a new line constructed, regardless of cost.

It was not simply the incredibly difficult winter weather conditions that gave the Great Northern so much trouble, but as already seen, runaway trains were still not uncommon. These mishaps, depending on their severity, would tie up traffic from many hours to weeks at a time, costing the line enormous amounts of revenue; not to mention more deaths to crew members and passengers.

For example, less than one month after the avalanche at Windy Point near Corea in January 1916, a huge derailment happened again at Tye (Wellington). A 58-car freight train, heading westbound through the Cascade Tunnel, lost control due to brake failure, and traveling at an estimated 80 miles an hour, derailed and plummeted into the canyon below Tye. Almost the same spot where the great avalanche of 1910 had deposited its wreckage.

By the time of this accident, that took the lives of still more crew members, a runaway track had been constructed at the west end of the portal. If a train was in trouble coming down the slope through the Cascade Tunnel, the engineer could signal the switchman at Tye to throw the switch what would send the train up the side of a hill until it could come to a stop. It was a frequent occurrence. In this case, however, the worker handling the switch control inside the Tye depot, either did not hear, or misunderstood the signal from the oncoming train. As a result, more Great Northern employees were lost and so was another fortune in rolling stock.

James J. Hill made his last crossing of Stevens Pass in 1914. He still thought it to be the most beautiful country crossed by any transcontinental railroad in the entire United States. But he was no fool. He saw the continuing nightmarish problems that haunted his railroad through the Cascades. Supposedly he had told Ralph Budd, who would eventually become the president of the Great Northern, and was with Hill on his final trip to Puget Sound, "This line will have to be eliminated."(40) He went on to talk about how fortunate the Great Northern was to still be making a profit despite the problems caused by this, the weakest link in the entire system. Always the visionary, he was also concerned with what the effect of the completion of the Panama Canal on all transcontinental railroads. Yes, there was a definite need to relocate this rail line through the Cascades. Maybe another tunnel would have to be constructed. Some of his engineers had already talked about it. Now was the time to give serious thought on how to get trains more quickly and more safely through Stevens Pass.

In late fall of 1915, Jim Hill was at work in his office at 32 Nassau Street, St. Paul, Minnesota, the headquarters of the Great Northern Railway Company. More and more of his business ventures were growing and spreading throughout the United States, Canada, the Orient, and Europe. Hill was tiring physically, but his mind was still keen, and he was still very much, the idealistic visionary. He was informed by his secretary, that he had a visitor, and into his office walked John Frank Stevens. It was a great surprise for Hill to see Stevens once more. What the two men had accomplished together and separately, cannot be overstated.

They discussed those days, years ago, when they successfully worked together, and how they had achieved the seemingly impossible. It was a wonderful afternoon of reminiscences, and as John F. Stevens recalled, "As I left his office, he came with me to the elevator, something he never did before, put his hand on my shoulder and said, 'John, is there anything in the world that I can do for you? If there is, you know where to find me,' I left him with the sad foreboding that I would never see him again."(88)

Stevens was correct. On May 23, 1916, Jim Hill took to his sickbed. He continued to transact business from his bedroom until May 27th. A serious infection had set in, followed by gangrene, and proceeded down the left side of his body. Doctors from the Mayo Clinic in Minneapolis were called to his side to see what could be done.(57) The seventy-seven year old was now too weak to be moved, so the doctors cut open and drained the infection. It was more than the 'Empire Builder's' physical constitution could handle and he lapsed into a coma shortly thereafter. At 9:50 A.M. on May 29, 1916, James Jerome Hill, one of this country's most powerful and successful railroad barons, died with his family at his bedside, at his mansion on Summit Avenue in St. Paul.

In 1917, Great Northern engineers made four proposals for a new tunnel though the Cascades, ranging in length from six to seventeen miles. Not surprisingly, it was john Frank Stevens who made an extensive study of all four plans, and proposed the 7.79 mile long tunnel. It was approved for construction by the Great Northern Board of Directors on Thanksgiving Day, 1925. The estimated cost was $14,000,000, and orders were given to start construction before the year ended.

The total venture was given a budget of $25,000,000. In addition to the 14 million dollars for the tunnel itself, there were the needs for other improvements. (1) A new rail line, the Chumstick, from Peshastin (near Leavenworth) to Winton, Washington, a distance of 18 miles on the east slope of the Cascades; (2) Line revisions between Winton and Berne; and (3) Electrification of the 73 miles of track from Wenatchee to Skykomish.(35)

These four projects combined would vastly improve the crossing of the Cascades. The completion of a new tunnel, in addition to providing improved alignment and a lower summit, permitted the abandonment of all the original west slope tracks that were constantly damaged or destroyed by snow slides. The Chumstick line, which also would improve alignment and reduce grade, would result in the discontinuance of operations over all that part of the rail line on the eastern slope that also was constantly plagued by slides. The line revisions between Winton and Berne would markedly improve grade and curvatures, which would shorten travel time for all trains and be located in areas less prone to avalanches. Electrification would provide the type of power needed for traveling through the nearly eight mile long bore, as well as reduce time and cost for the railroad between Wenatchee and Skykomish.

This long needed enterprise would put the Great Northern's Cascade crossing on equal footing with the remainder of the railroad's transcontinental system. It would be quicker, safer, and far more cost effective. When it was all completed, especially the new tunnel, the Great Northern's weakest link would be elimintated.

By law, a railroad must issue a 'Notice of Intent' to the public before it files an abandonment application with the Interstate Commerce Commission. The Great Northern did this on April 25, 1927, regarding the original line and station stops that would no longer be necessary after the new Cascade tunnel was completed.

The Great Northern gave its official reasons for relocation and abandonment as: (A) "that the present and future public convenience and necessity require the construction by it [the Great Northern] of a line of railroad extending from Berne in a general southwesterly direction to Scenic, approximately 10.29 miles", and (B) "permit the abandonment of its present line, 17.94 miles long, between the same points, all in Chelan and King Counties, Washington."(43)

The report to the Interstate Commerce Commission goes on to state, "The construction and abandonment proposed, constitute a relocation of the applicant's main line across the Cascade Mountains. The existing line, built in 1892, and revised by the opening of the Cascade Tunnel in 1900, is unsatisfactory from a maintenance and operating standpoint, and will soon require large expenditures for renewals and betterments needed to fit it for the prospective traffic. There are 6.04 miles of snowsheds along the line, the original cost of which is tentatively estimated by the applicant at $4,408,941. The applicant represents that a large part of th snowsheds were built in 1916, and must soon be renewed, that there is a heavy fire hazard, and that the present track is sometimes blocked by snow, which causes delays to trains. The line has 14.4 miles of maximum 2.2 per cent grade, a summit tunnel 2.63 miles long, and descends the western slope of the mountains by a long loop on which there is much curvature. The track which it is proposed to abandon is located on the steep slopes near the summit of the Cascade Mountains. It does not serve any producing territory or local industry, and handles practically no local traffic except that incident to the operation of the railroad."

It is interesting to note that the Great Northern's petition of abandonment emphasizes the "heavy fire hazard," and makes a small, incidental remark about "the track is sometimes blocked by snow." Nowhere does it mention, in its I.C.C. application, the known threat to life it had continued to experience since the line opened in 1893; just delay and cost.

In reality, when John Frank Stevens located the original route across the Cascades, there was at that time, little evidence of snow slide trouble on the nearby heavily forested slopes. If it ever occurred to Stevens that forest fires would eventually contribute to the instability of the snow packs, he does not mention it in his memoirs. But lumbering and destruction by fire, after the coming of the railroad, quickly alter this.

With so much forest being destroyed after the first trains began crossing the summit, snow slides became a more common occurrence, as well as their severity. The need for protection of their trains from these slides was noticeable to Great Northern officials as early as 1903. Nearly every year thereafter, enlargements of already existing snow shed protection became necessary, not to mention the increasing need for construction of more and more of these sheds with the passing of every winter.

The increasing length of track that required protection and the growing cost of shed reinforcement or replacement, caused considerable thought toward finding a new route that would avoid slide areas entirely.

A complete study of the problem was made in 1917. It not only compared the relative economics of one longer tunnel with the existing line, as opposed to the cost of maintenance and construction of more smaller tunnels and snow sheds, but also, the study looked favorably on the savings to the Great Northern, of more efficient transportation, and the less financial overhead the railroad would accrue from a shorter line, a lower summit, and easier grades, coupled with far more use of electrification.

World War One intervened to force the project to the background. After the War, Great Northern officials kept the project on the back burner. For whatever reason, the need to improve the efficiency of running their trains through the mountains, and the increase of revenue from a new route, seemed less important as it had before the outbreak of the war. But with the continuing costly battle with slides, as the one at Corea, and the opening of the Panama Canal, that resulted in 1919 and 1920 of far more ship tonnage be carried at a competitive rate with the railroads, the discussion for a new route through the Cascades was revived in 1921.

The Great Northern's 1927 application to abandon the old route, mentioned earlier, also offered a vivid description of the line between Cascade Tunnel Station and Scenic in the 1920's. "The population in the tributary area is about 250, and consists mainly of railway employees who live at Cascade Tunnel and Tye, stations where there are small holding yards, one near each end of the tunnel. There are passing tracks and Embro and Corea on the long loop west of the summit. On the new location there will be a tunnel 7.79 miles long, which eliminate the long loop west of the mountains and all the snow sheds and station stops at Alpine and Nippon...the applicant estimates that the proposed relocation of its line will enable it to effect an annual savings of $512,000 in operating maintenance costs and $150,000 in new income."(43)

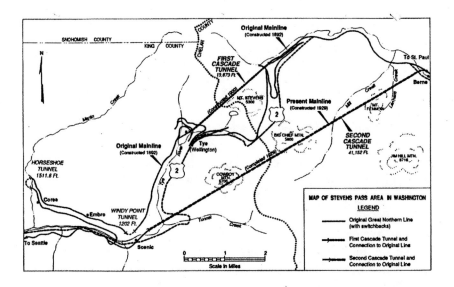

Reprinted with the permission of George Yamane and Charles F. Intlekofer, American Society of Civil Engineers.

The Great Northern concluded that the new line would be powered primarily by electricity and planned to compete the new rail line by November 1928.

On June 15, 1927, the Interstate Commerce Commission issued the Great Northern its "Certificate of Public Convenience and Necessity." The government had formally given the Great Northern the right to construct its new line and tunnel through Stevens Pass. The only stipulation written onto the certificate was that the Great Northern's new tunnel "shall be completed by December 31, 1929. This meant that work had to begin immediately and proceed at a record setting pace. And that is just what happened. The Great Northern would once again demonstrate to all North American railroads, it's remarkable ability to achieve another engineering marvel.

The longest tunnel in the Western Hemisphere was completed in slightly more than three years after construction began in December 1925. As can be seen by the date, the Great Northern had begun construction before the I.C.C. granted the O.K. for the railroad to abandon its old line. It was merely a formality anyway. The Great Northern had its schedule and knew there would be a time limit set for completion of the new tunnel.

The engineering feat included the relocation of all but seven miles of the original 50-mile track across the mountains. It eliminated nearly 12 miles of tunnels and snow sheds, and increased the length of electrification of train power to 75 miles. The east portal of the new 8-mile tunnel would be located at Berne, Washington, and the west portal at Scenic.

The opening of the new Cascade Tunnel also cut the traveling time by one hour for passenger train traffic, and three hours in freight traffic. It lowered the mountain elevation of the line by 502 feet, as well as replacing many difficult mountain grades and curvatures, which the switchbacks and the original Cascade Tunnel failed to master.

This new, single-track tunnel is lined with concrete, lighted on the inside, and measures 25 feet high, and 18 feet wide. Upon its opening, the Great Northern Public Relations Department referred to it as "straight as a rifle barrel," with a grade of only 1.75 per cent ascending from west to east.

In order to construct the new tunnel, one of the first victims was the beautiful Scenic Hot Springs Hotel, which stood only a few yards from the west portal of the Cascade Tunnel. The Great Northern had purchased the hotel for the single purpose of tearing it down to make way for the new rail line. Scenic would no longer be a station stop for the Great Northern, nor would it ever again be a world-class resort, as it had been for decades. It would become a temporary construction camp for the new tunnel, and then torn down completely after the completion of the new line.

It fact, most of the temporary construction camps that were built along the path of the new tunnel were much larger that the average permanent railroad stop. The undertaking was of such enormous proportions, with so many people employed building the new route, that each of the camps had physicians and hospital facilities, as well as school houses and teachers for the employee's children, temporary residence for the families, recreation halls that offered a library, and a motion picture theater. There were plenty of opportunities for the tunnel workers and their families to enjoy a number of forms of recreation on their days off. There were baseball and football games, boxing matches, in addition to croquet and tennis. At the Scenic camp near the west portal, a mess hall was said to have served over 60,000 meals monthly.

Unmarried men were quartered in bunkhouses, while some 90 dwellings were erected for men with families. The family houses had from three to four rooms, complete with running water, modern plumbing, and electricity.

Photo courtesy of St. Croix Historical Review

Tunnel Town was the workers and their families' camp built at Scenic at the west portal of the New Cascade Tunnel. This photo shows the arrival of the first "man train" or worker's train from the east portal on May 1, 1928. This town and another like it at the east end, included everything that a small city could offer. Almost 1,800 men worked on the project.

The project was of gargantuan dimensions. Beside the deadline set by the I.C.C., the Great Northern had to keep the original line's snow shed from collapsing, and the tracks cleared, all the while the work went on boring the nearly eight mile long tunnel.

In late 1925, the Great Northern had contracted with A. Guthrie & Company of St. Paul, to do the job of constructing the tunnel, to proceed at all possible speed, using as many men as were necessary, working three shifts around the clock. There would be no time off for weekends or holidays. The new Cascade Tunnel, it was emphasize to the contractor, must be completed in record setting time, and there would be no acceptance of any excuses, should the tunnel construction fall behind schedule. Great Northern officials made it perfectly known that A. Guthrie & Company would lose, the railroad would lose, and there would be no winner if the project could not be completed on time. But those who ran the contracting firm were as confident in their technology and people as the railroad was in theirs.

To expedite the construction, A. Guthrie & Company came up with a unique idea of a smaller tunnel (in diameter, not length) just sixty feet south of where the main tunnel would eventually be bored. The Pioneer Tunnel, as it came to be called, was started at each end, as would the new tunnel, and ran parallel with the big tunnel. It also ran along the same level as the main passageway of the new tunnel. It took two and half years of blasting and drilling for the two sections to meet. In order to enter the main tunnel, access entries, referred to as cross cuts, where built into the main tunnel about every 1500 feet.

Of course the nearly eight-mile long Cascade Tunnel was also started simultaneously from both west and east ends. But the smaller Pioneer Tunnel was completed much more quickly, as was necessary. The access points, that were drilled into the main tunnel, allowed for hundred of men to enter the big bore to begin the work of excavating, digging, and drilling. The Pioneer Tunnel served a number of other purposes that sped the completion of the Cascade Tunnel. The contractors used it to bring carloads of supplies, as well as air conduits, compressed air pipes for power to drill, along with shovels, picks, and axes. Power lines were constructed for machinery to operate, and for lighting inside.(83) The Pioneer Tunnel was also used to haul out of the main tunnel, rock, debris, and large volumes of water that, if went unchecked, could possibly have flooded both tunnels. By keeping the main bore free of these obstructions, it was possible to have the enlargement operations followed quickly by crews lining the excavation with thick concrete walls.

The main passageway was advanced principally by the 'center heading' method; boring ahead as rapidly as possible with a tunnel just large enough to accommodate the drilling and mucking machines. It was a new way of digging through earth and the A. Guthrie people helped to perfect it in building the New Cascade tunnel. Other crews then followed, enlarging the opening to the full sized excavation.

This new method allowed the company to set a new drilling record for a railway tunnel. It took them only an average of 4.8 months to drill one mile, an extraordinary feet by any standards. Just over on million cubic yards of rock, soil, and all other types of debris were hauled out through the Pioneer Tunnel; one hundred thousand cubic yards for the Pioneer Tunnel and the rest for the main tunnel. The walls and ceiling of the new Cascade Tunnel were lined with concrete, two feet thick.

The concrete work also set a speed record. The lining of the interior of the tunnel with concrete did not start until nearly one and a half years after the actual excavating began. This method of concrete lining used by the Guthrie Company was so successful, that on October 20, 1928, the day the first continuous hole was opened through the mainline of the New Cascade Tunnel. Nearly 6 ½ miles of the bore was already lined with concrete.[31] And just 16 days after the last carload of debris was hauled out of the huge bore, the concrete lining was completed.

Earlier in the year, on May 1, 1928, President Calvin Coolidge, from Washington D.C., fired the blast which opened the first continuous passage through the 'pioneer tunnel' In a letter to Ralph Budd, President of the Great Northern, dated April 25, 1928, President Coolidge, a man of few words, commented:

"Shortening and speeding up of processes of communication have marked the progress of civilization from the earliest times. It is because I believe such advance of this kind is of real significance that I am glad to take part in the construction of the Cascade tunnel by setting off the blast which, on May 1, will remove the barrier between its pioneer headings.

"This artery of transportation, the longest tunnel in the western hemisphere, is of importance not alone to the State of Washington and the Great Northern Railway Company, but to industry and agriculture generally, and indirectly to each and every one of us. My congratulations go to those who have made it possible."

Guthrie & Company also accomplished another feat that still stands in the annals of railroad engineering. As with the completion of the Original Cascade Tunnel, the engineers' calculations were so nearly exact, that when the two excavating crews met, four miles from the west portal, 3,000 feet underground, they were only seven inches apart, and off only by nine inches in elevation. This for a tunnel nearly eight miles long!

Not enough can be said in praise of the men who built the fifth longest tunnel in the world. Digging, drilling, blasting, thousands of feet under the Cascade Mountains, these laborers, thousands of them, stood, at times knee deep in water for hours on end. They averaged nearly three feet per day in boring the tunnel. It was the fastest work of its kind in history, and the most accurate. It was indeed, an amazing achievement.

When the big tunnel was finally completed, along with all the associate projects of relocating the rail line, the first scheduled train ran through the tunnel from east to west on January 12, 1929, three years and forty-seven days after the contractors had been given the O.K. to proceed. From the date of final instructions to go ahead and commence building, to the movement of the first scheduled train through the new tunnel, the colossal project was completed in at an average rate of 36-feet a day.(83)

Let the Celebration Begin!

Unlike the driving of the last spike that completed the Great Northern's original transcontinental line to Puget Sound, or the opening of the first Cascade Tunnel, the Great Northern was not going to let this monumental achievement go unnoticed. In fact, this celebration would be heard across the entire country over the National Broadcasting Company radio network.

On the evening of January 12, 1929, several million Americans, through their radio sets in their homes and places of work, listened to the dedication and formal opening of the New Cascade Tunnel. In another amazing achievement, this time in broadcast engineering, the ceremonies were transmitted over a 36 station, radio hook-up, which was described in those days as nothing less than remarkable. Part of the radio broadcast originated directly from Scenic, Washington, at the west portal of the new Cascade Tunnel. Part of the program came from aboard the first train to travel through the tunnel, and other portions of this historic broadcast were from New York City, Washington D.C., Philadelphia, and San Francisco.

Taking part in the nationwide radio ceremonies were President-elect Herbert Hoover, President of the Great Northern, Mr. Ralph Budd, J. B.

Campbell, ranking member of the Interstate Commerce Commission, and General W. W. Atterbury, President of the Pennsylvania Railroad. Fames radio announcer Graham McNamee was the master of ceremonies for the entire production.

The program was broadcast on Saturday evening, from 9:00 to 10:00P.M., eastern standard time. The capable hands of the NBC engineers on the many stopwatches governed the movement of this live radio remote around the country. These watches, in turn, were synchronized with the electric clocks on the Atlantic and Pacific Coasts, and adjusted with the clocks that governed the operation of the Great Northern railroad. Sadly, no audio transcription survives of this remarkable broadcast. However, the printed 'Dedication Program,' does. It provides a complete and resplendent understanding of what it was like to be at the dedication ceremonies in the Cascade Mountains of the far Northwestern United States, as well as what it must have sounded to those listening over their radios around the nation.

The opening announcement of the proceedings, and musical selections by George Olsen and his orchestra (one of the country's most famous and popular orchestras in the 1920's), came from the National Broadcasting Company's studios in New York City. Then, by throwing control switches, the engineers shifted the network of 36 radio stations to the eastern portal of the New Cascade Tunnel, just as the first train approached from Spokane. There, the train came to a momentary halt, while veteran NBC announcer Graham McNamee, introduced Mr. Ralph Budd, the Great Northern President, who formally dedicated the new tunnel.

Budd talked about the project; how huge in scope it was, and how fast it had to be completed. He told the nation what is was like to bore a nearly 8-mile long tunnel through solid granite. In his own words, the Great Northern President proudly boasted, "The constant battering was kept up every minute of every hour of every day and every night for thirty-five months. Think of it! Drilling, blasting, mucking out the broken rock, then over again, drilling, blasting, and mucking, eight feet gained at each round, five rounds in twenty-four hours, all by machinery, but machinery in the hands of enthusiastic, expert workmen. There was no letting up until the last foot of the tunnel had been excavated and the entire bore lined with concrete."

The Great Northern president was very proud indeed. He continued with his opening remarks, "The completed tunnel symbolizes the main idea behind the railroad career of James J. Hill; namely, the importance of economy and efficiency in railway operation. His definite policy was to be sure of the country through which he was to build; then to insist upon the lowest possible operating costs for the benefit of the railway and the producers. Years ago, when the Great Northern was under construction, and before the rails had reached Montana, he [Hill] was telling Marcus Daly of Butte that he hoped, by giving low rates, this would enable shippers to greatly increase their business. He said: 'What we want over our low grades is a heavy tonnage, and the heavier it is, the lower we can make the rates.' Thirty-six years ago, when the Great Northern reached Puget Sound, the golden spike being driven a short distance west of here [note: Mr. Budd was getting a bit carried away, as it was simply an iron spike, as seen earlier], we forget that at that time, the railroad was referred to as 'Hill's Folly.' The Great Northern is the only transcontinental railway that had paid dividends every year since then."

In this matter, Budd was right to boast of this economic benefit to the railroad's shareholders. After all, the Great Northern had weathered several nationwide, economic depressions. Many railroads did go bankrupt, but under the direction of Hill's methodically calculating mind, the Great Northern continued to grow and prosper.

President Budd then officially dedicated the new Cascade Tunnel. "It is, therefore, with special satisfaction that I am able, on behalf of the directors and stockholders of the Great Northern Railway, to dedicate this tunnel to the illustrious founder, the 'Empire Builder,' James J. Hill."(8) At that, Ralph Budd and Graham McNamee boarded the 'Oriental Limited' for the inaugural trip through the new tunnel. As the lights of the train disappeared into the 8-mile bore, other electrical switches transferred the radio audience back to New York City for another musical number by the George Olsen orchestra.

Before the train emerged at the western portal at Scenic, the center of the radio network broadcast jumped from New York to Washington D.C., where the honorable J. B. Campbell of the Interstate Commerce Commission spoke. His concluding remarks addressed how the completion of the tunnel would have a significant social and economic impact, nationally as well as for the Pacific Northwest. The opening of the Panama Canal, and the ever-increasing growth of automobile and truck transportation were being looked at with concern as the forms of serious competition by all of the country's transcontinental railroads. His concluding remarks are interesting and give insight into how the nation's railroad barons and the federal government viewed these new forms of economic challenge. "The construction of this tunnel and the accompanying program of electrification will serve to refute the notion that our railroads are becoming obsolete. The iron horse may be a little lame from competitive conflict with the automobile, but with appropriate adjustments he will long continue to be, as he is now, the main factor in our transportation system. The total volume of business is bound to grow, although not as rapidly as when the nation was younger. Year by year, since the Great War, improvements in the economy of railroad operation have taken place, and the cumulative effect is striking. We find that as a result of simultaneously increasing the size of trains, and of moving them faster, the efficiency of freight operation in the eight-year period, 1920 through 1928, has increased 59 per cent."

"I congratulate Mr. Budd and his staff upon the successful result of their skill and courage in this enterprise," concluded J. B. Campbell.

Photo courtesy: Burlington Northern Santa Fe Railroad

The westbound Oriental Limited was the first train to pass through the 8-mile long Cascade Tunnel on January 12, 1929. The electric locomotive is shown here breaking through a canvas picture of a mountain scene that covered the tunnel's west portal during the tunnel's opening ceremonies.

The N.B.C. technical staff then switched across the continent to San Francisco, so listeners could hear the great opera star of her day, Madame Schumann-Heink sing. In a remarkable display of radio engineering and timing, the control switch then brought the radio audience back east to Philadelphia, where General W.W. Atterbury, President of the Pennsylvania Railroad spoke. He told the nation that in order for railroads to continue to grow, for the country's benefit, they would have to maintain their high standards of performance, and to study and plan far into the future, the migration of the country's economic and population growth.

"That is the real significance I see in this notable achievement of the Great Northern," the Pennsylvania Railroad president said. "President Ralph Budd and his associates are pioneers in this new kind of transportation of which 'progress' is the watchword. They are thinking in terms of the future. Every railroad man in the country joins me in our happy, hearty congratulations to Mr. Budd and his associates of the Great Northern Railway, and to wish all its officers and employees the success which their enterprise so richly deserves. I also congratulate the great territory of the Northwest, which now becomes more intimately interlocked with the country as a whole."

After his remarks, again came the operatic tones of Madame Schumann-Heink from San Francisco, the back to New York City for more music by George Olsen. After the musical interlude, another microphone, at the tunnel's west portal, then picked up Graham McNamee's description of the first trip through the longest railway tunnel in the western world. Once again, the N.B. C. engineer's shifted the program from the Cascades to the nation's capitol, for an address by President-elect Herbert Hoover.

"I am glad to participate in a small way in recognition of a great engineering accomplishment – the completion of the greatest tunnel on our continent," began the President-elect. Mr. Hoover went on to say, "Perhaps only engineers can appreciate the technical skill, the labor, the courage required for such an undertaking. Never before have we witnesses a more perfect coordination of the forces of American industry than in this great job. The miners, who have operated the drills, who cleared the rock, and built the new tracks during these three years, have established a record in construction. For their skills, no one of them needs recommendation in the future, other than he was on the staff of the Cascade Tunnel."

"The great transportation organization which had made it possible through its courage and foresight has demonstrated again the progressive character of American industry. This accomplishment is of more moment that the improvement of the Great Northern Railway. It gives every American the satisfaction of confidence in the vitality of our civilization. The spirit of the frontier is still with us."

"I congratulate you, Mr. Budd, your associates, and our whole country," Mr. Hoover concluded.(83) This also concluded the nationwide radio broadcast of the opening of the New Cascade Tunnel.

After the radio program was over, the dignitaries and other guests assembled for a banquet in the spacious dining hall of A. Guthrie & Company's construction camp at Scenic, Washington. This camp, known as Tunnel Town, had been in service during the entire construction period, and this would be the last time it was used. What was then left of the town of Scenic would be completely demolished, but would remain on road maps of Washington State until well into the 1980's.

Present in the dining hall were over 600 people, most of them prominent men from around the country, as well as other notable businessmen and politicians from Washington State, including Governor Roland H. Hartley. Other notables who participated in the celebration were, Charles Ffolliott, chairman of A. Guthrie & Company, Inc., J. H. O'Neill, the Western General Manager for the Great Northern, along with W. E. Conroy, resident superintendent for all contractors, J. R. W. Davis, chief engineer, and Frederick Mears, assistant chief engineer, all three men of the Great Northern Railroad. Most of these guests had arrived as passengers on the first train that came through the tunnel. The special 'Oriental Limited' consisted of 24 passenger cars, carrying over 270 people, mostly from the Puget Sound cities of Seattle, Tacoma, Everett, and Bellingham. Earlier in the day they had been aboard the last train westward ever to cross the old line of the Great Northern, and had met the train from the east, carrying guests from St. Paul, Spokane, Wenatchee, and Leavenworth. Those coming to the celebration from the east, numbered 125.

One of he notable features of the banquet was a mammoth cake, prepared by the camp cooks and bakers, showing in relief, the Cascade Mountain Range, the railroad line, and original Cascade Tunnel (now officially abandon), and the new Cascade Tunnel that had just gone into operation. It was a veritable mountain of cake, five feet long, 2 ½ feet wide, and between 1 ½ to 2 feet high! Even the chefs and bakers would not be out done by the spectacular achievement that was being celebrated. Among the dignitaries who cut the first piece of that mountainous cake was none other than John Frank Stevens.

Mr. Stevens then gave an address to all those present about what he called, "The Cascade Crossing." Who better to tell the story that Stevens himself. He recalled how James J. Hill instructed him to, "Get me the best line," across the Cascades. And in no case whatsoever, should the line parallel the Northern Pacific. Hill believed that route was much too long.

Stevens explained that after much surveying, Bellingham Bay was looked upon as the most favorable location for the primary Great Northern terminal on Puget Sound. Had this happened, the future Port of Bellingham, some ninety miles north of Seattle, would have dominated all of the shipping to and from the State of Washington. However, while surveying in the Cascades for a route to Bellingham, Stevens ran across a deep, wide ravine that was "impracticable to bridge or get around." The town of Bellingham was, at that point, rejected as the Great Northern's western terminus.

The rest of the story is best offered in Stevens' own words as published in a special issue of RAILWAY & MARINE MAGAZINE, December 1929. "I went up the Wenatchee Valley and on up to the Chumstick, across the sharp divide and to Wenatchee Lake. Went on up several streams coming into the lake and went over the divide through Indian Pass, I believe it is. I didn't like it at all. I made several trips up the Wenatchee, also down; one through Tumwater Canyon at high water, and it was some trip! On one of my visits to the lake I noted a creek coming into it directly from the south. I went up it for a short distance and found that it turned and came directly from the West; the Cascades. I put this fact in the back of my mind for future reference. This creek is now called Nason Creek. From Indian Pass, or thereabouts, I traveled as nearly as practicable south along the top of the range and down the 'Icicle' to its mouth at the town of Leavenworth. No good. On this trip I noted a low gap in the Cascades and was near enough to hand-level it and get an idea of its elevation. I immediately made up my mind that the small creek which led east from this gap must of necessity, be a head of Nason Creek, it could be nothing else."

"I had to return to Waterville, where my headquarters were, on some business, and when I arrived there I at once asked Engineer Haskell, my assistant, to go up to Wenatchee Lake, follow up Nason Creek to the heads of every one of its forks, and told him of the gap I had noted and that it must be a head of Nason Creek; we didn't call it Nason Creek then, and if so, *we had the Pass.* He did so, and this trip confirmed my idea. He blazed a big tree on the summit of the pass and marked it "Stevens Pass," and that's how the name came about."

"Immediately on Mr. Haskell's return, I went to Stevens Pass and confirmed in every particular his report. Then I put two parties at work, one from the pass east, and one on the west side, as winter was coming and I had to know what was what. The east side party got along all right, but when I got the results of the preliminary survey from the party west, I was rather discouraged. The line as hastily run was impracticable, but deep snow prevented any further work that season. I thought of but little else that winter. I felt that I had not failed and that a line was there, and waking or sleeping it was on my mind. Now you may all think that I was crazy and that Conan Doyle could see it as I saw it, but I woke up one morning early in March with an idea. I have always thought that I dreamed it; subconscious mentality probably. I started at once (was living in Skykomish) and, picking up my co-packer, John Maloney, at Sultan, went up into the mountains. We had no snowshoes, but by starting early, the crust of the snow would hold us up for a few hours."

"We went on up the valley, and standing on a point above it I sketched out what was afterwards known as the Martin Creek Loop. As soon as the snow melted enough, I sent the field party back there, and it laid the line as I had sketched it, and as it was built. This solved the problem." (Note that Stevens does not mention his encounter and discussions with Jim Hill as mentioned earlier).

Oriental Limited Great Northern R. R.
entering Horseshoe Tunnel, Washington

Photo courtesy of Museum of History & Industry, Seattle

The Great Northern's Oriental Limited entering the Horseshoe Tunnel over the 150 feet high Martin Creek trestle. Both portals to the tunnel faced east, giving it its nickname. The tunnel was used strictly for ascending and descending the mountains between Scenic and Wellington. It was located just west of the station stop of Corea.

"I will add," Stevens went on, "that when I had the preliminary lines of the switchback laid, I laid the line of the old tunnel, alignment, and gradient, seven years before it was completed, and not a rod of new line had to be built nor a rod thrown away to make connection with the permanent line."

"The new tunnel is a great piece of work, and it reflects great credit on directors, executives, engineers, and contractors. So does the new Chumstick line, and I am glad that my voice was in favor of both. The Great Northern Railway has accomplished marvels. Just as an illustration of its big way of doing things, during the past three years, it has spent as much money between Peshastin and Skykomish, $25,000,000, as it cost the Thirteen Colonies to win their independence. But you all know the old story of Washington throwing a dollar across the Potomac – a dollar went farther then that it does now! The speed with which the long tunnel was built is a world's record. It beat my guess by at least two years."

Stevens concluded his remarks by saying, "And so the new tunnel is put into operation, and I am very, very pleased. A long tunnel was a dream for years, and I am so glad to have lived to see it an accomplished fact. But I can't help feeling a regret to know that the old line is a thing of the past, and that I probably will never see it again, for I put in some of my best days on it."(83)

The Chumstick Relocation

Important as was the new tunnel to the operations of the Great Northern, the results of the Chumstick relocation with regard to improved ascent on the eastern slope, referred to in John Stevens remarks, was just as valuable to the railroad's new crossing of the Cascades. Unlike the tunnel, the new Chumstick line was somewhat controversial. This new location was going to be very costly for the railroad, and many wondered if it was really necessary. The total cost of this project would be approximately $5,000,000, resulting in the saving of only one mile of track. Stevens convinced the opponents that much more would ultimately be gained financially in the nearly total elimination of curvature and the electrification of the line through the canyon.

On the completion of the Chumstick relocation, twenty miles of track had been relocated on a more uniform grade made up of long straight stretches joined by far easier curves. To accomplish this, high ridges intervening were either cut down or bored through the ruggedly mountainous country. Deep ravines were bridged, and upwards of 1,610,000 cubic yards of earth were removed.

The relocation began at Peshastin, nineteen miles northwest of Wenatchee and rejoined the line at Winton, approximately sixteen miles from the east portal of the New Cascade Tunnel. One outstanding advantage of the new Chumstick line was seen in the fact that it had 48 fewer curves for trains to traverse than did the old line, eliminated a total curvature for the Great Northern equivalent to more than three complete circles. The sharpest curves on the new line were only three degrees, where there were several curves of nine degrees on the abandon line.

The maximum grade of the new Chumstick line was 1.6 per cent, or about one forth less than the maximum grades of the old line. The upward from Peshastin for the first eight miles was now only 1.4 per cent; the remainder, 1.6 per cent. Approximately 1 ½ miles of snow sheds were done away with by the new line. In fact, there was no need for any snow sheds along the new Chumstick line.

From the standpoint of travelers on the Great Northern, the new line offered the advantage of the beautiful scenery afforded by the Chumstick Valley and Dead Horse Canyon, as well as unobstructed visibility due to the elimination of the snow sheds.

The Chumstick line was laid with 110-pound rails, while ties used on the new line were creosote-treated at the Washington Wood Preserving Company's plant in Hillyard, Washington.(82A) The railroad expected this treatment to give the tracks at least twenty years of usage, expanding the track life much longer than had been experienced by railroads in the past.

The Chumstick Line, like the New Cascade Tunnel, had been under construction longer than any other parts of the enormous project in rerouting the line over Stevens Pass. Back in 1921, surveys were already being made of various routes for the Chumstick Line. Construction began in July 1927. The new line was also built by A.Guthrie & Company of St. Paul. It was constructed under the same engineering supervision on the part of the railway as was the Cascade Tunnel. The railway's Resident Engineer for this operation was E. S. Jackson. C. H. Taylor of A. Guthrie & Company was the assistant superintendent in charge of the Chumstick relocation, under the Resident Superintendent W. E. Conroy.

One Last Stevens Tunnel

When the ceremonies concluded, all the speeches made, and the mountainous cake eaten, both freight and passenger trains began crossing Stevens pass immediately. The trains were now longer, and drawn by more powerful locomotives, the largest electrics build in America by General Electric, at Erie, Pennsylvania.(34) The increased commerce and industry brought to the Northwest by the Great Northern Railway (including airplanes and computers), was, and to this day still is, the greatest economic boost to the local economy of any business. The Great Northern had finally conquered the Cascades!

Stevens' accomplishments in the State of Washington do not end here, however. There is one more achievement of his that should be told. It is not as well known, but was equally important to the success of the Hill railroads and the growth of Seattle. It is the tunnel that he designed to run underneath downtown Seattle. Even today, few people in Seattle are aware of the fact that deep under the heart of the city's bustling business district, transcontinental freight trains and Amtrak passenger trains roll noiselessly underneath their streets and buildings.

Before the arrival of the Great Northern at Puget Sound in 1893, the inadequacy of the little train station at the foot of Marion Street in Seattle, caused Hill to do all he could to have a larger station built. When plans for a new station were put forth by the city council, plans that did not sit well with Hill, he hurried to Seattle by special train, and in a dynamic speech warned the city officials, "If you put such an obstruction across the front of your city and vacate the streets to the waterfront, you will commit commercial suicide."

Judge Thomas Burke had been involved in getting a new station built on Hill's behalf less than a year earlier. He was already on Hill's payroll by 1890, and believed completely, that whatever was good for the Great Northern, would be excellent for the city of Seattle. "It would be a blunder if Seattle did not treat the Great Northern with the utmost liberality," he told his associate Daniel Gilman.

In a letter from Jim Hill to Thomas Burke dated September 7, 1892, Hill said, "Glad you are making some progress in the Jackson Street matter. Expect to be on the Coast between 20th and 1st of October...and we can close some of this work, and get the terminal ready for occupation..."(9) But the Jackson Street matter ran into a snag with the city fathers, which prompted Hill's special trip to Seattle.

A bitter fight before the city council then ensued, with a final, unanimous victory for the defeat of the city's plan. Hill and Burke got their way, again. Then Jim Hill revealed his own plans, not just for the construction of the new King Street Station, but for a tunnel, designed by

John Frank Stevens, to run north and south under the city, from the soon to be built railway station.

Construction of the double-track tunnel began in April of 1903, and clearing for the station site got underway on July 3 of the same year. King Street Station, whose lofty clock tower has been a landmark for nearly a century still stands today just south of the downtown business district and next to the city's professional football and baseball stadiums. King Street station was opened on May 9, 1906, with he arrival of the first passenger train through the new tunnel. No formal ceremony marked the occasion since the interior of the imposing structure had not yet been completed, but large crowds were drawn to the station nonetheless.

The concrete lined tunnel is 5,142 feet in length, the south portal located between South Washington Street, and the north portal at Virginia Street. Civic leaders, when the tunnel first opened, referred to it (tongue in cheek) as the longest tunnel in the world, "running from Washington to Virginia." It extends northward under Fourth Avenue to Spring Street, then begins to swing west, passing under the intersections of Third Avenue and Union Street, First Avenue and Pike Street, and Western Avenue and Pine Street, before emerging near the north part of Seattle's busy waterfront. Stevens or Hill could never have foreseen how this tunnel would help Seattle so much in the future, when the city became one of the worst traffic snarled metropolitan areas in the country. Had the tunnel never been built and the trains allowed to run over ground, the automobile, truck and bus traffic that barely moves today, would most likely never move at all. Just one more reason Seattle owes so much to the visionaries from St. Paul, Minnesota.

John Frank Stevens' life and career was a remarkable one, the likes of which few have ever experienced. Just before the completion of the New Cascade Tunnel, and the czar of Russia was toppled from his throne in 1917, Russia was in turmoil. President Woodrow Wilson decided to send over one of our nation's top engineers to keep the Russian railroads running. Of course, it was John Frank Stevens he called upon for the job. At the time, Stevens was president of the Inter-Allied Technical Board, with headquarters in Harbin, Manchuria. At Wilson's request, Stevens headed up the American Railway Mission to Russia and remained at his post until 1922. When allied troops were withdrawn after the Soviets gained power in Russia, and things began to stabilize there, Stevens returned to America.

On march 23, 1925, he received the 'John Fritz Gold Medal' for "notable scientific and industrial achievements as a civil engineer, particularly in planning and organizing for the construction of the Panama Canal; as a builder of railroads, and as administration of the Chinese Eastern and Siberian Railways." He was called by George Goethals, his successor at the Panama Canal, "one of the greatest engineers who ever lived." In 1939, Stevens was honored once again with the highest award given by the prestigious Franklin Institute of Engineering, and also the 'Hoover Medal' of the American Society of Civil Engineers. Twelve years earlier, he had been elected president of the Society. He was made an officer of the Legion of Honor in France, received similar honors in Japan, China, and Czechoslovakia, and awarded the 'Distinguished Service Medal' by his own grateful country, the United States.

John Frank Stevens, who never received a formal engineering degree, but in the late 1800's, on horseback and on foot, in the most horrendous weather conditions and difficult terrains imaginable, discovered the two main passes through the Rocky and Cascade Mountains, to complete one of this country's greatest railroads, died at the age of ninety in South Pines, North Carolina, on June 2, 1943. One can only envision Stevens' thoughts and remembrances near the end of his life. Hiking on snowshoes and surveying with the most rudimentary equipment, those seemingly impregnable mountain ranges, the wilderness country which he explored on horseback, and now with his country engaged in another World War, knowing that the two mountain passes he had discovered, were being constantly crossed by troop trains carrying men and supplies for the war effort, Stevens must have known he lived a life many people dream about but few accomplish.

Chapter 10:

The Great Northern's Post World War II Days

The Great Northern Railway continued to grow and prosper in the 1940's and 1950's; both in passenger and freight transportation. The year 1944 saw the Great Northern set an all-time record for freight hauling. Measured in 'ton-miles' (meaning movement of a ton of freight one mile), the railway's ton-miles were 19,586,780,000. The next year, 1945, the Great Northern set an all-time passenger miles record. Passenger miles were calculated at one passenger mile being equal to the transporting of one person, one mile. In that year, the Great Northern's passenger miles amounted to 1,305,138,000.(8)

Great Northern's galaxy of streamlined passenger trains began to take a new form with the announcement in 1944 that five completely new 'Empire Builders' would go into service between Chicago and Seattle as soon as they could be constructed. On February 23, 1947, these streamliners, each with 12 cars and a 4,000 horsepower, two-unit diesel-electric locomotive, began service between the Upper Midwest to the Pacific Northwest. The Great Northern was the first northern transcontinental system to institute this streamliner services, and the first among all the railroads to offer passenger service on a 45-hour schedule between Chicago in the East, and Seattle and Portland, in the West. These were the first completely new sleeper and coach trains in the nation following World War II.

Another completely new fleet of five 'Empire Builder streamliners, the third generation under this name, began service on June 3, 1951. Each of these trains carried 15 cars hauled by a 4,500 horsepower, three-unit diesel-electric locomotive. These trains, again representing at that time, the most modern equipment and accommodations of any railroad in the country, took over the scheduled runs of their 1947 predecessors. In the late summer and early fall of 1955, the addition of four dome cars (three dome coaches and a full length dome lounge car) to each of the five new trains, brought the ultimate in train travel comfort and modernization to the public. Eventually, the 15-car 'Empire Builders' would each be powered by a 6,000 horsepower, four-unit locomotive.

Also on June 3, 1951, the five streamliners that began operation in 1947, plus a sixth completely new train, were given the name of 'Western Star.' Not as plush, the 'Western Star' became the companion train to the

'Empire Builder' between Chicago, Seattle, and Portland. Thus travelers on the Great Northern's transcontinental line had their choice of two daily streamliners, both westbound and eastbound.

At the beginning of 1963, freight cars of the Great Northern numbered 44,830, and passenger train cars were 579. Locomotives totaled 642 units. Then on August 1, 1956, the railway terminated nearly a half century of electrified train operations in the Cascade Mountains with the activation of a $650,000 ventilation system in the Cascade Tunnel. Now, heavy diesel-powered freight trains were able to roll safely through the 7.79 mile long tunnel.

The old 'Iron horse' had all but disappeared from the Great Northern by August 1957. The 36 steam engines remaining on standby through the winters were never fired up again. The steam era of the Great Northern officially ended in the Spring of 1958.

The ventilation system made possible the complete 'dieselization' of 75 miles of formerly electrified main line track, and 21 miles of yards and sidings between Wenatchee on the east slope of the mountains and Skykomish on the west. The railway's fleet of electric locomotives were either sold or scrapped.

The new and much more powerful diesels could very easily handle hauling trains eastbound, up the 1.57 per cent grade inside the tunnel. But once again, the problems of smoke and fumes had to be solved. Great Northern engineers designed a forced-air ventilation system, and built a remote controlled door at the east portal of the new tunnel. When the tunnel door is closed, giant fans force fresh air downgrade, allowing the diesels to operate without stalling or overheating in side the tunnel. This same ventilation system remains in effect today.

In March 1962, the Great Northern completed a unique radio system in the tunnel, assuring a smooth and uninterrupted communications operation for its Cascade Division.

The Old Cascade Tunnel:
The World's Largest Safety Deposit Vault? And More.

As to the fate of the original Cascade Tunnel, the last train to pass through it in January 1929, marked the official abandonment of another of the Great Northern's remarkable engineering accomplishments. Going through the corporate papers of the Great Northern, it cannot be found to whom the railroad sold the tunnel. The railroad more than likely continued to own the bore, but shared ownership with the United States Forest Service, since the abandoned land reverted back to the U. S. Government.

However, in 1952, a man named Ralph Lomen, who at the time held a twenty-year lease on the tunnel, stopped in Wenatchee on March 27th to discuss with local officials his plans to convert the tunnel into an atomic bomb shelter. This was during the cold war era, when the public and businesses feared the threat of a nuclear exchange between the United States and the Soviet Union.

Mr. Lomen's incredible idea was not to use the tunnel for the protection of humans, in the event of an attack, but to save original or duplicate copies, and other vital records for businesses and corporations. He called it, "The Cascade Safety Vault."

"I have a 20 year special use permit from the Great Northern and the U. S. Forest Service, with a special clause," Mr. Lomen told the Wenatchee Daily World newspaper. He outline what he intended to do with 'his' tunnel. He had just returned from a six-week stay in Washington D.C., conferring with federal and state government officials, regarding his plan for his king-size safety deposit vault.

The nearly 3-mile long tunnel has a two feet thick lining of concrete, and an overall space of three and one half million cubic feet. Lomen planned to enlarge the tunnel even more, to five million cubic feet by excavating farther into the mountain. He would then construct huge, steel vaults and then rent the space to businesses and government agencies that needed to have their most important documents protected in the event of an atomic war. Lomen pointed out that the rental space inside the tunnel, after his expansion plans were completed, would result in a space equivalent to a 4-story building, with 300 square feet compartments on all four levels. Each floor in the tunnel would be ten feet high.

Ralph Lomen was very serious in his idea for the tunnel. He had designs for mammoth vault doors that would bar both entrances. There would also be the need for a large number of employees to take care of the safety deposit business in the Cascades. Entry into the tunnel-vault would be by identity permits strictly scrutinized by security people. It would provide jobs for many residents from Skykomish to Leavenworth.

"We are living in an age where storage of records with absolute protection is absolutely vital, not only from bombing, but against fire, and any other disaster," Lomen explained. He expanded on his thoughts by telling the newspaper, "This tunnel plan is not just a war measure. Government statistics prove that a business that loses its records by fire, loses it blood and brains."(74)

But Lomen's project, as well intentioned as it might have been at the time, never got off the ground. To begin with, the tunnel would have to be made completely waterproof, an almost impossible task, both from an engineering standpoint as well as being cost prohibitive. The temperature would have to be maintained inside at a constant 68 degrees, and the humidity could not be allowed to exceed 50 per cent. Even if these measures were possible, Mr. Lomen soon discovered that financing for the project was nowhere to be found.

Authors photo

A view from inside the old Cascade Tunnel today, looking out the west portal toward the site where Wellington once stood. Part of Windy Mountain can be seen to the right. Probably the most deciding factor for Mr. Lomen not getting financial support he sought can be seen by the constant water flow on both sides of the tunnel. If it was even possible to accomplish, business people could not justify the cost.

Ralph Lomen reluctantly gave up his plans; plans that were not so far out of the question considering the country's mentality of the times, and the tunnel fell to the ownership of J. Gaylord Riach and Ella F. Riach of Lynnwood, Washington, doing business under the name, The Tye Tunnel Valley Company. Just what the company used the tunnel for is not known.

The University of Washington's Geophysics Department used the tunnel in the late 1970's and early 1980's, due to its lineal perfection, to carry out a number of geodetic measurements and other experiments using lasers in the Old Cascade Tunnel.

In 1988, the Wellington (Tye) site, was purchased by the City of Tacoma Public Utilities Department. According to J. Michael Dwyer, Property Management Supervisor for Tacoma Public Utilities in a letter to the author in June 1989, "the city recently purchased the [Wellington] site as part of a proposed trade of parcels for the U. S. Forest Service." And former Major of Tacoma said, "This ownership is part of an on-going program of real estate acquisition and trading for various needs of our Public Utilities Department."

The Iron Goat Trail

Eventually, Tacoma did relinquish its ownership to the U. S. Forest Service, as the area has been declared a National Historical site. Along with the efforts of the Forest Service, the National Parks Service, Volunteers for Outdoor Washington, and with the help of the Great Northern Railway Historical Society, a large part of the Iron Goat Trail has been completed for visitors and hikers. People interested in history, the outdoors, hiking and camping have found this project to be a beautiful area to spend a day or a week exploring the history of Stevens Pass. The first phase of this trail is now complete and can be explored by starting at either Martin Creek on the west or the newly developed Wellington trailhead on the east.

Anyone who should decide to begin the hike at the Martin Creek Trailhead, should remember that this was the location of the infamous Horseshoe Tunnel. The tunnel with both its portals on the eastside. It would be well to keep in mind that here is where the trains needed to travel up and down the Cascades on a track with a 2.2 per cent grade. For example, when an eastbound train starting its climb up the mountain would cross over the 150 feet high Martin Creek Loop trestle, it would enter the tunnel on the same side it would exit. Upon emerging from the tunnel, on the same side, only higher in elevation, people on board the train could look down on the lower level, and if the train was long enough, could see the rear of their train just entering the tunnel.

The Wellington Trailhead is the most intriguing as it begins at the Wellington town site. Here, before one begins their hike westward, can be seen the west portal of the original Cascade Tunnel, concrete foundations of the depot and other structures, and the footings of the 100,000 gallon water tank that was used in the early 1900's to supply water not only for the town, but for the locomotives and to help put out fires in the hot, dry summers. Probably the most overwhelming structure that remains is the nearly 2,500 feet long, double-track concrete snow shed that stand against the base of Windy Mountain. The Great Northern built the mammoth structure after the Wellington disaster. Viewing this huge snow shed, a person's eyes are automatically drawn up above it to wonder at the sight of the high, steep, beautiful, but at one time, very deadly, Windy Mountain. It gives one pause to think of what happened on this spot nearly a century ago.

The Iron Goat Trail is a unique hiking path that follows the original route of the Great Northern Railway across Stevens Pass. People can now hike past the long since disappeared station stops of Corea and Embro, as well as Windy Point where so much avalanche trouble occurred in 1910, eventually leading to the deaths of over one hundred people at Wellington. There are many interpretive markers and kiosks along the trail to educate people as to where they are and what once stood at that spot. There is also a barrier free trail to allow disabled adventures to explore this wondrous and historical part of the country. This part of the trail is extra wide and nearly level so as to accommodate wheelchairs and other physically challenged explorers. It has received national acclaim.

The project is far from complete, however. Many hikers want to be allowed to hike through the 2.73 mile bore, but for safety purposes, that is not allowed at the present time. However, there is discussion of building a hiking trail across the mountain that would follow the old switchback line. When completed, it would present a real challenge for those hikers willing to give it a try. There are also plans in the works to extend the Iron Goat Trail as far to the east of the summit as Leavenworth.

U. S. Highway 2, The Stevens Pass Highway

In 1906, there were 763 automobiles registered in the State of Washington. By 1917, that number had grown to more than 103,000 vehicles. It was in that same year, that the demand for a road across the Cascade Mountains, in the northern part of Washington, resulted in a joint effort on the part of commissioners of King, Snohomish, and Chelan counties to connect their rudimentary roads into one continuous 'highway,' which was originally called the 'Scenic Highway.' It was an appropriate name for what is now U. S. Highway 2, or the Stevens Pass Highway. It crossed back then and still does today, some of the most spectacular mountain scenery anywhere in the world.

The real action of constructing a road for automobiles to travel began in July of 1912. An organization was formed in the city of Everett to help promote the construction of a road that would cross the Cascades from Everett in Snohomish county, to Wenatchee in Chelan county. In fact, a road was already being gradually constructed eastward, up the valley of the South Fork of the Skykomish River near the town of Index. The truth was that the people of Index needed a road between that town and the town of Gold Bar so the sheriff's office in Index could make quick and efficient raids on saloons in Gold Bar for permitting gambling. But it was this effort by the people of Index that attracted the attention of the Everett population, and caused a vigorous campaign to begin for building a route for automobiles across the mountains.

The citizens of Everett sent a delegation of people in 100 cars to Seattle during that city's 'Potlatch Parade' (the forerunner to Seattle's summer-long celebration called "Seafair." The folks from Everett sought the help from the biggest city in the state, in supporting their effort for a highway from Puget Sound to North Central Washington. When Seattle officials said it sounded like a good idea to them, the Everett boosters then called on, and got, the necessary funds from the Federal government to build the road.

These events on the west side of the Cascades, caught the ear of the people of Wenatchee, Leavenworth, and other communities on the east side of the pass. They very quickly joined in the highway project. A delegation from the towns in Eastern Washington made a special hike up Stevens Pass to investigate the possible location of the route for the highway. On Sunday, August 18, 1912, they were joined by another large group of interested people from Wenatchee, Leavenworth, and Cashmere, took the early morning No. 3 train to the original Cascade Tunnel, arriving at the west portal at Tye, at 11 A.M.(67) They were met by nearly two hundred highway boosters, including many prominent citizens and engineers from Seattle, Everett, and other of the smaller towns along the way, that had arrived from the west side only hours earlier. They joined together to do some surveying and eventually, their eyes looked up at the abandoned switchbacks.

They determined that the best route for the roadway would be to follow the original switchbacks of the Great Northern Railway, as it seemed that this route would be the least cost to taxpayers. They also agreed that it would provide an easy grade for 'automobiling.' Both groups were also unanimous in the belief that it would become one of the most popular automobile routes crossing the Cascades, simply because of the magnificent scenic attractions it afforded everyone with the nerve to drive across the mountains in those days. The groups representing both sides of the state found the route to be perfectly feasible, and concluded that it could be made good and serviceable for an estimated $50,000.

All three counties put enough people to work on the roadway in order to have it open to traffic in the early 1920's. But the people at the Leavenworth Echo caught up in all the excitement believed the road could be finished much sooner as it reported two years later in its issue of August 14, 1914:

Work Will Commence This Fall On Road Over The Cascade Mountains
Open For Travel Next Year

County Commissioner Matt Hickey returned from the tunnel yesterday afternoon on No. 4 telling a reporter for this paper about his trip. He and Tom Henry, Joe Mooney, Fred Berry of Wenatchee, and L.A. Titchenal of Cashmere were in the party which divided at the tunnel and while some of them walked from the summit to Scenic hot Springs, down the west slope of the Cascades, he and others walked down the old G.N. roadbed to the east portal of the tunnel. He says those who walked down the west side reported that King County was actively engaged in work on the road and they found camps and gangs of men at work on the entire distance to be built on the west side to connect the highway with the road system of King County.

Mr. Hickey also said Chelan County would soon commence on her part of the work and would begin at the summit and try and get the switchback in condition for travel, but this was probably all that would be done this fall. Early in the spring, however, work would resume and an effort be made to have the road in condition for travel by midsummer. The road finances will not permit the work being completed this fall.

It was November 1, 1924 that the first automobile crossed over the Cascades on the Stevens Pass Road. It was not all "sunshine and roses" as reported in the papers back then. Many people considered it a publicity stunt, as the road was not yet fully completed.

The highway on the east side of the summit was in better condition that it was on the west side. Sure, there were a number of soft spots for autos to get stuck, but after all, it was November. However, on the other side, the west side, there was no road at all in some places.

Three daring men from Everett decided to take the chance and cross the pass to show everyone how well along the road construction was coming. They were concerned about the public enthusiasm being lost on the project. One, Mr. Collins of the Pacific Overland company drove the car, accompanied by Bailey Hilton and Abe Glassberg. The three started from Everett on October 31, 1924 at 5 A.M., and drove to Alpine where the passable road ended. At Alpine, their car was drawn up the incline by cable over a logging road used for dragging trees to the mill at Alpine. Undaunted, they continued their journey eastward, driving on the railroad tracks at times, until they reached Scenic. (If one were to look at a map of the area as it was in 1924, the route the three daredevils were taking can only be described as ridiculous). From Scenic to Tye, the new road was not yet completed for automobile traffic, but they were told by some of the locals that a wagon drawn by a horse just might make it.

Despite the cautions, and even the threats of the railroad workers, two of the travelers from Everett, Hilton and Collins, dropped in behind an eastbound freight train, and bumped along over the wooden ties, across a number of bridges, and through a few tunnels and snow sheds, all the way to Tye. They encountered gas and smoke inside the tunnels so dense that they were nearly overcome at times, they would later recall. Back at Scenic, Abe Glassberg didn't care much for the idea of following a train all the way to Tye, so he decided to walk. He hiked the new, but as yet incomplete highway, and met up with his companions at Tye where they spent the night recovering.

At 8 o'clock the next morning, Saturday, November 1st, the three motor-driven trailblazers got in their automobile to continue their travels over the 'hump.' It wasn't long before Collins and Glassberg were out of the car, pushing with all their might to keep their roadster moving through the mud and snow. Near the top of the switchback, where they unexpectedly encountered over two feet of fallen snow, they were successful in securing the help of Contractor Charles Monary and his team of horses, who pulled them out of the deep snow. The motorcar could now proceed under its own power again and reached Cascade Tunnel Station at about 11 o'clock. Here, they were joined by Steven Arnett, a reporter for the Seattle Times.

Before leaving Tye that morning, the three Everett men sent a wire to Leavenworth informing all the residents that they were on their way and to keep an eye out for their arrival. They failed to mention what time they planned to show up. At 9 o'clock that morning, a number of town people from Leavenworth filled three cars and headed west on what they were proud to claim was a much better strip of highway for which they were responsible. The caravan was doing just fine until they encountered an enormous tree lying across the new road near Nason Creek. Those in the lead car had no ax, and waited for the two other cars to catch up. Fortunately, someone in one of the other cars had brought along an ax, and with the assistance of most of the group, had the tree cut out of the way so they could continue west bound.

They reached Cascade Tunnel Station at 12:30 P.M., where they met the impetuous three from Everett. After lunch, they headed for Leavenworth. With periodic stops for taking pictures to promote the soon to be completed highway, they all reached Leavenworth at 6 o'clock in the evening. Mr. Collins of the Pacific Overland Company, who started the whole ordeal, was so excited at the end of the journey, he instructed all the newspapers in the area to play up the scenic attractiveness of the roadway, and how easy it will be to drive across when it is completed. "Don't forget to mention the easy grades of the road too," he told the reporters.(72) He also forecast that the completion would be ahead of schedule.

It was called Stevens Pass Road when it opened, and it cut travel distance by automobile between Spokane and Seattle by more than fifty miles. The crossing time from Everett to Wenatchee was just over six hours. At first, the highway was open only eight months of the year, if winter conditions were favorable and the completion of the Tumwater Canyon section was still a few years away. When that part was finished, it could truly be said the highway across Stevens Pass was finally complete. It did not become a year round crossing until 1942, when the name of the road was again changed to the Cascade Scenic Highway. It was just wide enough for one car, but pullouts for passing were constructed at periodic intervals. The surface was packed with earth and gravel.

Photo courtesy of Leavenworth Echo

In 1929, automobiles waited on the east side of the Cascades to be the first to cross the fully completed New Stevens Pass Highway. These motorists are seen heading west from Chelan County in Tumwater Canyon.

Over the next fifty years, the highway continued to be improved for safety and easier driving. It was rerouted with straighter alignments, the addition of guardrails, and that packed dirt and gravel was finally paved over with asphalt to further improve the road. Many people wanted to visit Stevens Pass now that they could drive there in their own car, not just for historical purposes, but also for the clean air and spectacular scenery. As the Wenatchee Daily World stated, "There is no advantage in having the finest scenery in the world, coupled with an ideal climate if people cannot come here and enjoy these blessings."

Driving across the Cascade Mountains on U.S. Highway 2 today, a number of small towns still remain, although the station stops for the original Great Northern line have long since vanished. Stops such as Tonga, Corea, Nippon (later: Alpine), Embro (later: Alvin), Drury, Gaynor, and Berne are only memories now. It is nearly impossible to locate the original sites of many of these once important stops. Their buildings, water tanks, and coal chutes are gone. At times, archeology students from the local universities, explore and search for relics in the area. They are often surprised to discover so many Japanese artifacts.

Chapter 11:

The Towns That Remain

Heading east along the Stevens Pass Highway, it isn't long before a traveler encounters the towns that still remain; towns that owe their existence, at least in part, in large part, to the Great Northern Railway. The Great Northern's history is also their history.

Sultan, located where the Sultan River meets the Skykomish River, like many of the small towns that still remain along the western side of Stevens Pass, began as a combination mining and lumbering village. In 1870, years before the Great Northern arrived, prospectors found scattered flakes and a few nuggets of gold in the Sultan River.

No roads of any kind existed back then, and the area was densely covered by some of the largest trees in the world. The would-be gold miners, made their way along already established Indian trails. One prospector named John Nailor established a claim to the property he was working in 1878, and this would become the town of Sultan, incorporated in 1880. According to legend, Nailor named his town after a local Indian he knew as 'Sultan John.'

Shortly thereafter, some crude buildings were constructed and quickly the area was inundated with all sorts of rough and tough undesirables. Men who could not find jobs in the larger cities on Puget Sound, believed that their fortune rested at the foot of the Cascade Mountains. The town also served as a dock for small steamers that loaded up with supplies there, heading for the gold prospectors at Galena and Monte Cristo. Sultan's reputation spread as a town to avoid, despite the prospect of getting rich panning for gold. Unless one enjoyed constant fistfights and no-holds-barred brawls, it was best to avoid the town.

However, Sultan really boomed when the Great Northern finally crossed the Cascades. Its impact on Sultan, in becoming a timber town was staggering. The once rowdy mining camp disappeared, and became a thriving lumber mill town and railroad stop. People moved there to stay to work in the mill and for the railroad.

In the early part of the 1900's, Sultan, due to its rapid growth thanks to lumbering and arrival of the Great Northern, found itself in need of an educational system. The one- room schoolhouse of that era became too small for Sultan, as well as other towns in the Skykomish Valley. More and more families were moving in, and homesteaded the region, and more of the small towns began to grow. Sultan joined with neighboring communities to form a school system that would be run more economically, "and with a common approach to education."

One of the towns that partnered with Sultan to form a respectable school district was Startup, founded in 1900. Only four miles east of Sultan, it was originally named Wallace, but quickly had to change its name, as the postal service kept getting it confused with the larger town of Wallace, Idaho and persisted in delivering all the residents mail to Idaho. So the people renamed their town after George Startup, the owner of the town's largest mill and also its largest employer. Mr. Startup also built a 4-mile long flume (an man made chute down a mountainside carrying an adequate stream of water to convey cut logs to his mill. Besides the mills, Startup consisted of a few stores and one gas station.

In 1922, Sultan and Startup formed the Sultan Union High School District that combined all the high school students into one school at Sultan. Since it already had a high school that was built on ten acres of donated land in 1909, it seemed the logical choice. Startup kept its elementary school.

Today, Sultan is a quiet, simple and respectable town. With the development of today's modern freeway system, it is not unusual for many of the residents to work as far west as Monroe, Everett, and even Seattle. Many of the buildings from Sultan's early, wild period, with their false fronts, remain today on the back streets of the town. They are reminders of what a typical mining and railroad town looked like. It is well worth stopping at Sultan to talk with the locals and relive the history of railroading.

The town of Gold Bar did not participate in consolidating all the students of the Skykomish Valley into one high school at Sultan. It had a high school of its own and maintained it until 1933. Arrangements were then made to have Sultan Union High School educate Gold Bar's high school students. It is possible that an incident at a meeting of the Gold

Bar School Board caused the decision for Gold Bar to join Sultan in the education business

The meeting was called to discuss building a gymnasium for the students and the town people. Supposedly, an older gentleman rose to his feet when the matter of funding the gym was about to be voted on, and offered his thoughts. "Don't know what a gymnasium is, I've never seen one, wouldn't know one if I met it coming down the street, but if we need one, let's build one."(12) But the funds available did not match the enthusiasm of the old timer. Later, the town of Index also joined up with Sultan High School, and in 1942, began sending its student's to Sultan.

Gold Bar, located less than six miles east of Sultan, was platted on September 18, 1900 by the Gold Bar Improvement Company, and incorporated on September 13, 1910. One story has it that a man named John McKay was given train fare by the town to travel to Olympia to take the official papers of incorporation to the Secretary of State. But the people of Gold Bar neglected to give McKay any money for the incorporation fees, so he paid for it out of his own pocket. There are no records in the clerk's office that the town ever paid reimbursed Mr. McKay for his good deed.

Gold Bar was originally explored in the mid-1880's by many of the same prospectors that traveled to Sultan, as the gold mining craze in the area continued to heat up. Many of the Chinese and Japanese immigrants working on the Great Northern would, on their day off, when they got one, would hurry to the Skykomish River's 'gravel bar,' to pan for gold. Hence the name, Gold Bar.

In November of 1912, after working around the clock, including Sundays and holidays, workers for the Great Northern Railway completed its assembly yards at Gold Bar. At this time, the station town boasted a large sawmill built in 1898, two mercantiles, a meat market, bakery, two barbershops, three poolrooms, three hotels, and only one saloon. Real estate was offered for as little as $55.00 per city lot, and $15.00 an acre just east of town. Gold Bar also had the distinction of a fully operational arsenic mine nearby, which stayed in business through World War I.

As with many other settlements along Stevens Pass, Gold Bar was primarily a Great Northern town. Its rail yard included a roundhouse, besides its depot and a number of passing tracks. In the early part of the

20th century, Great Northern Silk Trains had priority over any other trains on its lines. Raw silk was a very rare and expensive commodity, and needed to be transported to the East Coast as rapidly as possible, before deterioration set in. These trains also carried armed guards to protect the silk and discourage would-be train robbers. There are many people (affectionately referred to as the 'old timers' by the residents) at Gold Bar, who were mostly children back then, who still remember hearing the unique steam whistles of the silk trains, as they began blowing far away, down in the valley. This was an indication for all other trains to move to a sidetrack for the special silk trains to pass quickly through without stopping. The sounding of the whistle continued constantly until the train had passed Gold Bar and was still heard as far away as Skykomish, nearly fifteen more miles east of town.

The residents were optimists. They believed their town would eventually grow to a population of over 10,000 people. Like Skykomish, Gold Bar had its misadventures and unique railroad incidents too. For example, there was a wreck of the Great Northern Silk Train in the early 1920's just east of Gold Bar. Floyd Collins, a young boy of 14 would hang around the depot during his spare time and heard of the accident. He hopped on his bicycle and rode "hell bent for leather out past the Reiter pits." At this point, the road ended and young Collins had to walk the rest of the way to the accident scene carrying his bike. He recalled hearing a train coming by and figuring he shouldn't be there, he hid in the bushes until the train passed. To his surprise, as the train passed, a brakeman in the caboose gave him a hearty wave. Encourage by this pleasantry, Collins continued on his way to the wreck of the silk train. When he finally reached the scene, he was not greeted in the cordial manner of the brakeman who had earlier waved to him. Instead, an unknown Great Northern official sternly told the boy, "Nothing for you here boy." That was all it took for Floyd Collins to turn around and carry his bike back home to Gold Bar.(12)

Gold Bar had its share of misbehavior and lawbreaking also. One night, there was a big stakes poker game going on at Shelton's Pool Hall & Card Room. The big winner went home that evening with about $800 in his pocket. He was found the next morning, halfway up the stone steps leading to his house, shot dead. A search for an itinerate miner, who was seen hanging around the pool hall that night, was briefly conducted and then given up. It should not be surprising by the manner in which records were kept in those days that the dead man has never been identified. However, many long time residents have always heard that the chief suspect was actually a Great Northern engineer. The murder went unsolved, and Gold Bar being a Great Northern town, led many locals to believe that was the sole reason that the crime was never fully investigated.

More than Sultan and Startup, Gold Bar retains more of its rich history of the Great Northern glory years, and is well worth a visit.

Seven miles east of Gold Bar is probably the most popular town for travelers and the curious. Index is spectacularly situated in what the pioneers called a 'Hole.' Surrounded on one side by towering mountain peaks, in a wild and beautiful section of the Cascades, it is bounded on the other side by the rushing and rapids of the North Fork of the Skykomish River. The backdrop of the town is Mt. Index. Imposing as can be, with its almost perpendicular slope densely covered with forest, the spectacularly beautiful mountain gives Index a setting unparalleled in the Cascades or anywhere else in the country. It can easily be considered the 'jewel' of the railroad towns that remain in the Skykomish Valley.

Miners were exploring the steep mountainsides along the Skykomish River in the 1880's. Following the path made by the Skykomish Indian fisherman, they hacked their way even farther up the mountainsides in search of gold, silver, and copper. Some struck it rich in ore, while others, not so lucky, made their living in the traditional way by opening up establishments that offered the explorers, food, drink, shelter, and supplies. Two of these people were Persis and Amos Gunn who brought their family to homestead on a former squatter's claim in 1898, building the first hotel to serve the transient population and to run the post office. The post office had actually begun business in 1891, before the arrival of the Great Northern.

The Gunn's knew that the railroad was on its way and saw all kinds of opportunities to benefit from its eventual arrival. Soon the area would swell with railroad workers who would join the miners and homesteaders who had already been there for several years. Recognizing the inevitable growth the Great Northern would soon bring, Amos Gunn filed a plat for the Town of Index in 1893, just before the railroad arrived.

Where did the town of Index get its name? Officially, it is named after the beautiful mountain that forms the backdrop to the town. But then, how was Mt. Index named? No one seems to know the true story. But the most popular is that two of the peaks that surrounded the town were first noticed by the Gunn's upon their arrival. They decided to unabashedly name them after themselves; Mt. Persis and Gunn's Peak. Mrs. Gunn, was so impressed with the beauty of one other specific ragged peak, told her husband that it resembled the looks of a giant index finger. And so the legend goes.

Logging, not mining, was actually the first and most economically foundational industry for Index. Timber mills were necessary for helping complete the new railroad, and the construction of new homes and businesses. But mining continued to grow and prosper also in and around Index. By the time the Great Northern arrived, there were several mines in full operation. Some taking out high grade copper known as 'bornite.' More mines were being discovered and opened all the time. One of the largest, the Sunset Copper Mine, operated continuously. The miners worked around the clock, and in an effort to make as much money as quickly as possible, safety measures were not considered. As a result, many men were killed over the years in its tunnels and shafts.

The fortunes of Index rose and fell in proportion of the rise and fall of ore and timber prices. But the Great Northern helped to stabilize the economy. Index suffered the same growing pains as Gold Bar and Skykomish. The influx of laborers looking to get rich quick and the railroad people who knew they would not get rich quick, but had the assurance of steady work, led to numerous and legendary scuffles and all out fights constantly. By 1900, Index had a number of hotels, drug stores, supplies stores, a newspaper, and many saloons.

Records at the Index City Hall tell how the citizens became somewhat concerned with the social direction the town was heading. In order to help balance the rougher aspects of life there, influential town people built a church, school, open and fish and game club, along with a number of fraternal organizations. The landmark year for Index was 1907, when it was officially incorporated. Permanent residents now took a far more serious role in their community. In addition to electing a mayor and town council, they also hired themselves a Marshall and opened a fire department.

The fire department became the most important of all Index government agencies. Beautiful as the terrain was where Index was located, it also presented a constant danger of forest fires and floods.

The most disastrous fires occurred in 1893, 1902, and 1939. But there were many others. Floods were also a continuous threat. Several major floods took place in 1917, 1932, and 1980, destroying many homes and businesses along the riverbanks.

The decline of logging and mining, combined with the Great Depression of 1929, curtailed the growth of Index. But the town still survives and prospers today as its beautiful natural setting continues to offer a unique retreat for travelers, hikers, and vacationers. Across the street from the Index General Store, is a small wooden cabin that houses many artifacts and photographs of the bygone boom days of Index and Stevens Pass. Of major interest to anyone who wants to know more about this part of railroading American, is the collection of pioneering photographer Lee Pickett, who took thousands of images between 1912 and the 1940's. He was an official photographer for the Great Northern Railway who lived in Index and had his own studio in town. As a result, many of Mr. Pickett's photographs can be viewed at the small wooden cabin across from the general store. Most of the Pickett photography collection is now housed at the University of Washington in Seattle.

Travelers driving across Stevens Pass today like to make Index one of their stops. Still standing, are a number of buildings from the town's boom days. Tourists and travelers find here a number of fine restaurants, motels and unique stores. And surrounded by the steep, timbered slopes of the Cascades, Index remains probably the most popular town, both in summer and winter, along U.S. Highway 2.

Driving east from Index, the next town is Skykomish, written about earlier in this narrative. It is the last stop for food and fuel now that Scenic is no more, before arriving at the summit of Stevens Pass and the Stevens Pass Ski area. One of the most popular ski areas in Washington State, "Stevens Pass Winter Recreation Playground," is now more than seventy years old. The ski season opens up around mid-November and can run as late at early May. Its 37 major runs, covering over 1,125 acres, rests among an alpine wonderland, equal in beauty to any winter resort in the United States. The ski runs cover three sides of two high mountains, and offer every type of skiing, including cross country, backwoods, and downhill racing.

With a base area elevation of 4,061 feet, and an average annual snowfall of 415 inches, the ski district is located only 78 miles east of

Seattle, 65 miles east of Everett, and only 58 miles west of Wenatchee. Its three day lodges, four restaurants, two comfortable lounges, cash machines, child care facilities, and a repair center for skis, snowshoes and snowboards, attract tens of thousands of winter sports buffs every year.

Of course the Hot Springs, that once accounted for one of this country's finest resorts, still exist. However, the people of Skykomish do their best to keep it a secret. Scenic Hot Springs is no longer a hotel with all its amenities. The hot sulfur springs are located within the Snoqualmie National Forest. During recent years, the springs have been turned into four pools with plastic liners, surrounded by sturdy wooden decks and benches. People wishing to take advantage of the hot springs cannot get there by car, however. Those curious enough to get there must first locate the unmarked trail that begins just outside of Skykomish, and then must be prepared for a steep hike up to the hot springs. The four pools are kept scrupulously clean by a newly installed siphon hose. The site of these springs sits on a steep hillside overlooking Highway 2 and the Tye River Valley. The springs are maintained by a group of volunteers known as "Friends of Scenic Hot Springs." Even though, the springs are available to the public at no charge, those who take care of them are very much protective of what they have in the Cascades. They constantly express their concern over too much publicity for the hot springs, as they believe it will bring too many people to the site. However, they do have a Post Office Box and bank account in Skykomish, and welcome all donations to help maintain the hot springs.

Once over the summit, on the east side, there are fewer small towns left since the heyday of the Great Northern. Cashmere is one of those remaining towns well worth the visit. Although it existed before the coming of the railroad, Cashmere still owes much of its growth and success to the Great Northern.

Cashmere began as the small community of 'Old Mission' or simply, 'Mission' in 1873, named after the mission church built by a number of Catholic Jesuit Priests led by Father Grassi. They had come there from the Wenatchee River Valley to establish a mission for the Indians who lived there. In 1904 a name change was necessary because there was already a town in Washington State name 'Mission,' and like the town of Wallace, which had to change its name to Startup, the postal service was delivering all the mail to the original town of Mission. Judge James H. Chase suggested the name be changed to Cashmere by comparing the town's natural beauty to the Vale of Kashmir in India.

In the 1880's more white settlers began to make their homes in the valley. One of the first was a man named Alexander B. Brender, an immigrant from East Prussia who homesteaded 160 acres of land about four miles from what is the present town of Cashmere. In 1883 there was an influx of settlers to the valley. Many of these used there land for farming even though obtaining water was a problem. Indeed, the terrain was much different then. Many of the early writings describe the land as barren and desert like. These settlers, making their way to 'Mission, were struck but the numerous small orchards in the Wenatchee Valley. One of the orchards was owned by Sam Miller and Frank Freer, who also operated the Miller-Freer Trading post in Wenatchee.

In the late 1880's, these pioneers began constructing small irrigation ditches and by 1901 water was available to most of the farms in and around Mission. In 1903 the first apples were shipped out of the settlement and a number of warehouses and grower cooperatives were established including the Cashmere Fruit Growers Association, Cashmere Pioneer Growers, and the Cashmere Fruit Exchange.

It was not until 1904, however, that the settlement got its name, Cashmere and was incorporated that same year. Within the next decade, telephones were installed, as well as electric lights, and Cashmere became one of the first towns of its size to have both paved streets and sidewalks.

Today Cashmere is a major apple and pear supplier in North Central Washington and many people make a living in the fruit industry, by either working in the packing houses, as growers, or employed at Liberty Orchards which manufactures famous Aplets & Cotlets that are sold worldwide.

No apology is offered that this book ends as seemingly a travelogue to Washington's Cascade Mountains. The fact remains that these towns and historical points of interest continue as a testimony to the irrepressible determination of those proud and selfless explorers whose labors connected the Northwest with the rest of the United States. And the country is all around better off because of the Pass and the people who constructed it.

Stevens Pass has now entered its second century of service to the motoring public and business of rail transportation. This magnificent thoroughfare, cutting across a breathtaking and majestic mountain range, with all its history and natural wonderment, calls everyone to visit. To the culture, sophistication, and urbanity of today's American travelers, that prefer to see their country, no longer by train, but by automobile, Stevens Pass beckons everyone to visit. Not simply to experience and enjoy part of the ever depleting natural wonders of this country, and the towns that still remain, but to recall and reflect upon those times over a century ago, when thousands of people worked so arduously, and continuously, to near physical exhaustion, because of their dream of contributing to the growth and success of the Pacific Northwest.

Epilogue

Over a half million trains, both freight and passenger, have crossed Stevens Pass since the completion of the Great Northern Railway in 1893. Freight trains became larger, and longer with increased motive power. The realignment of track, with lower grades and less curvatures, prevented the Great Northern – now the Burlington Northern Santa Fe – from becoming the only major railroad in the country to go into receivership during the economic Panic of 1893. It also afforded Jim Hill to take control of the Northern Pacific.

An argument can easily be put forward that no other industry, not one, has had the impact on the economy of the entire State of Washington, as did the Great Northern Railway. Today, one can only wonder if there would have been a Boeing Company, a Microsoft, or the unparalleled success of Weyerhaueser, if Jim Hill had decided not to build his railroad from Minnesota to Puget Sound. No doubt, the aircraft and aerospace industry would have developed, grown and prospered, as well as the new era of the computer and its rapidly increasing impact on how the world does business today; but would Seattle and Puget Sound have been their home? One can only speculate.

Additionally, no other railroad actually created new settlements, towns and cities, as well as having a major impact on their economies, as did the Great Northern. Would the Seattle of today, be one of the world's great port cities, without Hill deciding on Seattle as the western terminus of the Great Northern? The answer is, probably not. And it should not be overlooked that with the ever growing and expanding economic global society, especially the Orient and the Far East, that this country finds itself, Seattle and the other ports on Puget Sound, Tacoma, Everett, and Bellingham, will play an even more significant role in this country's economic success.

Some say the glory days of the railroads are over. For passenger trains, this may be true. But then again, railroads continue to be the cheapest form of transportation. Therefore, the business of hauling cargo of any and all kinds continues to be by train. One can see this for them self by stopping at any port city in the United States and viewing the number of tankers and freighters in harbor, and unloading their merchandise directly onto the waiting trains to be transported around the country. And the opposite is equally true regarding this country's export business.

Think of this too. A person driving along U. S. Highway 2, the Stevens Pass Highway, will still pass, or will be passed by, freight trains coming and going, both east and west, hauling all types of produce and products. What will catch their eye is that many of these trains are more than a mile long!

And for the residents of the Puget Sound country, those commuters who refuse to give up their car and complain about the ever increasing traffic congestion; when they are far too often brought to a halt while on their way to work or home, by a lengthy freight train of the Burlington Northern Santa Fe, or the Union Pacific, it would do well to think (since there is nothing else to do but wait) of what they are seeing. Boxcars filled with computers and electronic components, flatcars hauling large logs and timber products, and other flatcars carrying aircraft engines and fuselages; here is the reason for the rapidly enormous growth of the Northwest. Not just in business and industry, but in the influx of people from around the country. It is a sort of reminder of the past when the Northwest held so much promise for a better job and a better way of life. People flocked here over one hundred years ago for these promises, and today, they are doing the same thing. Thanks primarily to the coming of the Great Northern Railway.

A final thought. Fewer trains cross Stevens Pass today. The BNSF prefers to make more use of its route along the Columbia River. But make no mistake, Stevens Pass remains a vital railroad crossing for freight, and even the two-a-day visits of Amtrak's "Empire Builder." The Pass is safer, with better, and more efficient operations. People can see this for themselves if they were to stop near the east portal of the New (1929?) Cascade Tunnel. If they can time it just right, they will experience a remarkable sight. Just before an eastbound train emerges, suddenly the massive tunnel door begins to rise, allowing the air that has been compressed inside the tunnel to escape. There is a powerful rush from the released air that can be felt and heard by anyone witnessing this unique event. Then a headlight appears inside the 8-mile tunnel, it is advisable to be nowhere near the tracks, and within minutes, a giant train emerges at a remarkable speed hauling its cargo to all parts of the eastern United States.

Today, Stevens Pass is stilled filled with excitement and wonder, drama and beauty. It is a constant reminder of the pioneers and visionaries who saw the Northwest as a future economic behemoth. They were right, of course. The Great Northern (in name) is gone, but Stevens Pass remains, a reminder of the triumph and tragedy that created and developed much of Washington State, Puget Sound, and the Pacific Northwest, in addition to the social and economic relations with the Pacific Rim of Nations.

For all this, people of today should remember, in fact they have an obligation to remember, the courage, vision, determination, and sacrifice of all those who labored so hard, and in far too many cases gave their lives, in the construction of the most important venturous endeavor that the people of the Pacific Northwest have ever been given and from which they now benefit.

THE END

Index of Resources

1. Abdill, George, THIS WAS RAILROADING, Superior Publishing, Seattle, WA, 1958

2. Academic American Encyclopedia, Vol. 12, Grolier Inc., Danbury, CT, 1994

3. AMERICAN WEST MAGAZINE, "John F. Stevens, Pathfinder of Western Railroads," by Earl Clark, Palo Alto, CA, 1971

4. Anderson, Eva, RAILS ACROSS THE CASCADES, Wenatchee World Publishing, Wenatchee, WA, 1952

5. THE ARGUS MAGAZINE, December, 18, 1909, "Scenic Hot Springs," by H.A. Chadwick, Seattle, WA

6. Binns, Archie, NORTHWEST GATEWAY, Binford & Mort Publishers, Portland, Oregon, 1941

7. Bladine, R.A., Seattle Monument Co., Records of tombstones order for or by the Great northern Railway, letter, 1989

8. Burlington Northern Santa Fe Railroad, Public Relations Dept., Seattle, WA and Houston, TX, interviews and letters

9. Burke, Thomas, personal papers, University of Washington, Manuscripts section, Seattle, WA

10. Butterworth, Manning, Ashmore Funeral Directors, death records of Wellington victims, Seattle, WA

10a Carsten Publishers, railroad articles from 1940's, Newton, N.J.

11. Case, Robert Ormond & Victoria, LAST MOUNTAIN, THE STORY OF THE CASCADES, Doubleday Publishing, New York City, N.Y., 1945

12. City of Gold Bar, Sharon Riley, Clerk/Treasurer, written correspondence and   interviews re: history of Gold Bar

13. Colliers Encyclopedia, Vol. 5, New York City, N.Y., 1997

14. CONCRETE-CEMENT AGE, "Concrete Snowsheds in the Cascade Mountains Built by Great Northern Railway, January, 1914

15. Consulate-General of Japan, Jun Yoshida, Consul for Consular Affairs, Seattle, WA, information of C.T. Takahashi and illegal Japanese Immigration, correspondence, 1989

16. Edwards, William N., President (retired), Mount Pleasant Cemetery, Seattle, WA, interviews and correspondence re: Great Northern Wellington Plot, 1989-1990

17. CORONET MAGAZINE, "Wreck of the Spokane Run," by Norman Carlisle, New York City, N.Y., December, 1955

18. El Hult, Ruby, author and Northwest historian, Puyallup, WA, numerous interviews, talks and correspondence re: Wellington, Great Northern Railway, and Japanese, 1988-1992

19. El Hult, Ruby, NORTHWEST DISASTER, Binford & Mort Publishers, Portland, Oregon, 1960

20. Encyclopedia Americana-International Edition, Vol. 6, Grolier, Inc., Danbury, CT, 1996

21. ENGINEERING NEWS, "Cascade Tunnel Nearing Completion," June 14, 1900

22. ENGINEERING NEWS, "Cascade Tunnel," March 14, 1901

23. ENGINEERING NEWS, "Problems in Cascade Tunnel," January 10, 1901

24. ENGINEERING NEWS, "Serious Difficulties in Operation of Cascade Tunnel," March 14, 1901

25. ENGINEERING NEWS, Letter from John F. Stevens re: March 14th article, March 28, 1901

26. ENGINEERING NEWS, "Accident in Tunnel," April 11, 1901

27. ENGINEERING NEWS, "Train Stalled in tunnel," February 13, 1903

28. ENGINEERING NEWS, "Tunnel and Snowsheds in Cascades," June 4, 1914

29. ENGINEERING NEWS, "A Thirty Mile Railway Tunnel Under the Cascades," November 16, 1916

30. ENGINEERING NEWS, "Progress of Cascade Tunnel," April 11, 1927

31. ENGINEERING NEWS, "Driving Second Cascade Tunnel," February 28, 1928

32. Federal Railway Administration, Bruce M. Fine, Director, Office of Safety Analysis, correspondence, Washington D.C., 1990

33. Fricken, Robert E. & LeWarne, Charles P., WASHINGTON: A CENTENNIAL HISTORY, University of Washington Press, Seattle, WA, 1988

34. General Electric Transportation Systems, J. William Sinclair, Service Development Program Manager, correspondence re: G.E. "Helpers," Erie, PA, 1989

35. Great Northern Railway Historical Society, St. Paul, Minnesota

36. HARPER'S WEEKLY, "Northwest Railroad Disaster," by Paul Hedrick, New York City, N.Y., March 29, 1910

37. HARPER'S WEEKLY, "Six Hundred Million Dollar Mortgage," New York City, N.Y., June 17, 1911

38. Haskell, Charles Frederick Beals, "On Reconnaissance for the Great Northern, letters of C.F.B. Haskell, New York Public Library, New York City, N.Y.

39. Hisashi, Tsurutani, AMERICA BOUND, "The Japanese and the Opening of the American West," translated by Betsy Scheinerm with assistance of Yamaura Marilo, The Japanese Times Ltd., Tokyo, Japan, 1977, first English translation, January, 1989

40. James Jerome Hill Reference Library, W. Thomas White, curator, personal corresponce, 1988-1989, St. Paul. MN

41. Hill, James J., HIGHWAYS OF PROGRESS, Doubleday Publishers, New York City, N.Y., 1910

42. Hutchinson, Cary Talcott, "The Electric System of the Great Northern Railway Company at Cascade Tunnel," A paper (including pictures and diagrams) presented at the 240th meeting of the American Institute of Electrical Engineers, in New York City, November 12, 1909.

43. Interstate Commerce Commission, Washington D.C.

44. Ito, Kazuo, ISSEI, "A History of Japanese Americans in North America", translated by Shinichiro Nakamura and Jean S. Gerard, Seattle, WA, 1988

45. Japanese Community Services of Seattle, help with history of Oriental Trading Company, Seattle, WA

46. Kalmbach Publishing Company, Milwaukee, Wisconsin

47. King County Medical Examiner's Office, Copy of Coroner's Jury Inquest in the Wellington avalanche disaster, Seattle WA

48. King County Dept. of Judicial Administration, transcript of "Topping v. Great Northern," Seattle, WA

49. Knechtges, David R., Chairperson, Dept. of Asian Language and Literature, University of Washington, help with translating many Japanese letters and burial stones, 1990, Seattle, WA

50. LABOR HISTORY, Vol. 21, No. 3, Summer, 1980, "Japanese Immigrant Contracts with Northern Pacific and Great Northern Railways, Seattle, WA

51. Lake View Cemetery Association, Daniel W. H. Griffith, Cemetery Manager, help in locating graves of Wellington disaster, 1989, Seattle, WA

52. Lambert, Dale A., THE PACIFIC NORTHWEST, PAST, PRESENT, AND FUTURE, 2nd edition, DMI Directed Media, Inc, Wenatchee, WA, 1986

53. Leavenworth Chamber of Commerce, interviews with staff re: history of Leavenworth, 1989-1991

54. LeWarne, Charles P., WASHINGTON STATE, University of Washington Press, Seattle, WA, 1986
55. Wing Luke Asian Museum, Kit Freudenberg, Director, personal correspondence re: Japanese immigration history, Seattle, WA 1990
56. Martin, Albro, Professor of American Heritage, Bradley University, Bethel, CT., personal correspondence re: biography of J.J. Hill, and coded G.N. telegram translation, 1988
57. Martin, Albro JAMES J. HILL AND THE OPENING OF THE NORTHWEST, Oxford University Press, New York City, N.Y., 1960
58. Martin, Albro, RAILROADS TRIUMPHANT, Oxford University Press, New York City, N.Y., 1992
59. McClelland, John, President Emeritus, Washington State Historical Society, personal correspondence, 1988
60. Merrill, Robert T., Chairperson and Professor, Graduate Program, Geophysics Dept., University of Washington, provided information of lazer experiments in Old Cascade Tunnel, 1989, Seattle, WA
61. Minnesota Historical Society, house all Great Northern and Northern Pacific corporate papers, St. Paul, MN
62. Morgan, Murray, Northwest author and historian, personal correspondence and conversations, 1988-1990, Trout Lake, WA
62a Museum of History & Industry, James Mattson, historical researcher re: biographies of Great Northern employees, Seattle, WA, 2004
63. Nakagawara, Jon, Administrative Assistant, King County Medical Examiner's Office, personal correspondence and interviews re: history and purposes of coroner's juries and information of Wellington disaster, 1989-1990, Seattle, WA
64. Nesbit, Robert, HE BUILT SEATTLE, University of Washington Press, Seattle, WA, 1961
65. NEW ENCYCLOPEDIA, Vol. 1, Chicago, Illinois, 1993

NEWSPAPERS:
66. Everett Herald
67. Leavenworth Echo
68. New York Times
69. Seattle Post Intelligencer
70. Seattle Standard
71. Seattle Star
72. Seattle Times
73. Tacoma News Tribune
74. Wenatchee World

75. Nippon Kan Society, Elizabeth Burke, Mgr., assistance with history of Asian Americans in Pacific Northwest, 1990, Seattle, WA

76. North Central Washington Museum, Mark Behler, curator, personal correspondence and discussions re: Basil Sherlock and Raymond Starrett

76a Polk City Directory, addresses of Oriental Trading Co., Burke, and Takahashi, Seattle, WA 1900-1915

77. Puget Sound Power & Light Company, information re: Raymond Starrett, 1991, Seattle, WA

78. Puget Sound Railway Historical Society, North Bend, WA

79. RAILROAD GAZETTE, "Location of Pacific Extension of the Great Northern," October 13, 1893

80. RAILROAD GAZETTE, "The Cascade Switchback and Tunnel of the Great Northern," October 15, 1897

81. RAILWAY AND ENGINEERING REVIEW, "Electric power Equipment for the Cascade Tunnel," September 18, 1909

82. RAILWAY AND LOCOMOTIVE ENGINEERING, "Rotary Snowplows & Snowsheds Ready for Winter," January 1916

82a. RAILWAY AND MARINE NEWS, "Opening of New Cascade Tunnel," Special Edition, January 1929

83. St. Croix Historical Review Museum, P.W. Stafford, provided much information on construction of switchbacks and original Cascade Tunnel, 1988, River Falls, Wisconsin

84. Sale, Roger, SEATTLE, PAST AND PRESENT, University of Washington Press, Seattle, WA 1976

85. Seattle Betsuin Buddhist Temple, N. Horikawa, secretary, person interview, 1989, Seattle, WA

86. SEATTLE MAIL & STANDARD, "The Cascade Tunnel," April 27, 1901

87. Speidel, William, SONS OF THE PROFITS, Nettle Creek Press Publishing, Seattle, 1967

88. Stevens, John Frank, AN ENGINEER'S RECOLLECTIONS, McGraw Hill, New York City, N.Y., 1936

89. Sutherland, Doug, former Mayor of Tacoma, 1989 correspondence re: ownership of Wellington site

90. Tacoma Public Utilities, help with tracking ownership of Wellington town site before Tacoma purchase, 1989

90a. TECHNICAL WORLD MAGAZINE, January 1911

91. Topping, Edward William, son of Ned Topping, 1988-1990 personal correspondence and telephone conversations re: letters of his father from Wellington

92. TOWN CRIER MAGAZINE, "Scenic Hot Springs Hotel," Seattle, WA, January 21, 1921

93. TRAINS MAGAZINE, "How the Great Northern Conquered the Cascades," by D.W. McLaughlin, November 1961, Milwaukee, Wisconsin

94. WASHINGTON MAGAZINE, "A Resting Place in the Mountains," by Robert W. Boyce, July 1906, Seattle, WA

95. WASHINGTON STANDARD, "2,000 Men Are at Work in the Mountains," September 16, 1892

96. WASHINGTON STATE HISTORICAL MUSEUM, correspondences of some victims trapped at Wellington, Tacoma, WA

97. Wenatchee Chamber of Commerce, Brook Murray, information specialist, history of Wenatchee

98. Wolverton, James, retired Great Northern employee, 1917-1960, personal correspondence and conversations from 1988-1990, Nordland, WA

99. Wood, Charles & Dorothy, THE GREAT NORTHERN RAILWAY, A PICTORIAL STUDY, Pacific Fast mail Publishing, Edmonds, WA, 1979

100. Wood, Charles, LINES WEST, Superior Publishing, Seattle, WA 1967

101. CASHMERE VALLEY RECORD and Cashmere Library, Cashmere, WA

102. Historical Societies and Chambers of Commerce of Gold Bar, Index, Skykomish, Sultan, Peshastin, and Monroe, Washington

About The Author

Gary Sherman has spent more than 20 years researching the history of the Great Northern Railway and it's crossing the Cascade Mountains in Washington State.

He majored in history and social geography at the University of Washington. He is a free-lance writer with numerous stories printed in magazines in the United States and Canada. Mr. Sherman serves as a historical researcher for numerous museums, historical societies, and has contributed to a number of biographical television programs.

This is his first novel. Mr. Sherman lives in Seattle.

Printed in the United States
23754LVS00006B/73-81